ASIAN ENTREPRENEURIAL MINORITIES

NORDIC INSTITUTE OF ASIAN STUDIES

Recent Monographs

ASIAN ENTREPRENEURIAL MINORITIES

Conjoint Communities in the Making of the World-Economy 1570–1940

Christine Dobbin

RoutledgeCurzon
Taylor & Francis Group

LONDON AND NEW YORK

Nordic Institute of Asian Studies
Monograph Series, No. 71

First published 1996 by RoutledgeCurzon Ltd.,
St. John's Studios, Church Road
Richmond, Surrey TW9 2QA

Transferred to Digital Printing 2005

ISBN 0-7007-0404-3 [hardback]
ISBN 0-7007-0443-4 [paperback]

British Library Catalogue in Publication Data
A CIP catalogue record for this book
is available from the British Library

For Jack McManners

Contents

List of Maps

Preface

This is a book about what I have called, in the context of the historical development of the world-economy, conjoint communities. Its protagonists are five Asian minority commercial communities which entered into economic collaboration with three European polities from as early as the sixteenth century and which played a vital entrepreneurial role in the evolution of the world-economy from that date through to its florescence in the late nineteenth and early twentieth centuries. Each community constituted what Abner Cohen has called a trading diaspora, defined as the commercial organization of 'a nation of socially interdependent, but spatially dispersed, communities'.[1] Cohen sees the members of such a diaspora as culturally distinct from both their society of origin and from the societies among which they lived. Marked by their possession of common values and principles, these evolved as the diaspora aged into an ideology – usually a 'universal' religion – mirroring the collective consciousness and permitting the organization of interdependent communities for commercial purposes.[2]

The origin of the book lies in my own previous work on both India and Indonesia. The suggestion that I try to view major themes in these two societies from a comparative perspective came from the Cambridge-Delhi-Leiden-Yogyakarta Project on the Comparative Study of India and Indonesia, whose organizers invited me to speak at the final conference of the Project in Cambridge in September 1987. My theme was 'middleman minorities'. I am extremely grateful to the participants in that conference for their comments, and also for the comments I received afterwards on the published paper.[3]

To make more apparent my debts, I should like to thank Chris Bayly for inviting me to the Cambridge conference and for suggesting to me a theme on which I might possibly write. I should also like to thank Claude Markovits, who later pointed out a flaw in my scheme of things. My work could not have been pursued without the kind invitation of Cees Fasseur to join the research nucleus 'Agrarian and Economic Processes of Development in Southeast Asia in Historical Perspective' at the Netherlands Institute for Advanced Study in the Humanities and Social Sciences as a Fellow-in-Residence for the academic year 1988–89. Thanks are owed to the Director of the Institute, Dirk van de Kaa, and to the other members of my research nucleus, Peter Boomgaard, Robert Cribb, Frans Hüsken, Nico Kana and Willem Wolters, for their encouragement and for their readiness with both discussion and source material. Debts are owed too to other Fellows resident at the Institute during my time there, in particular the late Robert Cohen and Walter Heinz who discussed with me Sephardic Jewry, Werner Sombart and Georg Simmel.

During 1989 and again in 1993 I had the opportunity to test my ideas at several seminars. I should like to thank Jan Breman of the Centre for Asian Studies Amsterdam, Denys Lombard of the École des Hautes Études en Sciences Sociales, Dietmar Rothermund and Jürgen Lütt of Heidelberg and Bernhard Dahm of Passau for inviting me to speak and exposing my themes to critical scrutiny. I should also like to thank the late Jennifer Cushman, Mary Heidhues, Ann Kumar, Merle Ricklefs, Claudine Salmon, Heather Sutherland and André Wink for their encouragement, manifested in varying ways.

For library services – without which nothing can be achieved – I must thank Dinny Young of the Netherlands Institute for her pursuit of books even beyond the borders of the Netherlands and certainly beyond the call of duty. Gratitude is also owed to the librarians and staff of the Koninklijk Instituut voor Taal-, Land- en Volkenkunde in Leiden, of the India Office Library in London, of the National Library and of the Australian National University Library in Canberra.

My daughter Julia Wright agreed to accompany me to the Netherlands for a year. I thank her for her companionship. Norma Chin deciphered my manuscript. I thank her for her professionalism. The person to whom this book is dedicated helped me at the outset of my historical studies and has continued to do so.

Portions of Chapter 7 were previously published in my article 'From Middleman Minorities to Industrial Entrepreneurs: The Chinese in Java and the Parsis in Western India 1619–1939', *Itinerario* 13, no. 1 (1989): pp. 109–132. These are reproduced with permission from the editors.

C.D.
Canberra

Notes

1. A. Cohen, 'Cultural strategies in the organization of trading diasporas', in C. Meillassoux (ed.), *The Development of Indigenous Trade and Markets in West Africa*, London, Oxford University Press, 1971, p. 267. Cohen defines a diaspora as 'an ethnic group in dispersal', *ibid.*, fn. 1

2. Cohen, 'Cultural strategies', *passim*; for further discussion see P.D. Curtin, *Cross-Cultural Trade in World History*, Cambridge, Cambridge University Press, 1984, *passim*.

3. C. Dobbin, 'From Middleman Minorities to Industrial Entrepreneurs: the Chinese in Java and the Parsis in Western India 1619–1939', *Itinerario* 13, no. 1 (1989), pp. 109–132.

Note on Spelling and Abbreviations

Chinese and South Indian names have been spelt in accordance with contemporary Spanish, Dutch and English sources. For Western India I have standardized spelling to conform with the spelling of my earlier writings. For ease of reading, all diacritical marks other than those in authors' names have been removed from the body of the text. Where a word of foreign origin is encountered frequently, pluralization with the English 's' has been used.

The following abbreviations have been used:

BKI   *Bijdragen tot de Taal-, Land- en Volkenkunde van Nederlandsch Indië*, uitgegeven door het Koninklijk Instituut voor Taal-, Land- en Volkenkunde.

BR   E.H. Blair and J.A. Robertson (eds), *The Philippine Islands 1493–1898*, 55 vols, Cleveland, Arthur Clark Co., 1903–07.

Opkomst   J.K.J. de Jonge *et al.* (eds), *De Opkomst van het Nederlandsch Gezag in Oost-Indië*, 13 vols, The Hague, Martinus Nijhoff, 1862–88.

The Problematic: Classical Formulations

The founders of the first permanent European mercantile settlements in Asia recognized from the beginning that collaborators were needed both to maintain these settlements and to assist in acquiring the desired commodities for export. Experience made it attractive to acquire the assistance of commercial groups who were ethnically different from the local population and who had a tradition of successful trade in the region of the new settlements.

A Spanish expedition to Manila in 1570 instantly comprehended the importance of gaining the commercial collaboration of the Chinese, whom the Spaniards found trading in the port from four junks, whilst a number were settled in the town. Manila and the Chinese, it was reported, carried on an extensive trade, which must be maintained for the benefit of Spain and the continuation of the Manila settlement. In 1574 Manila proclaimed:

> The Chinese, in view of the kind treatment that they have always received and do receive at our hands, continue to increase their commerce each year, and supply us with many articles as sugar, wheat, and barley flour, nuts, raisins, pears and oranges; silks, choice porcelains and iron; and other small things which we lacked in this land before their arrival.[1]

A little later, at their settlement of Batavia, the Dutch were of the same opinion as the Spaniards. Ending his mission four years after the founding of Batavia, Governor-General Jan Pieterszoon Coen noted on 20 June 1623 that: 'There is no race which serves us better than the Chinese, nor one which is so easily to be had'.[2] His immediate successors were of the same opinion and held it to be an important plank of policy that Chinese should be encouraged to join the Dutch in their settlements.[3]

The British in Western India were also taught by experience to look favourably upon racial distinctiveness when seeking commercial collaborators. On 21 November 1676 Governor Aungier of Bombay urged Surat to encourage as many Parsi weavers as possible to settle in his emerging town.[4] It was recognized that Parsis were originally immigrants to India, and that they had kept themselves apart as a unique community, with a religious identity which could be appreciated by their European would-be partners.[5] Considerably later, in the period of florescence of Britain's formal empire, a similar policy was followed. From the early days of the British endeavour in Burma efforts were made to attract both Indian labour and Indian service personnel, particularly from the Madras area.[6] Somewhat later still, when European politics had given much of East Africa to Britain without the means to develop it, Sir Harry Johnston, Special Commissioner for Uganda, wrote in 1901:

> On account of our Indian Empire we are compelled to reserve to British control a large portion of East Africa. Indian trade, enterprise and emigration require suitable outlets. East Africa is, and should be, from every point of view, the America of the Hindu [native of Hindustan].[7]

British imperial control of Burma and East Africa was comparatively brief. Other empires, in other places, radiating out from those earliest settlements to which it had been so important to attract collaborators, survived longer. By 1949, however, retreat was final. But, looking at the next forty years by means of some snapshots, what is clear is the persistence of the economic importance of these outsider communities which had for so long existed in a conjoint role together with European power. In the Philippines, for example, in the early 1950s Chinese formed a little over one per cent of the population and yet they controlled the greater bulk of the retail and wholesale trade, which was the principal economic activity outside of commercial agriculture at that time. By the 1980s they had emerged as a serious element on the big business scene. Further, Filipinos of Chinese mestizo background remained an additional important group economically, both in agriculture and industrial entrepreneurship.[8] In Indonesia in the 1980s a Chinese population representing 3 per cent of the total was estimated to own, at the very least, 70–75 per cent of private domestic capital, while Chinese business groups, the so-called conglomerates, continued to dominate medium and large-scale corporate capital.[9]

In India the Parsis, together with several other traditional business communities, continued in the important economic role designed for them in the seventeenth century. A comprehensive study conducted by a government commission in 1965 found that the modern corporate private sector was dominated by 75 business houses which controlled almost half of the non-governmental, non-banking assets in the country. The top 37 houses were drawn predominantly from families who belonged to the major traditional trading communities of India. The dominant position was occupied by Marwari houses, which controlled Rs 7.5 billion in assets, followed by the Parsis with Rs 4.7 billion and Gujaratis with Rs 3.8 billion. By 1978, 40 per cent of the aggregate assets of the top twenty houses were controlled by two groups, the Parsi Tatas – the largest business group in India – and the Marwari Birlas.[10] Yet in 1971 the total Parsi population for the whole of India was only 91,266.[11]

The other two Indian communities which feature in this analysis are also microscopic. Britain's major conjoint community in Burma was that of the Nattukottai Chettiars of Tamilnad, whose financial acumen made possible the opening up of the Burma rice frontier. Returning, after the departure of the British, to Southern India as a population of only 80,000 in the 1950s, they came to control the major business combines of the south, the largest banks and, in particular, a considerable portion of the region's cotton textile industry.[12] In East Africa, one of the most important conjoint communities was that of the Muslim Ismailis, who organized a network of retail outlets throughout the territory and also undertook early industrial enterprises. Many, together with their Bombay brethren, ultimately found an abode in Pakistan where they and a number of other very small Muslim trading communities, representing under 1 per cent of the population, controlled over half of the country's industrial assets by 1959.[13]

With this progression from 1570 to 1940 and beyond we have claimed the period and the subject of our central concerns. But no amount of historical exposition can take the place of well-judged formulations. The issues dealt with in this book are not a byway in the history of Asia. They are themes – the connection between ethnicity and commerce; the relationship between religion, capitalism and industrialization; the sources of entrepreneurial creativity; the place of conjoint communities of the periphery in the making of the world-economy – as old as the discipline of sociology itself, and particularly sociology in its German form.

Sociology, as is well known, started somewhat late in Germany because there the philosophical tradition was particularly firmly rooted. The philosophical tradition of German thought gave sociology in Germany a historical and theoretical bias so that it is not surprising to find that two of the greatest sociologists of all time, Max Weber and Georg Simmel, were scholars profoundly attuned to historical issues and at the same time important philosophical thinkers. It is vital to address the major sociological questions raised by our subject matter in order to recognize that what we are investigating here is not a curiosity in the history of Asia but rather the larger sociological question which aims to understand the changes brought about in society by embryonic industrial capitalism in which two partners, Asia and Europe, were involved.

Georg Simmel: Commerce and the Stranger

The five communities which form the subject of this book were minorities in the countries in which they carried out their commercial activities. The classical sociological consideration of this situation is to be found in 'The Stranger', published by

Georg Simmel in 1908. This concept Simmel intended to apply to a variety of social situations; the stranger, he considered, was a social type who appears in different societies at different times. As in much of his other work, his aim was to formulate propositions about the stranger which would be very general and which could be filled with varying historical content or applied to other aspects of social reality.

The stranger, as Simmel conceived him, differed from the wanderer who comes today and goes tomorrow. The stranger is a person who comes today and stays tomorrow. Into the group which he penetrates, he imparts qualities which do not and cannot stem from the group itself. The unity of nearness and remoteness involved in every human interaction means, in relation to the stranger, that 'he, who is also far, is actually near'.[14] The stranger is an element of the group itself, and his position involves being both outside it and confronting it. This is his essential quality, his spirit.[15]

Simmel argued that the archetypal stranger was the trader who, due to economic circumstances, was largely restricted to intermediate trade. The classical example was the history of the European Jew, who everywhere occupied the formal position of the stranger, in contact with every individual at some time, but not organically connected with any single one. For our purposes it is important that Simmel hints at the notion that not merely an individual stranger but also a stranger group can be near and far at the same time. For this reason 'strangers are not really conceived as individuals, but as strangers of a particular type: the element of distance is no less general in regard to them than the element of nearness'.[16] As an individual, however, another important characteristic of the stranger, in addition to his trading, is his 'objectivity', his not being committed to the peculiar tendencies of the host community. This objectivity comprises both 'distance and nearness, indifference and involvement';[17] it does not imply non-participation, but a positive and specific kind of participation.

> Objectivity may also be defined as freedom; the objective individual is bound by no commitments which could prejudice his perception, understanding, and evaluation of the given ... he

is freer, practically and theoretically; he surveys conditions
with less prejudice; his criteria for them are more general and
more objective ideals; he is not tied down in his action by
habit, piety and precedent.[18]

Our intention throughout this chapter is to add a counterpoint to the major theme. In 1911 Werner Sombart published
The Jews and Modern Capitalism, elaborating 'stranger theory'
quite considerably in the course of addressing a range of
issues. In particular his argument was that Jews, as strangers,
made good traders because they were likely to be objective in
the marketplace. The argument then proceeds that objectivity
in the marketplace is desirable in the sense of being rational
and that a stranger group is at the base of modern capitalism's
principle of economic rationalism; it is, indeed, the pioneer of
modern capitalism. As Sombart writes:

> I really believe that the rationalization of life which the Jewish
> religion effects cannot be too highly estimated for its influence
> on economic activities. If it is at all to be accounted a factor in
> Jewish economic life, then certainly the rationalization of con-
> duct is its best expression.[19]

Sombart then continues that the Jewish characteristic of rationalism is also the leading characteristic of capitalism.[20]

Other stranger characteristics, Sombart writes further,
assisted the Jews to succeed as modern capitalists. Of importance to us is the fact that they were dispersed over a wide
area, living in a diaspora which played a key role in Jewish
success because of family business ties.[21] Jews were also
psychological strangers, not bound by tradition, not held in
check by other than personal considerations. The spirit is
formed which becomes suited to that of the capitalist
entrepreneur.[22]

Max Weber: Capitalism and Its Spirit

It is apparent from its themes that Sombart wrote his book as
part of the debate aroused by the appearance in 1904–05 of
Max Weber's *The Protestant Ethic and the Spirit of Capitalism.*
Sombart reinforced Weber's views on the active 'rationality' of

modern capitalism. The capitalist era, Weber wrote, betokens 'the rational utilization of capital in a permanent enterprise and the rational capitalistic organization of labour'.[23] Further, 'it is one of the fundamental characteristics of an individual capitalistic economy that it is rationalized on the basis of rigorous calculation, directed with foresight and caution toward the economic success which is sought'.[24]

What was the unique spirit which had brought about this trend to rationality? The argument Weber constructed is well known. Just as Simmel was looking for the 'essence' of the individual who, among other things, trades objectively in the marketplace, so Weber was trying to document a particular spirit, a peculiar ethic, in its classical form. In so doing, he would document one source of rationalization in Western societies. He found what he was looking for in a particular form of the Protestant ethic, particularly the ethos of Calvinism. Weber made it clear that he did not consider Protestantism to be the direct cause of capitalism, nor was it a requirement of capitalism after its establishment. But the Protestant ethos did encourage a culture which emphasized individualism, achievement motivation, legitimation of entrepreneurial vocations, opposition to magic and superstition, rational conduct, asceticism and self-reliance. This ethic, then, had an 'affinity' with early capitalism.[25] Weber also dug somewhat deeper, into the psychology of the individual entrepreneur. He produced a psychological analysis of the effects of the Calvinistic doctrine of predestination or election on individual Puritan believers, postulating a 'salvation anxiety' which is allayed by a rational, methodological dedication to success in one's 'calling'. Evidence of success in the form of wealth or expansion of enterprise symbolizes that the believer may be on the right path to salvation and this reinforces his devotion to his 'calling' and the pursuit of success; this in turn reduces his 'salvation anxiety' still further.[26] The 'unprecedented inner loneliness of the single individual'[27] was assuaged.

What is important to us is the fact that Weber's *Protestant Ethic* was only part of a much larger work, the study of other major world religions for which he analysed the divergent modes of the rationalization of culture in order to trace the significance of divergencies for socio-economic development.[28] The five communities we are dealing with here represent not only minority communities, but communities that generally espouse several of the world's greatest religious traditions. What Weber has had to say on the ethos of these traditions and their relationship to the development of the rationalization which, he felt, characterizes the development of modern capitalism has been influential and will be raised again in the body of the text. The essence of his argument is that the specific ethos which characterized the first European capitalist entrepreneurs was absent in other civilizations. This ethos, of course, was not the cause of capitalism, but it was one of the fundamental elements of the spirit of modern capitalism. Individualism and capitalism remained indissolubly linked in Weber's thought, so that he saw not only rationalization as lacking in other spiritual traditions but, further, observed what was present to be a sort of collective conformity and adjustment to social relations.[29]

In his studies of these spiritual sources, Weber dismissed Judaism as a bearer of the capitalistic spirit and wrote a fragment, 'Judaism and Capitalism' in response to Sombart.[30] Weber argued that Judaism lacked the decisive hallmark of the inner-world type of asceticism, an integrated relationship to the world from the point of view of the individual's conviction of salvation which nurtures everything else.[31] There was no conception of self-fulfilment in a calling,[32] and Jews failed to engage in one element particularly characteristic of modern capitalism, the organization of industrial production in domestic industry and in the factory system. Jews, in fact, 'were relatively or altogether absent from the new and distinctive forms of modern capitalism, the rational organization of labor, especially production in an industrial enterprise of the factory type'.[33] Nor could anything else be anticipated, as the legally and factually precarious position of the Jews hardly permitted continuous and rationalized industrial enterprise with fixed capital, but only trade.[34]

In his study of India, Weber located the alleged irrational spirit of Hinduism in the caste system and the theodicy of fate (*karma*), rebirth and duty (*dharma*) as well as in excessive ritualism and reliance on magic.[35] These he saw as obstacles to capitalistic development. But it must always be remembered that Weber's concern was for origins, not for the subsequent adoption of capitalism. Writing of the caste system, he notes that the core of the obstruction to capitalism was embedded in the 'spirit' of the whole system. It must be considered extremely unlikely 'that the modern organization of industrial capitalism would ever have *originated* on the basis of the caste system'.[36] Modern industrial capitalism, in particular the factory, was introduced by the British.[37] Even the Jains, a clearly mercantile community, lived a ritualistically isolated existence and remained confined to commercial capitalism, failing to create an industrial organization; nor did a rational economic ethic develop in Buddhism.[38] In general, all faiths constructed for themselves a 'magical garden'[39] whence the 'personality' so crucial to Western economic achievement could not emerge.[40]

Confucianism, too, failed to generate a particular economic mentality and a moral dynamism in economic activity;[41] its ethic stressed rational adjustment to the world as it is, and so was in no sense comparable to that characteristic of the spirit of European capitalism. The spirit of Confucianism was the spirit of familism, in which the individual was tied to family members or 'persons' instead of to functional tasks or 'enterprises'. It could be said to be of considerable economic consequence whether or not confidence, basic to business, can rest upon purely personal, familial or semi-familial relationships as was largely the case in China. The great achievement of the ethical and asceticist sects of Protestantism was to shatter the fetters of the extended family, basing business confidence upon the ethical qualities of the individual proven in his impersonal, vocational work.[42]

Taoism, too, failed to develop towards rational capitalism. Certainly mercantile circles adhered to Taoism and cultivated their special god of wealth, the vocational god of merchants. But Taoism's centre of gravity was its promise of health, wealth and happy life in this world and the beyond, and naked magic was rampant. Not only was there no path leading from Taoism to a rational method of life, but Taoist magic necessarily became one of the most serious obstacles to such a development.[43]

Weber's ambitious set of comparative studies concluded that, at the relevant stages in the development of cultures, material conditions in India, China and Judaea compared favourably from the point of view of capitalistic and bureaucratic potentialities with those of European medieval and early modern times. But in each culture the economic ethic of the dominant religious tradition concerned was directly antagonistic to the development of modern rational bourgeois capitalism. In Protestantism, on the other hand, the economic ethic was directly favourable.[44]

The counterpoint here is once again Sombart's *The Jews and Modern Capitalism*. Sombart, we have seen, argued that there was a transition from the objectivity of the stranger to the rationalization necessary for modern capitalism, which he attributed to certain facets of the Jewish religion. Sombart also identifies a Jewish ethic, running through Jewish moral theology, which regards the getting of money as a means to an end and lauds possessions as a means of doing what is pleasing in the sight of God. It is in fact a duty to obtain possessions as a way of doing God's will on earth, and indeed Talmudic doctors preached the getting of gain.[45] 'The more pious a Jew was and the more acquainted with his religious literature, the more he was spurred by the teachings of that literature to extend his economic activities.'[46] Moreover, the rationalization of Jewish economic activities did lead to industrial enterprises, despite Weber's denial. Sombart names a range of Jewish manufactures from the earliest capitalistic period in support of his argument that Jews were the 'pioneers of capitalism'.[47]

Joseph Schumpeter: the Entrepreneur and Creativity

We have described our conjoint communities both as minorities and as entrepreneurial. Weber introduces in *The Protestant Ethic* the entrepreneur of a new type, 'men who had grown up in the hard school of life, calculating and daring at the same time, above all temperate and reliable, shrewd and completely devoted to their business, with strictly bourgeois opinions and principles'.[48] Such an entrepreneur avoids ostentation and unnecessary expenditure and carries on a manner of life characterized by a 'certain ascetic tendency'.[49] But the founder of the sociology of entrepreneurship is Joseph Schumpeter, whose *The Theory of Economic Development* was originally published in German in 1912. Here, and in his numerous later works, Schumpeter stressed the leading role of the entrepreneur in economic development under capitalism.

What Schumpeter looked for were not ethical qualities, but a certain personality type. In 1912 Schumpeter sees the entrepreneur as less tradition-bound than any other type in society, because his characteristic taste was to break up old and create new tradition.[50] Schumpeter runs through the psychological motivations of the entrepreneur. He sees him as wanting to found a private kingdom, and even a dynasty. Then he has 'the will to conquer',[51] the impulse to fight, to prove himself superior and to succeed purely for the sake of success.

> Finally, there is the joy of creating, of getting things done, or simply of exercising one's energy and ingenuity. This is akin to a ubiquitous motif, but nowhere else does it stand out as an independent factor of behavior with anything like the clearness with which it obtrudes itself in our case. Our type seeks out difficulties, changes in order to change, delights in ventures.[52]

Schumpeter saw the entrepreneur as carrying out new combinations in order to make a profit, the characteristic entrepreneurial function. He argued that, for economic life, everything outside the boundaries of routine involved a new element and so the psyche of the businessman was of considerable importance, with his effort to do something new, to conceive a new combination.[53] The entrepreneur possessed a rare characteristic, 'mental freedom',[54] whilst furthermore he was prepared to undertake 'deviating conduct'.[55]

In his later writings Schumpeter constantly emphasized the creativity of the entrepreneur. Coterminous with the study of entrepreneurship was the study of 'creative response'.[56] The entrepreneur did something that was outside the range of existing practice; he did new things or things that had already been done but in a new way. He was a person who can be characterized as 'getting a new thing done'.[57] Schumpeter's examples include enterprise that introduces 'new' commodities; enterprise that introduces technological innovation into the production of 'old' commodities; enterprise that introduces new commercial combinations such as the opening up of new markets for products or new sources of supply of materials; enterprise that consists in reorganizing an industry.[58] It is not simply the increase of the existing factors of production but the incessantly different use made of these factors that matters.[59]

Schumpeter's argument, like Weber's, emphasizes the centrality of individualism and individual entrepreneurial activity to the whole economic process. Only the psychological motivation is different. The chief contribution to this debate by a professional psychologist was made by David McClelland in *The Achieving Society*, published in 1961. McClelland concluded that a particular psychological factor, the need for achievement, is responsible for economic growth.[60] McClelland's debt to both Weber and Schumpeter is obvious. To behave 'like an entrepreneur' or 'in an entrepreneurial way' implied possession of certain characteristics which included moderate risk-taking as a function of skill not chance; decisiveness; energetic or novel instrumental activity; individual responsibility and self-confidence.[61] All these characteristics, McClelland found, were possessed by those with a high need for achievement, and where this was at a high level in a society, more rapid economic development would follow.[62]

McClelland also addressed the question of whether certain minority groups which had obvious entrepreneurial success possessed an achievement motivation different from that of individuals. He argued that a reasonably high need for achievement was required by group members, but that this must also be accompanied by a certain class status and by an ideology – generally a religious ideology – which favoured the achievement motivation. The religious ideology he found most congruent was one with an individualistic spirit and without religious experts prescribing the minutiae of behaviour. The person with a high achievement motivation, wishing to be responsible for his or her own decisions and able to accept uncertainty of outcome, is like a believer in individualistic religions.[63] Weber's emphasis on individualism as essential to entrepreneurial activity is therefore confirmed by McClelland and extended to the role of minority groups.

André Gunder Frank: Allies at the Periphery and the World-Economy

The final theoretical issue we have to raise is what happens when we move the locus of the argument on economic development quite clearly outside of Europe. In 1967 André Gunder Frank published *Capitalism and Development in Latin America*. While fighting on several fronts, Frank reversed the orthodox theory of economic development: trade, he said, did not spread wealth but poverty; gains from productivity increases were not spread evenly throughout a free trading system but rather free trade increased polarization and concentrated such gains on those best endowed initially.[64] Most importantly, from our point of view, Frank argued that the capitalist system historically developed a polarization between metropolitan centre and peripheral satellites, which generated underdevelopment in the peripheral satellites – their economic surplus being expropriated – and development in the metropolitan centres:[65]

> Capitalism produces a developing metropolis and an under-developing periphery, and its periphery – in turn characterized by metropolis and satellites within it – is condemned to a stultified or underdeveloped economic development in its own metropolis and inevitably to underdevelopment among its domestic peripheral satellite regions and sectors...[66]

What is important for us is Frank's argument that the capitalist world metropolis undoubtedly has allies in the peripheral metropolises. But these allies, these interest groups, he does not see in any sense as dynamic and entrepreneurial leaders of economic growth; their interests were rather in policies producing underdevelopment at home, inevitable because their metropolis was at the same time a satellite. These allies in fact supported an economic structure and policies which maintained the exploitation to which they themselves were subject by the world metropolis, championing their own exploitation in order to be able to continue their exploitation of people in their own periphery.[67]

Frank elaborated this idea, which was intended to apply to all underdeveloped countries, in *Lumpenbourgeoisie: Lumpen-development*, published in 1972. Using arguments drawn from Latin American history, he saw the so-called lumpenbourgeoisie as a junior partner in foreign capital, subjugating its own industrial sector and imposing new policies of lumpen-development in a situation of growing economic dependence in the single world system of expanding commercial capitalism.[68] They formed 'a satellized bourgeoisie',[69] eager to participate in an ultra-exploitative export economy.

A counterpoint to Frank's 'dependency theory' is provided by the work of Immanuel Wallerstein, who owes clear intellectual debts to Frank and to Fernand Braudel. It is not possible or desirable here to give a general analysis of Wallerstein's 'world-system' approach. Suffice it to say that the approach considers that it is the peculiarity of the modern world-system to have survived as a world-economy for 500 years, a global economic system which made possible the flourishing of capitalism because the world-economy has had within its bounds not one but a multiplicity of political systems. The world-economy is divided into core-states and peripheral areas, with semi-peripheral areas in between the core and the periphery. This world economic order began to develop in Europe in the fifteenth century with the slow evolution of capitalist agriculture.[70]

What interests us here is what Wallerstein has to say about the world-economy's allies or collaborators in the periphery. In general he follows Frank in perceiving these groups as non-entrepreneurial and non-dynamic. Despite willingly sacrificing their local cultural roots for participation in 'world cultures' from the sixteenth century, they were unable to constitute an international class without the cooperation of the capitalist strata in the core-states, and this was not forthcoming. They lapsed into somnolence,[71] though struggling to remain in the world-economy.[72] Unfortunately Wallerstein does not elaborate this theme, although he deals with vast new zones being incorporated as periphery into the world-economy between 1750 and 1850. To use the example of India, this he deals with in terms of commodities being produced, not the communities which handled them as allies of the metropolis.[73]

The Sociological Contribution

Historical sociology has always been a central element of sociology as a whole.[74] Much work that is still pivotal in the discipline was inspired by the rapid rate of social and economic change which was brought down upon Europe in the early decades of industrialization. The earliest writers in the field were fascinated by the 'spirit' inspiring these new enterprises and the entrepreneurs who created them. Throughout this survey we have seen used over and over again the words 'essence', 'spirit' and 'ethos', and the concepts 'objectivity', 'rationality' and 'creativity'. These terms are applied both to individuals and to groups.

In our own day, too, the rapid industrialization of East Asian societies has attracted sociological analysis possessing historical depth. Peter Berger speaks of these societies as 'a "second case" of capitalist modernity'.[75] Here, however, instead of terms denoting individualism, the concepts used are 'collective solidarity',[76] 'collectivism',[77] 'post-Confucian ethics'[78] and 'familism'.[79]

Our own concern is with what we have labelled the conjoint communities of South and Southeast Asia, which have assisted in making possible the growth of the world-economy. In relation to these communities our central concerns have been set out by means of addressing some of the iterated themes of classical sociology. In developing our argument we will characterize our protagonists as stranger communities, as deriving their essence from a variety of spiritual sources, as exhibiting clear entrepreneurial creativity, and as collaborating with European enterprise on the periphery. It must be conceded at the outset, however, that the historical evidence – particularly for the sixteenth, seventeenth and eighteenth centuries – is simply not adequate to answer all the questions one would wish to formulate. What follows is an *excursus* on a somewhat larger scale than may be justified.

Notes

1. De Lavezaris to Philip II, 17 July 1574, in E.H. Blair and J.A. Robertson (eds), *The Philippine Islands 1493–1898*, Cleveland, Arthur Clark Co., 1903-07, vol. 13, p. 276 (hereafter *BR*); see also 'Relation of the voyage to Luzón', *BR* 13, pp. 101–104.

2. J.K.J. de Jonge *et al.* (eds), *De Opkomst van het Nederlandsch Gezag in Oost-Indie*, The Hague, Martinus Nijhoff, 1862–1888, vol. 4, p. 280 (hereafter *Opkomst*).

3. Phoa Liong Gie, 'De Economische Positie der Chineezen in Nederlandsch-Indië', *Koloniale Studiën* 20, no. 5 (1936), p. 104.

4. G.W. Forrest (ed.), *Selections from the Letters, Despatches, and Other State Papers Preserved in the Bombay Secretariat, Home Series*, Bombay, Government Central Press, 1887, vol. 1, p. 110; this letter, which does not actually use the term Parsis, is explained in E. Kulke, *The Parsees in India. A Minority as Agent of Social Change*, Munich, Weltforum Verlag, 1974, pp. 33–34, fn. 71.

5. J.R. Hinnells, 'British Accounts of Parsi Religion, 1619–1843', *Journal of the K.R. Cama Oriental Institute* 46 (1978), pp. 20–41.

6. P. Siegelman, 'Colonial Development and the Chettyar: A Study in the Ecology of Modern Burma, 1850–1941'. Ph.D., University of Minnesota, 1962, pp. 26–27.

7. M. Mamdani, *Politics and Class Formation in Uganda*, New York/London, Monthly Review Press, 1976, p. 110, fn. 21.

8. K. Yoshihara, *Philippine Industrialization. Foreign and Domestic Capital*, Quezon City, Ateneo de Manila University Press, 1985, pp. 83, 108, 143; E. Wickberg, 'The Chinese Mestizo in Philippine History', *Journal of Southeast Asian History* 5, no. 1 (1964), p. 99; R. McVey, 'The Materialization of the Southeast Asian Entrepreneur' in R. McVey (ed.), *Southeast Asian Capitalists*, Ithaca, Cornell University Southeast Asia Program, 1992, p. 17.

9. R. Robison, *Indonesia: The Rise of Capital*, Sydney, Allen and Unwin, 1986, pp. 276–277.

10. S.A. Kochanek, 'Briefcase Politics in India. The Congress Party and the Business Elite', *Asian Survey* 27, no. 12 (1987), pp. 1280–1281; see also H.B. Lamb, 'The Indian Business Communities and the Evolution of an Industrialist Class', *Pacific Affairs* 28, no. 2 (1955), pp. 109, 116.

11. Kulke, *The Parsees*, p. 35.

12. S. Ito, 'A Note on the "Business Combine" in India – with Special Reference to the Nattukottai Chettiars', *Developing Economies* 4 (1966), pp. 369, 372–375.

13. G.F. Papanek, 'Pakistan's Industrial Entrepreneurs – Education, Occupational Background, and Finance' in W.P. Falcon and G.F. Papanek (eds), *Development Policy II – The Pakistan Experience*, Cambridge, Harvard University Press, 1971, pp. 238, 250; H. Papanek, 'Pakistan's Big Businessmen: Muslim Separatism, Entrepreneurship, and Partial Modernization', *Economic Development and Cultural Change* 21, no. 1 (1972/73), pp. 7, 13–14; S.R. Lewis, *Pakistan. Industrialization and Trade Policies*, London, Oxford University Press, 1970, pp. 46–48.

14. G. Simmel, 'The Stranger' in K.H. Wolff (ed.), *The Sociology of Georg Simmel*, New York, The Free Press, 1950, p. 402.

15. Simmel, 'The Stranger', pp. 402–403. I am grateful to Werner Kraus for giving me Simmel's work in the original German; see G. Simmel, 'Exkurs über den Fremden', in A. Loycke (ed.), *Der Gast, der Bleibt. Dimensionen von Georg Simmels Analyse des Fremdseins*, Frankfurt, Campus Verlag, 1992, especially p. 9.

16. Simmel, 'The Stranger', pp. 403–404, 407.

17. *Ibid.*, p. 404.

18. *Ibid.*, p. 405.

19. W. Sombart, *The Jews and Modern Capitalism*, New Brunswick/London, Transaction Books, 1982, p. 234.

20. *Ibid.*, pp. 205–208.

21. *Ibid.*, pp. 169–170, 175.

22. *Ibid.*, pp. 162, 177, 245.

23. M. Weber, *The Protestant Ethic and the Spirit of Capitalism*, London, George Allen and Unwin, 1976, p. 58.

24. *Ibid.*, p. 76.

25. *Ibid.*, pp. 53–54, 69, 71, 162, 174.

26. *Ibid.*, pp. 54, 97–98, 108, 112, 119, 124, 172.

27. *Ibid.*, p. 104.

28. A. Giddens, 'Introduction', in *ibid.*, p. 5.

29. N. Abercrombie, S. Hill and B.S. Turner, *Sovereign Individuals of Capitalism*, London, Allen and Unwin, 1986, pp. 16–17, 25.

30. M. Weber, *Economy and Society. An Outline of Interpretive Sociology*, New York, Bedminster Press, 1968, pp. 611–615.

31. *Ibid.*, p. 622.

32. *Ibid.*, pp. 497–498.

33. *Ibid.*, p. 614.

34. *Ibid.*, p. 615.

18   ASIAN ENTREPRENEURIAL MINORITIES

35. M. Weber, *The Religion of India*, New York, The Free Press, 1958, pp. 24–25, 112, 119, 123.
36. *Ibid.*, p. 112.
37. *Ibid.*, p. 113.
38. *Ibid.*, pp. 199–200, 216.
39. *Ibid.*, p. 336.
40. *Ibid.*, p. 342.
41. M. Weber, *The Religion of China. Confucianism and Taoism*, New York, The Free Press, 1951, pp. 77, 104.
42. *Ibid.*, pp. 236–237.
43. *Ibid.*, pp. 204–205.
44. C.K. Yang, 'Introduction' in *ibid.*, p. xviii. Weber's work on Islam remained a fragment. An excellent survey is B. Turner, *Weber and Islam. A Critical Study*, London, Routledge and Kegan Paul, 1974.
45. Sombart, *The Jews*, pp. 192, 212–213, 220.
46. *Ibid.*, p. 222.
47. *Ibid.*, pp. 111, 234.
48. Weber, *Protestant Ethic*, p. 69.
49. *Ibid.*, p. 71.
50. J.A. Schumpeter, *The Theory of Economic Development*, Cambridge, Harvard University Press, 1949, pp. 88–92.
51. *Ibid.*, p. 93.
52. *Ibid.*, pp. 93–94.
53. *Ibid.*, pp. 84–85, 132, 137.
54. *Ibid.*, p. 86.
55. *Ibid.*
56. J.A. Schumpeter, 'The Creative Response in Economic History', *Journal of Economic History* 7, no. 2 (1947), p. 150.
57. *Ibid.*, pp. 153.
58. *Ibid.*; J.A. Schumpeter, *Capitalism, Socialism and Democracy*, London, George Allen and Unwin, 1943, p. 132.
59. J.A. Schumpeter, *Essays of J.A. Schumpeter*, Cambridge, Addison Wesley Press, 1951, p. 257.
60. D.C. McClelland, *The Achieving Society*, New York, The Free Press, 1967, pp. vii, 36.
61. *Ibid.*, pp. 206–207, 222.
62. *Ibid.*, pp. 211–212, 224, 226, 228–229, 238–239. McClelland argued that parental encouragement of self-reliance and mastery in early childhood was responsible for need for achievement in adults.
63. *Ibid.*, pp. 280, 339, 369–370, 372.

64. D. Lehmann, *Dependencia: An Ideological History*, Brighton, IDS University of Sussex, 1986, p. 3.

65. A.G. Frank, *Capitalism and Underdevelopment in Latin America*, New York/ London, Monthly Review Press, 1967, pp. 1–8.

66. *Ibid.*, p. 53.

67. *Ibid.*, pp. 67, 72, 94–95, 116.

68. A.G. Frank, *Lumpenbourgeoisie: Lumpendevelopment. Dependence, Class and Politics in Latin America*, New York/London, Monthly Review Press, 1972, pp. 13–15.

69. *Ibid.*, p. 70; see also p. 14.

70. See, for example, I. Wallerstein, *The Modern World-System I. Capitalist Agriculture and the Origins of the European World-Economy in the Sixteenth Century*, New York, Academic Press, 1974, pp. 348–350.

71. *Ibid.*, p. 353.

72. I. Wallerstein, *The Modern World-System II. Mercantilism and the Consolidation of the European World-Economy, 1600–1750*, New York, Academic Press, 1980, p. 129.

73. I. Wallerstein, *The Modern World-System III. The Second Era of Great Expansion of the Capitalist World-Economy, 1730–1840s*, New York, Academic Press, 1989, pp. 127, 140, 167.

74. For a discussion of some of these themes, see P. Abrams, *Historical Sociology*, London, Open Books, 1982 and D. Smith, *The Rise of Historical Sociology*, Oxford, Polity Press, 1991.

75. P.L. Berger, 'An East Asian Development Model?' in P.L. Berger and H-H.M. Hsiao (eds), *In Search of an East Asian Development Model*, New Brunswick and Oxford, Transaction Books, 1988, p. 4.

76. *Ibid.*, p. 6.

77. N. Abercrombie *et al.*, *Sovereign Individuals of Capitalism*, London, Allen and Unwin, 1986, pp. 121–131.

78. Berger, 'East Asian Model', p. 7.

79. Yeu-Farn Wang, *Chinese Entrepreneurs in Southeast Asia: Historical Roots and Modern Significance*, Stockholm, Center for Pacific Asia Studies, 1994, pp. 8, 14.

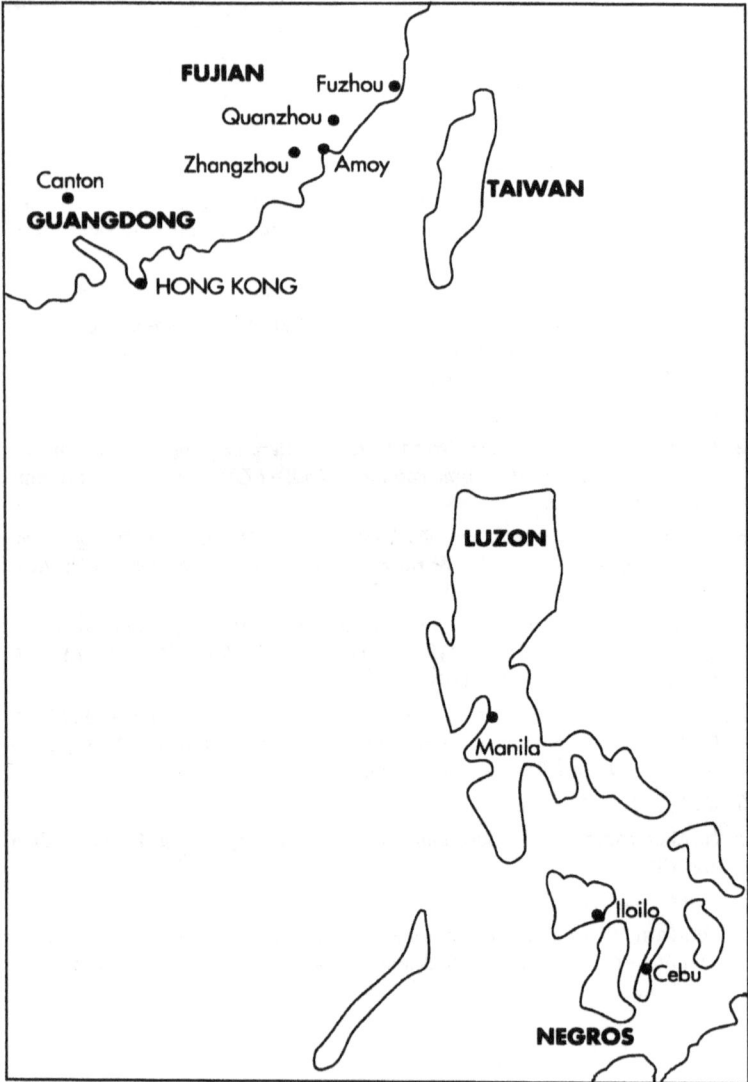

Map 1: South China and the Philippines c. 1850

2

Manila and the Creation of a New Chinese Identity 1570–1830

The Spanish expedition which arrived at Manila in 1570 found four Chinese junks in the harbour. Manila, the Spaniards reported, 'was large and carried on an extensive trade. In the town lived forty married Chinese and twenty Japanese'.[1] They discovered that the Philippines was part of the easterly route of the Chinese junk trading system, the junks passing through the western part of the Philippines archipelago on the way from South China's Fujian province to Sulu, Borneo and the Moluccas. As direct commercial connections with China were soon found to be fraught with difficulty, the Spanish, after establishing their headquarters in Manila Bay in 1571, made every effort to attract Chinese junks. Initially the goods the junks brought were inferior to the ones destined for the Indies because the Chinese considered the Spaniards had little to offer in return.[2] This problem was quickly resolved by the shipment of American silver from Acapulco. Thus began the Manila galleon trade, which was the lifeblood of the colony at least until the end of the seventeenth century and which tied Manila and her overwhelmingly Chinese inhabitants not merely to Mexico but to the commercial world of the Atlantic and the Christian expansionism of Seville.[3]

The Fujian junk trade, largely originating in Amoy, was everything the Spaniards had hoped for. By the 1580s some 20 to 30 junks were arriving each year; 48 came in 1588 and the total between 1571 and 1601 was 630. Their highly prized merchandise was satin, damask, taffeta and fine silk and cotton cloths in addition to items of daily use such as furnishings, ironware, foodstuffs, wooden goods and crockery.[4] With the exception of members of Spanish religious orders, Spaniards who came to the Philippines gravitated to Manila as the Asian hub of trans-Pacific commerce. There they could obtain loans from Chinese junk traders to cover the cost of the merchandise they wished to ship on to Acapulco as part of this lucrative economic venture. Antonio de Morga reported in his *Sucesos de las Islas Filipinas* of 1609 that Spaniards had given up all other forms of economic endeavour for the galleon trade;[5] the entire Spanish community in the Philippines came to depend for its sustenance on profits from the galleons.[6]

But not all the cargo of the Fujian junks was so highly prized or, if prized, then equivocally so. Fujian, with its narrow coastal strip and hilly terrain, was a region of emigration. Each junk carried 200 to 300 would-be immigrants to Manila; an estimated total for 1571–1601 was 190,000 to 200,000. In 1586, fifteen years after the foundation of the commercial hub, at least 10,000 Chinese had settled in the city, contrasting in their ever-growing numbers with the 800 Spaniards and Mexican creoles occupying the entire colony.[7] By 1603 it was reported that there were more than 16,000 Chinese in the Manila region, augmented to 20,000 when the China fleet came in.[8]

Indubitably Manila was a Chinese town, the Chinese furnishing the Spaniards not only with their means of livelihood but also with the very sinews of their everyday existence. Chinese artisans and craftsmen became indispensable to the Spaniards as skilled labourers, domestic servants, market gardeners and intermediaries in transactions with the native Filipinos; they engrossed the entire retail trade of the settlement.[9] 'We rely on the Chinese', the Audiencia in Manila wrote to the King in 1686, 'for the economic existence of our country. They control the supply of prime commodities, retail trade and the crafts necessary to the life of the community.'[10] But for a long time this was not fully accepted. The Spanish authorities conceived the idea of a 'necessary' number of

Chinese, and beyond that junk passengers were to be turned around and sent home. The 'necessary' number in 1603 was decreed to be 3,000.[11] Yet a Dominican could write in the mid-seventeenth century:

> A surprising thing that we see in this land is that although the city is small, and the Spaniards are few, nevertheless, they require the services of thousands of Chinese, Chinese mestizos and natives who earn a living through these services so that in the Chinese Parian, there must be some 200 carpenters and all trades exist likewise; and their business in Manila is with the Spaniards. There are 200 Chinese and Chinese mestizo barbers who earn a living from Spaniards like all the others.[12]

The Spanish response to this partially recognized indispensability of the Chinese was threefold: segregation, expulsion coupled with massacre, and conversion. In 1581 the Spanish established a sort of ghetto called the Parian outside the Manila city walls, distant enough for military security but near enough to supply the city's economic requirements. All Chinese, except converts, were expected to reside within its walls and, very soon, to submit to the authority of a Chinese *gobernadorcillo* – a 'petty governor' – who acted as intermediary with the Spanish government.[13] The Parian, which lasted for many decades, was described in 1590 as an economic jewel in the Spanish crown. In addition to serving as the silk-market, it had assumed the role of manufacturing locally whatever could be brought from China, including gold and silver jewellery, shoes and clothing. Chinese in the Parian offered their services as doctors and apothecaries; tavern-keepers; market-gardeners; leather manufacturers; barbers; butchers; sellers of fish, chicken, eggs and firewood; and builders.[14] In 1745 the situation was the same.[15]

The Chinese in the Parian were extremely homogeneous. They were Hokkien-speakers originating from the two prefectures Quanzhou and Zhangzhou adjacent to Amoy.[16] The significance of this will be discussed later, in the context of the concept of 'preadaptation'. Suffice it to say that, partly because of the instability surrounding Spanish policy and the frequent recourse to expulsions, the Chinese community in the

Parian was not able to build up the strong lineages character-istic of Southern Fujian. Rather it was organized in Spanish-style 'corporations', having something of the characteristics of guilds and numbering at various times anything between twenty and forty. As an example, a census of Manila Chinese establishments in 1745 noted that the sugar dealers' guild consisted of sixty shops and the sweetmakers' guild contained twelve.[17]

But despite the indispensability of the Parian – or, perhaps better, because of it – accumulated mutual distrust and hostility also led to Chinese revolts over measures of Spanish policy, Spanish reprisals and massacres, and ultimate Chinese expulsion. The major episodes took place in 1603, 1639, 1662 and 1686. Expulsion was always followed by gradual Chinese return, by a renewed estimation of the number of 'necessary' Chinese, and by the continuing fear that the number might rise to an uncontrollable degree.[18] As with Batavia later, the revolts were usually instigated by newly arrived Chinese without yet a propertied interest in the community. Their situation was such that they could expect no assistance from the Fujian authorities with any problems, such as the 1639 Spanish attempt to make them farm outside of Manila, and violence appeared an appropriate reminder that they were not impotent guests in the colony.[19]

The Making of the Catholic Chinese Mestizo

But Spanish policy had another dimension. Although the small merchant and bureaucratic oligarchy of Manila made a successful living, the Philippine colonial government produced an annual deficit, only made up in Mexican silver bullion. However, a religious and missionary commitment – initially fastened on the prize of China itself – kept the Spanish state in the colony and led it to pursue a religious-cum-cultural mission to Catholicize and Hispanicize the inhabitants.[20] Members of the Dominican Order arrived in Manila in 1587 and to them was given the task of converting the Chinese of the Parian. This was of particular significance, because the Dominicans had been founded to preach against heresy and they later took an important part in converting Muslims and Jews in Spain, ultimately being entrusted with the execution of the Inquisition there. Partly through them, Spanish attitudes and policies towards the Chinese were conditioned by this Iberian experience, as the construction of the Parian itself indicates.

But success in the Parian in terms of absolute numbers was never very great,[21] possibly because much of the population there was transient. What is important is that attempts to Catholicize were complemented by attempts to create a Hispanicized mestizo community of Chinese origin. While the Dominicans were about their work in the Parian and elsewhere, members of other orders were Christianizing the native Filipinos, particularly in the provinces around Manila. The Filipinos' Catholicism was eclectic; while the sacraments had limited attraction, the colourful ceremonies of the fiesta system – Holy Week (Semana Santa), Corpus Christi and the feast of a locality's patron saint – exercised mass appeal and brought flocks into the local town. Catholicism appealed through its splendid ritual and colourful pageantry; Filipinos could be selective in their response to Catholicism and, as John Phelan notes, they endowed the new religion with a unique emotional and ceremonial content. It was a folk religion, existing side by side with the Catholicism of the Spanish clergy and the Spanish colonists.[22]

It was the females among them, converted Filipinas, who were used by the missionaries to create a community with a new identity, a community which would identify itself with Catholicism, the Philippines and Spain: a community rising from Chinese soil and with every Chinese commercial talent, but tied through Spain to the world of Seville. The almost complete lack of Chinese women in Manila made intermarriage of the new Chinese converts with Catholic Filipinas both unavoidable and desirable. But the model the clergy aspired to was not assimilation to *indio* culture but towards a Hispanicized Filipino culture where Spain took the place previously held by China.[23]

Both the Dominicans and the Jesuits maintained forcing-houses for this experiment. The Dominicans' Binondo town was founded in 1594 across the river from both the Spanish city of Manila and the Parian. It was a community of married Catholic Chinese; by 1600 the group possessed 500–600 souls. Ultimately it was intended to be an all-mestizo community, possibly available for the increasingly distant dream of the China mission field. The Jesuits established a similar mission settlement primarily for Catholic Chinese also across the river at Santa Cruz between 1619 and 1634. Both these communities were segregated from the non-Catholics of the Parian. Mestizo offspring, as had been hoped, identified themselves with the Philippines and Spain. Their support for Spain was consistent, even to the extent of assisting in the suppression of Chinese outbursts.[24]

The Chinese Mestizo Economy and Mestizo Catholicism

Over one hundred years passed between the earliest conversions and the legal recognition of Chinese mestizos as a distinct element in various towns of Luzon, with their own taxation classifications and their own *gremios* (corporations). Their right to move freely was, of course, far greater than that of the Chinese.[25] But in this period it is sometimes difficult to identify Chinese mestizos commercially and what follows is merely the outline of an argument which comes more clearly into focus with the economic changes that were introduced into the Philippines in the late eighteenth century.

From the beginning Catholic Chinese were associated with the friar estates of Central Luzon, where they initially carried out improved methods of agriculture.[26] Throughout most of the Spanish colonial period these ecclesiastical estates occupied nearly 40 per cent of the surface area in the four Tagalog-speaking provinces of Bulacan, Tondo, Cavite and Laguna. The larger estates included entire towns within their area. They owed their origin to land grants given to early Spanish *conquistadores* from the late sixteenth century; these gradually passed into friar hands as their original owners betook themselves to Manila and the galleon trade.[27] Just as there was a collaborative economic policy for the Chinese in the Parian,

so too was there one for the nascent class of Chinese mestizos.
Philip III decreed on 25 August 1620:

> Whereas in the Philippines many Sangleys [Chinese] are con-
> verted to Catholicism and they marry Indians who are natives
> of those islands and they live in the suburbs of the City, there-
> fore, they should be given lands where they may settle and
> establish a town of farmers to till the soil so that they may be
> useful to the country and they may forego the trade of buying
> and selling supplies, thus increasing their stability and domes-
> ticity and rendering safe the City of Manila although their
> number may increase.[28]

Chinese mestizos were particularly heavily represented on
Dominican estates. Gradually, however, they became non-
cultivating tenants, spreading further afield in the early
eighteenth century and becoming active in the municipal
centres of the estates, buying and selling wherever the Filipino
tenants produced agricultural commodities or needed particular
goods.[29] By 1729 certain Manila citizens were already com-
plaining that Chinese mestizos derived large profits from this
domestic trade in which they could be said to be middlemen.
In detail, they bought up products such as wax, cocoa, abaca,
trepang and wheat, funnelled them to the Parian, and in return
sold in the towns China goods with which the Parian supplied
them.[30] By the early 1740s a Spanish Justice visiting the
provinces could say that, however necessary the Chinese
mestizos may be for Manila, they were even more essential for
the provinces. Inspecting the regions nearest to Manila, he
found that those towns where Chinese mestizos were living far
surpassed the remainder in prosperity. Through their purchases
they stimulated the cultivation of Filipino products and, in
exchange for rice, chickens and lumber, they supplied the rural
inhabitants with all their needs, forwarding on what they had
bought to Chinese in the Parian. As a sign of what was to
come, he also noted that Chinese mestizos owned sugar mills.
By the 1760s there was talk of a mestizo monopoly over the
domestic trade in the provinces, particularly in the buying up
of agricultural products.[31]

From the latter part of the eighteenth century mestizos'
fortunes were favoured by Spanish attempts to reform the

finances of their colony. This involved, among other things, the encouragement of the production of cash crops such as sugar, indigo and tobacco for export. The galleon system was also modified, as an increasing number of products were loaded for Mexico, superseding the old exchange of silks for silver and depriving the junk trade of its *raison d'être*. In 1789 Manila was opened to non-Spanish vessels. Opportunities for middlemen – both wholesale and retail – expanded rapidly and by this time Chinese mestizos were reported to be dwelling all over the provinces, occupied with retail trade and living in towns with a manner of life, in relation to food, housing and general behaviour, modelled on that of Spaniards.[32]

The well-known 1800 account of the Augustinian friar Joaquin Martinez de Zuñiga is explicit, if not very favourable, concerning the role of the Chinese mestizos. Zuñiga found them actively involved in the retail trade of the provinces, especially those nearest Manila. At Tambobong in the province of Tondo adjacent to Manila, half the population of 15,000 consisted of Chinese mestizos:

> Many people live here because the place is suitable for storing the provisions to be carried to Manila when the prices rise. Those who come from Pampanga and Bulacan pass through the place. The people of Tambobong buy all their products and keep them. As if this were not enough, they themselves go with their boats to these provinces and gather everything that Manila consumes. Indigo, sugar, rice, and other goods are available in this town. The Chinese mestizos who hoard these goods do not sell them, but store them up so that there will be a scarcity of supply in Manila ... Without any doubt, this town is the richest in the Islands. It has among its residents several mestizos whose assets each total P 40,000 ... Everyone is engaged in business. They gather cocoa, oil, wax, sugar, indigo, wheat, pottages, *achuete*, wood and everything that comes from the provinces. They purchase by the lot from the foreigners or from the Spaniards goods from the Atlantic coast and China. They store up salt, rice, and whatever is consumed in Manila, all of which they hoard, and sell little by little.[33]

Elsewhere it was a similar story. At most places in the Luzon rice plains Chinese mestizos formed the wealthiest inhabitants of the towns. At the regular weekly town markets they would offer for sale all kinds of cloths from Europe and China, while on other days travelling in their boats to any province they could reach to gather imperishable local products. By now their activities in the rice trade had become as important as their part in the textile trade.[34] Tomas de Comyn concluded in 1810 'that the whole of the interior trade is at present absorbed by the principal Indians, the Sangley [Chinese] Mestizos of both sexes, and a few Chinese peddlers'.[35]

There is a lack of family histories for this period, but a slight one is available for a somewhat later time when other economic factors had already become important. The Chinese mestizo Don Pedro Paterno was one of five children of the Catholic Chinese pharmacist and trader José Mong Lo from Santa Cruz, across the river from Manila. Mong Lo in the early nineteenth century married a Filipina and built up a wide commercial network all over the Philippines. He would take his children along with him on his visits to different towns to train them in the proper administration of the family interests. Paterno married a Chinese mestiza, had eight children, and continued to assist in his father's enterprises while building up his own mercantile business which included a fleet of small boats used for inter-island transportation. His own and his father's business took him throughout the Philippines, enabling him to acquire considerable agricultural land in Laguna and Batangas, as well as several other provinces, including areas as far distant as the extreme north of Luzon. On his father's death Paterno maintained both business houses, now initiating relationships with those foreign firms which new policies had permitted to enter the Philippines. His son Maximo, born in 1839, had also been trained in the family business as a young boy by accompanying his father on commercial trips, and he subsequently took over the enterprise.[36]

The conclusion must be that Chinese mestizos were the key economic force in the Spanish colony, at least outside Manila. The question arises, in what manner was this economic mentality influenced by Hispanicized Catholicism? To answer this it is necessary to go back to the economic role of the Manila Spaniards in relation to both the Chinese and the Chinese mestizos. In about 1800, at the height of the Chinese mestizo retail activity throughout the provinces, both Chinese and mestizos purchased goods imported from abroad from Spanish-owned warehouses in Manila while at the same time selling the produce of their area to Manila Spaniards for export abroad. Capital, however, was always a problem and credit was undoubtedly the lifeline of the local economy. This is, as Edgar Wickberg notes, a difficult subject and one lacking in documentation.[37] It seems, however, that at this period the Chinese of Manila – the mestizos are not mentioned – borrowed money at high rates of interest from many Spanish merchants, who had full confidence in their creditworthiness. All Spanish citizens of Manila, it was alleged, were engaged in credit transactions with the Chinese, often for quite humble activities such as supplying a household with vegetables or chickens.[38]

For Chinese mestizos the situation was somewhat more complicated. Having entered the Catholic Church, they found religious institutions which were beneficial both for the moral economy of the family and its creditworthiness. To return to the early days of the Spanish mission, we find conversion providing considerable financial and social advantages to the new convert. The Dominicans possessed one church in the Parian and one, somewhat later, in their mestizo colony of Binondo. The first entry in the baptismal register of the former is 19 November 1618. Catholicism requires each person at baptism to have two sponsors, a godfather (*compadre*) and a godmother (*madrina*). What is interesting is that high-ranking officials in both the civil and military branches of the Spanish administration vied to become godfathers to the Chinese. From 1627 they also transferred their names to their godchildren.[39]

These *compadrazgo* (co-parenthood) ties were extremely important economically. In contemporary Mexico they were an important feature of the credit system and research in the Philippines also assumes this to have been the case.[40] The relationship stressed was that between godparents and parents rather than that between godparents and godchildren, so creating a functional relationship between equals in age which was readily visible. Further, in both the Americas and the Philippines the tendency was to expand the number of people involved, extending the relationship to relatives of the participants in order, so an ordinance of the 1590s proclaimed, 'to have them ready for any emergency that may arise … exchanging with them favors and assistance in their affairs'.[41]

In other ways, too, the institutions of the Catholic Church were favourable to economic development. The orders were of course involved in agricultural pursuits and even in mercantile operations which they hoped would bring them profit.[42] But research in contemporary Mexico has also shown that the social institution which was the principal source of credit was the Church. There a variety of important religious institutions participated in the credit market (for example, parish churches and fraternities), access to ecclesiastical funds being facilitated by an individual's position as a lay official in the Church or through a functional relationship with relatives or *compadres* who themselves had direct access to these funds.[43]

For example, by around 1800 in the Philippines, sanctuary funds were quite clearly being used as collateral for economic activities. Entire provinces were in the hands of Filipino and Chinese mestizo clergy, as were half of all towns, leading to Spanish complaints that use was being made of sanctuary funds other than for the expenses of festivities and worship for which they were collected.[44] As in Mexico, brotherhoods (*cofradías*) of laymen also lent out sums of money. These brotherhoods were voluntary associations with the religious goal of carrying out charitable works and practising piety. They also functioned as welfare agencies, offering insurance to members and their families during personal crises. Moreover, as their funds multiplied beyond what was needed by their members, they obtained additional income through money-lending.[45] In 1810 Comyn reported on two Chinese mestizo brotherhoods – the Brotherhood of the Sanctuary of Binondo and the Brotherhood of the Holy Sepulchre of Binondo – which lent out funds.[46]

Much of the credit available in the colony at this period can be traced to the needs of the Acapulco galleon trade, and from the very earliest days much of the financing of this depended on a religious institution, the *obras pias* (pious foundations). Indeed, the principal sources of loan capital for sizeable ventures in the pre-nineteenth century Philippines were the *obras pias*.[47] The foundations usually originated in the wills of charitable merchants or prosperous churchmen who would leave funds to be administered for various charitable ends. Influential laymen – who of course had kin and *compadrazgo* ties – often sat on the boards of trustees. These bodies lent out funds at interest, particularly for the Acapulco trade, and Chinese mestizos were reported to be part of the chain of credit. Even the richest merchants often applied for their loans, and they certainly furnished much of the money for the investments of lesser traders. It should be made clear that not all the cargo shipped to Acapulco consisted of silk; Filipino produce such as wax and cottons was also shipped, though in varying quantities at different times.[48]

To conclude, one additional aspect of Chinese mestizo religious life may have had some economic bearing. This was the infusing of the spirit of the Catholicism to which they adhered with the essence of 'collectivity'. The Dominicans made some allowances for Chinese customs[49] and they, like the Filipinos, gravitated towards a Catholic community consciousness which was made manifest in the fiesta system – particularly the three main fiestas of Holy Week, Corpus Christi and a locality's patron saint – where their religious processions could be accompanied by Chinese musicians and fireworks and their festive days by Chinese theatre and Chinese feasts. One of the major religious festivals of Binondo, for example, was La Naval, an eight-day celebration financed and dominated by Chinese mestizos.[50] This outlet for 'collectivity' and its economic bearing will be discussed more extensively later.

Chinese Mestizos as a Landed Elite

In about 1810 the population of the Philippines was recorded as consisting of 2,395,687 Filipinos and 119,719 Chinese mestizos, the latter representing a total of about 5 per cent of the population. The Chinese mestizos were concentrated in the most Hispanicized and most economically advanced parts of the Philippines. Their numerical strength was now in the three Central Luzon provinces of Tondo, Bulacan and Pampanga, where over 60 per cent of the Chinese mestizos of the Philippines resided. The province of Tondo alone accounted for more than 30 per cent of the mestizo population in the Philippines, and they also made up about 15 per cent of the province's total population. In other less-populated provinces in the same general region of Central Luzon the mestizos, although not numerous in absolute terms, were an important percentage of the provincial population; in Bataan, for example, they were 15 percent and in Cavite 12. About 90 per cent of all mestizos in the Philippines lived in Luzon and in a few centres in other islands, usually linked to places of Spanish settlement.[51]

This period represented a turning point in Chinese mestizo economic activity. It was only necessary for land to become economically valuable for them to diversify their commercial activities into landholding and agricultural production for the market. Government encouragement of the development of cash crops for export dated from the late eighteenth century, but these crops became more important with the ending of the Manila galleon trade in 1815 and the independence of Mexico – whence subsidies had come for the colony – in 1821. Mestizo diversification into agriculture and land acquisition, having begun on friar estates in the eighteenth century, speedily increased. The result was the evolution of the Chinese mestizos into a landed elite, and the ultimate metamorphosis of their identity.

Because of their accumulation of commercial capital, the Chinese mestizos were in a position to finance agricultural production, particularly on friar estates where tenants had to pay rent. The Dominican estate of Biñan in Laguna, for example, was one with which Chinese mestizos had had a long connection. Rice was raised in large amounts on the extensive irrigated rice fields of the estate. Chinese mestizos cultivated

Map 2: Central Luzon c. 1850 (based on Wickberg, *The Chinese*, p. 26)

land on a lease-rent basis, paying rent in rice for the arable land allotted to them. In so doing they interposed themselves above the original Filipino tenants, who now became sharecroppers. It was reported by 1800 that the greater part of the Biñan estate was in the hands of wealthy Chinese mestizo tenants, while the town of Biñan was well known for its 4,000 opulent inhabitants:

> Their houses are well furnished, with an assortment of tables and other pieces of furniture. There are movable chapels adorned with gold-filled niches, in which are encased their favorite saints. Most of the residences belong to the Chinese who have settled and married in Biñang and the Chinese half-breeds who compose the main pillars of the town.[52]

Zuñiga also reported on other estates in Tondo and Bulacan where Chinese mestizos had moved into an intermediary role in the rice fields. Elsewhere mestizos had acquired land outright, taking it from Filipinos by means of the *pacto de retrovento* – a contract of sale with the right to repurchase – under which the Filipino could borrow money from the mestizo using land as a pledge of repayment.[53] Since the Filipino could seldom repay the loan and redeem the land, it went by default to the original lender. The practice, Zuñiga concluded, 'if not remedied on time, will soon make the Chinese mestizos the owners of all the lands of this archipelago'.[54] Sinibaldo de Mas, sent to Manila by the Spanish government to investigate economic conditions, warned in his 1842 report:

> The Chinese mestizo will within a century have grown to at least one million by natural increase and immigration from China; and will possess the greater part of the wealth of the islands. They are the proprietors, merchants, and educated people of the country, and will dominate public opinion.[55]

The landed interests of the Chinese mestizos soon became dominated by the cultivation of export crops. One mentioned quite early was the cultivation and manufacture of indigo. A member of the Augustinian order taught the Chinese mestizos of Tambobong to extract the dye from indigo and these neophytes chose to sow their first plants in Bataan province, where there was a large amount of land available for planting, and water to extract the dye. By 1800 the province had already produced many thousands of kilograms of indigo dye and the Chinese mestizos were selling the finished product to Manila at a considerable profit. Friar estates assisted mestizos with other crops. In the eighteenth century the Augustinian estate at Pasay was famous for its sugar production, based on the best contemporary practice of the sugar mills of Mexico. The 200 Chinese mestizo tenants on the estate were reported in 1800 to be attracted to sugar production, which they could carry on together with their commerce.[56] Everywhere that sugar became established from the mid-eighteenth century Chinese mestizos gained for themselves a place as provincial middlemen between Filipino labour and Chinese or European agents and Iberian managers who did the processing, warehousing and retailing.[57]

More research has been carried out on sugar and the making of the Filipino elite than on any other crop. It was the export of sugar, claims John Larkin, that brought the Philippines into direct contact with the outside world and it was the sugar barons, to a great degree, who shaped Philippine social and economic life from the nineteenth century. At some stage in the second half of the 1820s sugar began its rise in output that continued, with occasional interruptions, until the end of the nineteenth century.[58] This was due not to the official opening of Manila to world trade, but to the growing demand for sugar in England and the United States. By 1836 sugar had surpassed rice, abaca and indigo as the main Philippine export and had become one of the mainstays of the economy, in some provinces the principal source of revenue and the largest crop.[59]

Larkin has traced the rise of a sugar-growing Chinese mestizo-*indio* elite in the province of Pampanga close to Manila. He calls this elite a new entrepreneurial class.[60] Pampanga began making sugar in the seventeenth century, using a restructured prehispanic social system which mobilized the population in the service of the *indio* elite and the Spanish establishment, a patron–client system very adaptable to the needs of the sugar industry. By 1786 Pampanga was already the largest sugar-making area in the Philippines. Chinese fled to the province after the 1603 Manila massacre and settled in Guagua, the chief provincial outlet to Manila Bay. Like many Chinese elsewhere, their occupation was trade in the products that came out of Central Luzon destined for Manila. With marriage to Filipina wives, a mestizo society developed, first in Guagua and then in the capital of the province Bacolor, forming by the mid-eighteenth century mestizo corporations (*gremio*) with their own leaders. For a considerable period commerce remained their occupation. They acted as collecting agents for established Chinese merchants in Guagua, buying, for example, the sugar that was then sent on to the small refineries operated by the Chinese in Manila. As Pampanga began the transition to a cash-crop economy, the mestizos showed considerable entrepreneurship. They were able to respond to the need to trans-ship sugar and indigo from the interior to various markets. They provided the capital to enable farmers to switch from rice to sugar and indigo farming and supplied cash for new machinery, cane cuttings and indigo seed. They lent money for the purchase of Western goods as these penetrated the province from Manila, taking advantage of new economic circumstances. Finally, they themselves began to buy up land, making loans to farmers and using the *pacto de retro* to become landowners. But their landowning functions, under the conditions of the sugar industry, were those of entrepreneur, estate manager and land speculator.[61]

As landowners, these Chinese mestizos gradually merged into the dominant official class of the province known collectively, as elsewhere in the Philippines, as the *principalia*. Spaniards in Pampanga never numbered more than fifty before the second half of the nineteenth century and municipal government had perforce to be undertaken by the local elite, the descendants of those prehispanic headmen who were prepared to cooperate with the new regime. Larkin notes that Pampanga town officials' lists show a marked continuity in the families that composed the earliest *principalia* down to the middle of the eighteenth century; then, from 1765 to 1820 Chinese mestizos infiltrated and assimilated the old *principalia*.

By 1799 there were more than 13,000 Chinese mestizos in the province and the dominant economic position of the original *principalia* weakened as the lands which they had acquired over two centuries passed into the hands of the mestizos. Here too, as on the friar estates with tenants, the *pacto de retro* was used, together with moneylending for farm implements, work animals and house lots, to acquire land. The lenders soon controlled most phases of agricultural life in the province. Municipalities and offices rapidly became heavily infiltrated with newcomers; town records show new, Hispanic-ized Chinese names appearing in the major offices, especially after 1765. The local *principalia*, to preserve their position, intermarried with them.[62]

Often this new class was created with the movement of the sugar frontier. In the 1820s and 1830s the sugar frontier moved north in Pampanga. The town of Angeles developed when Don Angel Pantaleon de Miranda organized his tenants to clear land in this out-of-the-way district. In 1822 he erected the first sugar mill in the town, together with an alcohol distillery. De Miranda's heirs married local Chinese and Chinese mestizos and their offspring in turn became the *principalia* of the newly founded town, constituting the leading officials and landowners in succeeding generations. Gradually a handful of families came to control local social, political and economic life.[63] This was a landholding elite — in Pampanga geared for large-scale sugar production — and there as elsewhere it was mobile, business-oriented, aware of the need for contact with Manila and, all in all, to repeat Larkin's summation, 'a new entrepreneurial class'.[64]

Chinese Mestizos outside Central Luzon

The two other Spanish settlements to which Chinese were chiefly attracted were Cebu City, the earliest Spanish settlement in the Philippines lying at the very heart of the Visayas and surrounded on all sides by islands, and Iloilo, again an early Spanish settlement, located in the western Visayas on the southeast coast of Panay facing Negros. Cebu was a major population centre, primarily due to its central location astride the archipelago's main trade routes. Although extensive details are not known, from the late sixteenth century it was the site of a Parian second only to Manila's. Spanish policy, as in Manila, was to convert the Chinese and marry them locally, and for that purpose a secular parish was established in 1614.[65]

By the early eighteenth century the Cebu Parian was already a predominantly mestizo community and, by the end of the century, it was entirely so. The community had also been considerably Hispanicized, the heart of the community at that time being the parish church of San Juan Bautista. The parish had considerable wealth and the church was decorated with beautifully carved wooden images and gold and silver inlaid walls. Records from the 1830s put the Parian's total population at 1,200 mestizos and 6 Chinese, in a total urban population of 10,078: as usual, there were only a handful of Spaniards.[66]

The elite of the Parian comprised approximately thirty wealthy mestizo families, representing about 10 per cent of the population. These *principalia* were alleged to exercise more influence over the urban area than did the colonial authorities.[67] They were closely knit and socially interrelated, tending to intermarry. Culturally and linguistically they were similar to the Cebuano *principalia* of the area. But, according to Michael Cullinane, unlike the Cebuanos they developed an identity beyond their families;[68] they were 'a powerful and cohesive ghetto elite',[69] forming the earliest identifiable 'Filipino' urban elite. The rise of export agriculture, which will be discussed later, led to intermarriage with Cebuanos but did not result in the emerging provincial elite being any less dominated by established Parian mestizo families.[70]

These Parian mestizos showed no interest in acquiring land until the 1840s. They were a commercial community and rivalled the Spanish governors in their economic activities. There is a lack of information about their earlier endeavours, but by the 1820s Cebu was starting once again to resume its position as the major entrepôt for the central and eastern Visayas and northern Mindanao. The demand for Visayan products was increasing in Manila, and Parian mestizos extended their earlier activities, placing commercial agents throughout the region and initiating trading voyages for the distribution and collection of a variety of products. The wealthiest owned vessels as well as stores and warehouses located in the Parian, and occupied the position of both wholesale and retail merchants.[71]

The initial tie between the Chinese mestizos and Spain in Iloilo was equally apparent. At the beginning of the seventeenth century there were in Iloilo more than a hundred Chinese married to local women, together with a Spanish garrison and a shipyard for the construction of ships. Evolving into a mestizo community, they resided in the Parian at Molo, an urban township, and became distinguished by the mid-eighteenth century for their commercial involvement in the local weaving industry in Molo and nearby Jaro. The local industry had reached a high level of sophistication and cloth was collected by the Chinese mestizo merchants of Molo and Jaro and put on board their own vessels for transport to market in Manila. With the sale profits they acquired the raw materials needed to make the cloth, which included Chinese silk and Batangas cotton.[72] A British observer in the 1850s reported that the textile productions of Iloilo had reached 'a remarkable degree of development',[73] with local women working in a form of debt bondage and each mestizo family keeping a considerable number of looms at work.[74] Of the Iloilo Chinese mestizos, Bowring noted:

> I found nowhere among the natives a people so industrious, so persevering, so economical, and, generally, so prosperous … They are more active and enterprising, more prudent and persevering, more devoted to trade and commerce, than the Indios.[75]

In addition Chinese mestizos monopolized the retail trade and, with the gradual opening up of export commerce, they used their vessels to collect and export leaf tobacco, sugar, sapanwood, rice, hemp and hides. They left for Manila in groups of six to twenty coasting vessels and there, after disposing of their products, bought up foreign – chiefly British – manufactures purchased at cheap rates from Chinese shopkeepers in Manila. Their agents then sold these goods by travelling with large buffalo carts to the regular interior markets.[76] Like the Chinese mestizos of Cebu – and like their fellows in Luzon – they gradually became a landed class, and this will be discussed subsequently.

Reprise

We have been dealing with a community on which was imposed – by the policy of a European power – a dual identity, an overlap of Hispanicism and Catholicism varnished on a South China entrepreneurial personality. This is a community which, in its entrepreneurial activities, exhibits Simmel's objectivity of the stranger, an objectivity comprising both 'distance and nearness, indifference and involvement'.[77] Surrounded by virtual economic quietism, the creative tension of duality is apparent.

Simmel, of course, did not elaborate his theory. We have noted that he intended it to be applicable to a range of situations. In fact, the concept of dual identity appeared in varying guises in the work of Simmel's followers. With his 1928 concept of the 'marginal man',[78] Robert Park – a student of Simmel's in Berlin[79] – adapted his teacher's work to the zones of culture contact in American cities experiencing extensive migration. The 'marginal man' concept was further developed and clarified by Everett Stonequist in 1930.[80] Neither used the concept in a way that is identical to Simmel's stranger but, as part of a broader argument, both provide important insights into the idea of duality.

Stonequist in particular explored 'those individuals who are unwittingly initiated into two or more historic traditions, languages, political loyalties, moral codes or religions'.[81] With a duality of social connections, such an individual will, in fact, 'be a kind of dual personality'.[82] Stonequist returns again to the concept of a 'dual personality', and also to another concept of 'double consciousness'.[83] In such an individual the clash of two images of the self gives rise to 'a dual self-consciousness and identification'.[84] It can also, and this is crucial for our argument, 'release individuals for creative thought'[85] and give rise to 'creative types of personality'.[86]

It is not intended at this point to pursue the sociology of the stranger well beyond Simmel. But since the notion at the core of this book is that the economic creativity of our subjects is made possible by the possession of a dual identity rather than of one particular religious spirit, the writings of Simmel's first anglophone followers are important and can provide us with pertinent insights. Stonequist looks at the objectivity of his version of the stranger in a way that is applicable to our theme. Speaking of the type of social change which results from the sudden contact of two or more societies with different cultures, Stonequist writes:

> The clash of codes and philosophies is profound. The effect upon the subordinate group which must do the major share of adjusting is particularly severe ... As a result the individual may have to readjust his life along several points: the language in which he communicates, the religion he believes in, the moral code he follows, the manner in which he earns his living, the government to which he owes allegiance, as well as the subtler aspects of personality. The duality of cultures produces a duality of personality ... It is one fact of cultural duality which is the determining influence in the life of the marginal man.[87]

The duality here is that of Amoy and Seville. Seville conquered, but its dependency was considerable.

Notes

1. 'Relation of the Voyage to Luzón', *BR* 3, p. 101.

2. De Lavezaris to Philip II, 17 July 1574, *BR* 3, p. 276.

3. P. Chaunu, *Les Philippines et le Pacifique des Ibériques (xvie, xviie, xviiie siècles. Introduction methodologique et indices d'activité*, Paris, S.E.V.P.E.N., 1960, pp. 15–20.

4. 'Ordinance Forbidding the Indians to Wear Chinese Stuffs, 9 Apr. 1591', *BR* 8, pp. 85, 90; R. Bernal, 'The Chinese Colony in Manila, 1570–1770', in A. Felix Jr. (ed.); *The Chinese in the Philippines*, vol. 1, Manila, Solidaridad Publishing House, 1966, pp. 43–44, 46.

5. Morga's Sucesos, *BR* 16, pp. 177–180; see also S.D. Quiason, 'The Sampan Trade, 1570–1770', in Felix, *The Chinese*, vol. I, pp. 163–165, 167.

6. W.L. Schurz, *The Manila Galleon*, New York, E.P. Dutton, 1939, p. 154.

7. Bernal, 'Chinese Colony', pp. 43–44, 46.

8. De Santa Catalina to Philip III, 15 Dec. 1603, *BR* 12, p. 147.

9. Bernal, 'Chinese Colony', p. 42.

10. Quoted in *ibid.*, p. 62.

11. *BR* 12, pp. 148–149, fn. 29.

12. Quoted in A. Santamaria, 'The Chinese Parian (El Parian de los Sangleyes)', in Felix, *The Chinese*, vol. I, p. 108.

13. E. Wickberg, *The Chinese in Philippine Life 1850–1898*, New Haven/London, Yale University Press, 1965, pp. 11–12, 37.

14. 'Bishop Salazar's Report to the King', in Felix, *The Chinese*, vol. I, pp. 125–127.

15. L. Diaz-Trechuelo, 'The Role of the Chinese in the Philippine Domestic Economy (1570–1770)', in Felix, *The Chinese*, vol. I, pp. 198–199.

16. Wickberg, *The Chinese*, pp. 37–38.

17. *Ibid.*; J.A. Larkin, *Sugar and the Origins of Modern Philippine Society*, Berkeley/Los Angeles, University of California Press, 1993, p. 22.

18. Bernal, 'Chinese Colony', pp. 61–62.

19. M.C. Guerrero, 'The Chinese in the Philippines, 1570–1770', in Felix, *The Chinese*, vol. I, p. 33; Wickberg, *The Chinese*, pp. 242–243.

20. J.L. Phelan, *The Hispanization of the Philippines. Spanish Aims and Filipino Responses 1565–1700*, Madison, University of Wisconsin Press, 1959, pp. 13–14.

21. Wickberg, *The Chinese*, p. 16.

22. Phelan, *Hispanization of the Philippines*, pp. 71–84, 88.

23. Wickberg, *The Chinese*, p. 18.

24. *Ibid.*, pp. 18–20.

25. Wickberg, 'The Chinese Mestizo', pp. 63–65, 71.

26. De Benavides to Philip III, 5 Jul. 1603, *BR* 12, p. 109.

27. D.M. Roth, 'Church Lands in the Agrarian History of the Tagalog Region', in A.W. McCoy and E.C. de Jesus (eds), *Philippine Social History: Global Trade and Local Transformations*, Sydney/Manila, George Allen and Unwin/Ateneo de Manila University Press, 1982, pp. 131–132, 134.

28. Quoted in Bernal, 'Chinese Colony', p. 61.

29. Roth, 'Church Lands', pp. 144–145.

30. Diaz-Trechuelo, 'Role of the Chinese', pp. 192–193.

31. M.L. Diaz-Trechuelo, 'The Economic Background', in A. Felix Jr. (ed.), *The Chinese in the Philippines*, vol. 2, Manila, Solidaridad Publishing House, 1969, pp. 19, 23.

32. Diaz-Trechuelo, 'Economic Background', pp. 23, 32.

33. J.M. de Zuñiga, *Status of the Philippines in 1800*, Manila, Publications of the Filipiniana Book Guild xxi, 1973, pp. 233–234.

34. Zuñiga, *Status of the Philippines*, p. 268.

35. T. de Comyn, *State of the Philippines in 1810*, Manila, Filipiniana Book Guild, 1969, p. 37.

36. J. Merino, 'The Chinese Mestizo: General Considerations', in Felix, *The Chinese II*, pp. 61–63.

37. Wickberg, 'The Chinese Mestizo', pp. 75–76, 85.

38. Zuñiga, *Status of the Philippines*, p. 210; Diaz-Trechuelo, 'Economic Background', pp. 19, 36.

39. Merino, 'The Chinese Mestizo', pp. 53–55.

40. L.L. Greenow, 'Spatial Dimensions of the Credit Market in Eighteenth Century Nueva Galicia', in D.J. Robinson (ed.), *Social Fabric and Spatial Structure in Colonial Latin America*, Ann Arbor, University of Michigan, 1979, p. 276; Wickberg, *The Chinese*, pp. 16, 191–192.

41. Phelan, *Hispanization of the Philippines*, p. 78.

42. *Ibid.*, pp. 35, 38.

43. Greenow, 'Spatial Dimensions', pp. 234–235.

44. Comyn, *State of the Philippines*, pp. 108–113.

45. Greenow, 'Spatial Dimensions', pp. 242–243.

46. Comyn, *State of the Philippines*, p. 153.

47. *Ibid.*, p. 40; Zuñiga, *Status of the Philippines*, p. 215.

48. Comyn, *State of the Philippines*, pp. 39–40; Schurz, *Manila Galleon*, pp. 45, 167–169.

49. 'Bishop Salazar's Report', p. 129.

50. Phelan, *Hispanization of the Philippines*, pp. 72–73; Wickberg, *The Chinese*, pp. 178, 193.

51. Comyn, *State of the Philippines*, p. 145; Wickberg, 'The Chinese Mestizo', pp. 72–73.

52. Zuñiga, *Status of the Philippines*, p. 62; see also Roth, 'Church Lands', p. 145.

53. Zuñiga, *Status of the Philippines*, pp. 258, 276–277, 294, 299, 339.

54. *Ibid.*, p. 67.

55. 'Internal political condition of the Philippines, 1842', *BR* 52, p. 64.

56. Zuñiga, *Status of the Philippines*, pp. 38–41, 362–363.

57. Larkin, *Sugar and Philippine Society*, p. 43.

58. *Ibid.*, p. 1.

59. *Ibid.*, p. 24; J.A. Larkin, *The Pampangans. Colonial Society in a Philippine Province*, Berkeley/Los Angeles, University of California Press, 1972, pp. 47–48.

60. Larkin, *Pampangans*, p. 73.

61. *Ibid.*, pp. 48–52, 74; Larkin, *Sugar and Philippine Society*, pp. 27, 33–34.

62. Larkin, *Pampangans*, pp. 52–56, 74; Larkin, *Sugar and Philippine Society*, pp. 30–33, 35; for a further discussion see N.G. Owen, 'The Principalia in Philippine History: Kabikolan, 1790–1898', *Philippine Studies* 22 (1974), pp. 297–324.

63. Larkin, *Pampangans*, pp. 55–56; Larkin, *Sugar and Philippine Society*, p. 35.

64. Larkin, *Pampangans*, p. 73.

65. M. Cullinane, 'The Changing Nature of the Cebu Urban Elite in the 19th Century' in McCoy and Jesus (eds), *Philippine Social History*, p. 255; Wickberg, 'The Chinese Mestizo', p. 74.

66. Cullinane, 'Cebu Urban Elite', pp. 257–262; Zuñiga, *Status of the Philippines*, p. 434.

67. Cullinane, 'Cebu Urban Elite', pp. 257–258; Zuñiga, *Status of the Philippines*, p. 434.

68. Cullinane, 'Cebu Urban Elite', p. 260.

69. *Ibid.*, p. 282.

70. *Ibid.*, p. 282–283.

71. *Ibid.*, pp. 258–259.

72. A.W. McCoy, 'A Queen Dies Slowly: The Rise and Decline of Iloilo City', in McCoy and Jesus (eds), *Philippine Social History*, pp. 301–303.

73. J. Bowring, *The Philippine Islands*, London, Smith, Elder and Co., 1859, p. 396.

74. *Ibid.*, p. 397.

75. *Ibid.*, pp. 114–115.

76. *Ibid.*, pp. 115, 400–401.

77. Simmel, 'The Stranger', p. 404.

78. R.E. Park, 'Human Migration and the Marginal Man', *American Journal of Sociology* 32, no. 6 (1928), pp. 881–893.

79. Loycke, *Der Gast*, p. 113.

80. E.V. Stonequist, *The Marginal Man. A Study in Personality and Culture Conflict*, New York, Russell and Russell, 1961. The relationship between Simmel, Park and Stonequist is discussed in D.N. Levine, 'Simmel at a Distance: On the History and Systematics of the Sociology of the Stranger', in D. Frisby (ed.), *Georg Simmel. Critical Assessments*, vol. 3, London and New York, Routledge, 1994, pp. 174–177. It is often forgotten that, before Stonequist met Park, his interest in the subject was aroused in 1925 on hearing a lecture by the British colonial administrator, Lord Lugard, on the effects of European ideas and practices on indigenous life in Africa: Stonequist, *Marginal Man*, p. vii.

81. *Ibid.*, p. 3.

82. *Ibid.*, p. 4.

83. *Ibid.*, p. 145.

84. *Ibid.*, p. 146.

85. *Ibid.*, p. 218.

86. *Ibid.*, p. 156.

87. *Ibid.*, pp. 216–217.

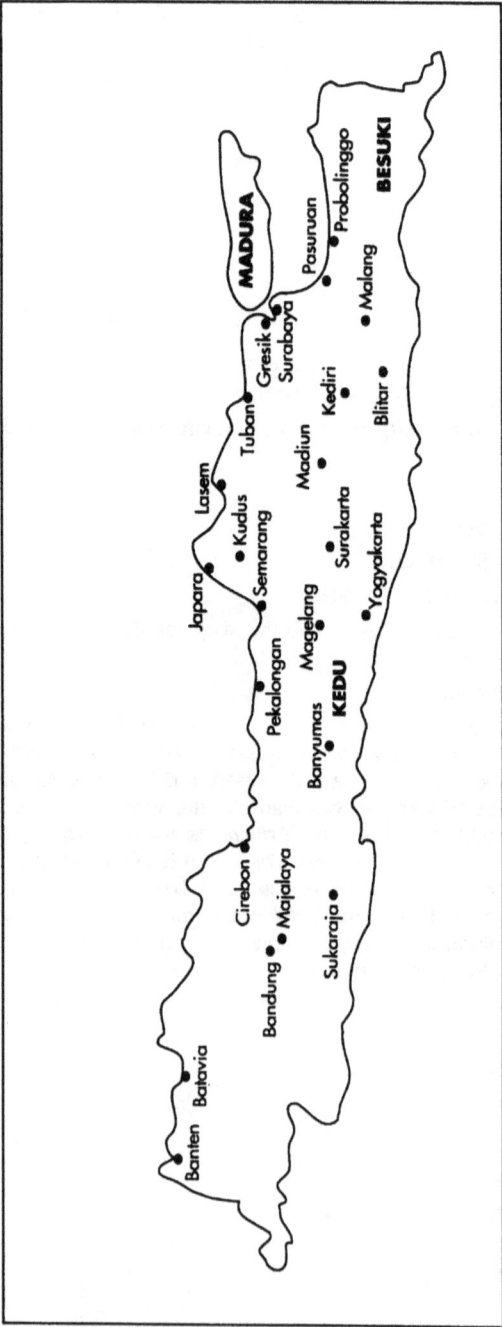

Map 3: Java c. 1900

Batavia and the Peranakan Chinese
1619–1870

When in May 1619 the Dutch entered into occupation of the town in West Java they called Batavia they found that the local population, with the exception of a small Chinese community, had fled. The port had its origin in the twelfth century and it owed its rise as a colonial city to the Dutch East India Company's need for an administrative headquarters in the Indonesian archipelago where ships could be built and repaired, goods could be stored, provisions acquired and local intelligence obtained.[1] To keep the settlement functioning in every respect the Dutch were required to follow Manila's example and attract Chinese residents. The first Dutch Governor-General, Jan Pieterszoon Coen, returned often in his letters to the success of Manila and the way in which that city was able to profit from its Chinese inhabitants.[2] Coen used every means possible to persuade the Chinese to leave neighbouring Banten, where they were active in pepper-growing and in the pepper trade; he highly prized their usefulness to the Company as artisans for building the new town and he wanted to ensure that Chinese junks coming to Java from the north used Batavia as their terminus.[3]

Chinese had been settled on the north coast of Java from at least the fourteenth century, with important colonies at Surabaya, Gresik and Tuban. By the late sixteenth century their most important locality was Banten. A large number of Chinese settlers were converted to Islam. Having come largely from Fujian, they not only found it advantageous to adopt the predominant religion of the Javanese port towns, but in fact were familiar with the role of Islam in Fujian's trade. In Quanzhou, Fujian's most important seaport by the late thirteenth century, both trade and administration were dominated by foreign Muslims and an Islamic diaspora promoted trade with the rest of Asia.[4] Immigrants coming to Java from Fujian were acculturated to the need to change identity in the course of trade, and this preadaptation was to their advantage as they later evolved into a special type of indigenous community on Java.

Coen's policy towards the Chinese bore fruit. He gradually planned that the Company should reserve to itself the position of wholesale dealer, whilst the Chinese should monopolize retail trade. Further they were to assist the settlement as artisans, agriculturalists, gardeners and fishermen. Unlike the Spaniards at Manila, with their background in the policies of the *reconquista*, the Dutch did not place the Chinese in a separate settlement. Although they built a fortress to act as the headquarters of the Company, they chose to live with the Chinese in one city, left their religion unhindered and cooperated with them in a manner different from that of the Spaniards. The Chinese population of Batavia, 400 in 1619, increased to 2,000 in 1629 and reached 10,000 after 1725.[5]

Chinese Commercial Society 1619–1740

After Coen's time East India Company policy towards the Chinese remained consistent for a considerable period. There was a certain mistrust of the Javanese; very few Javanese lived in the city, and the need for Chinese was so great that major efforts were made to increase their numbers. These policies included the granting of trade advantages and generous offers of credit. As the Spaniards had experienced, it was gradually found that large numbers of Chinese were arriving in the city whom it was difficult to accommodate or remove because the junks on which they came were highly desired. The failure of Dutch attempts to trade on the China coast made it desirable that Chinese junks carrying tea should terminate at Batavia, but without leaving behind too many settlers.[6] Less clearly expressed than by the Spaniards, Dutch policy after the 1660s also came to conceive of an optimal number of 'necessary' Chinese.

This number of 'necessary' Chinese came to be carefully calculated in the mid-eighteenth century. By the 1720s and 1730s most newcomers were going to the agricultural areas surrounding Batavia (ommelanden) and to the northeast coast or to Banten. Since the influx could not be halted, measures such as shop regulation were commenced against existing Chinese on the premise that only those of use for the trade of the colony should remain. Chinese in the agricultural areas were pursued for their residence permits, leading to their well-known 1740 rebellion and the subsequent European massacre of approximately 10,000 Chinese in Batavia and elsewhere. After the massacre it was found impossible to replace the Chinese. They were severely missed as provisioners of the city, especially of rice; their sugar exports were severely injured, the Company's cloth imports could not be sold for suitable prices and old ships, usually sold to Chinese, could not be disposed of. There was considerable fear that Chinese junks would not return.[7]

Chinese required for shops were almost immediately allowed back into the city and in March 1742 the government set in train an inquiry into how many Chinese were necessary for the sugar mills and arak distilleries in the lands surrounding Batavia and for other trades. On 1 August 1742 it was reported that the colony needed 5,934 Chinese, and a long list of trades in which they were required was appended.[8] These Chinese, however, were to live outside the city and, although this prohibition was later relaxed, most Chinese did not return to the city until the 1790s. Ultimately, as a result of this confirmation that the colony could not do without the Chinese, their position in Batavia and elsewhere became stronger, leading to a considerable Chinese economic expansion in the late eighteenth century. By 1814 they formed one-quarter of Batavia's population, comprising 11,854 out of 47,217 inhabitants.[9]

The Chinese community in Batavia contained from the early days of collaboration with the Dutch an upper stratum of elite merchants. But the majority of the community, as in contemporary Manila, practised a variety of occupations that made them useful to Europeans. Francois Valentijn, writing at the turn of the eighteenth century, gave high praise to the services of the Batavia Chinese. As well as running the import trade in tea, porcelain and silk goods, they were extremely impressive artisans, working as smiths, carpenters and makers of numerous domestic articles such as sunshades. They also distilled arak, dealt with the sugar coming from the sugar land around Batavia, ran revenue farms and made bricks. They ran tea-houses, fished, controlled water transport, unloaded ships and cultivated the entire agricultural area surrounding Batavia.

> There is nothing one can conceive of that they are not capable
> of undertaking and which they do not practise ... Were the
> Chinese not here, Batavia would be completely lifeless and
> lacking in many necessities.[10]

A 1742 report tallied the number of Chinese in Batavia at 3,431, including 1,442 merchants and traders, 935 farmers, gardeners, lime-burners and arak distillers, 728 sugar-millers and timber-cutters and 326 craftsmen.[11] By the turn of the eighteenth century the impression given was that nothing could happen in Batavia without the Chinese, not even the building of a church or digging of a canal. In addition to what has been mentioned already, they performed a variety of auxiliary services. On the one hand they were there to help if the Company wished to dispose of damaged or spoilt goods; on the other, if certain goods had to be acquired from Banten or Central Java, it was the Chinese who had the contacts to do it.[12]

While the whole settlement of Chinese may have been considered 'necessary' by the Dutch, the leading merchants among them existed in a symbiotic relationship to Dutch trade in the archipelago and beyond. Initially the Batavian mercantile elite consisted of individuals who had prospered in the pepper trade at Banten by processing pepper for the Company and who followed the Dutch to Batavia. They were immediately put on their feet financially by the servants of the East India

Company. In 1623 it was reported that Lim Lacco, an important merchant from Banten, had arrived in Batavia having lost everything and asked for money and cloth with which to trade, promising to increase commercial activity at Batavia. He was given 400 rials, together with 600 rials in cloth. Three years earlier So Bing Kong and Jan Con, arriving from Banten, were given 600 rials in cloth, and other Chinese merchants on whom great commercial hopes were pinned were treated likewise. This practice continued, Governor-General van Diemen in 1639 issuing a firm order that henceforth credit should be offered to a limited group of thirteen Chinese merchants, up to a maximum of 2,000 rials per person in the case of the two most prominent.[13]

The business interests of this Chinese commercial elite became more and more intertwined with the private business interests of the Company's servants. In addition they served directly the official interests of the East India Company. Their commercial activities were extensive, but in particular they comprised the China junk trade, revenue-farming and the sugar-milling industry. By the late sixteenth century Banten had become the most important terminus on Java for junks coming from South China for pepper and to sell goods in what was an important stapling place for traders originating in the Indian Ocean, the South China Sea and the Indonesian archipelago. Batavia was founded to be accessible to the Chinese junks and the use of Chinese merchants from Banten to act as a lure for the junks was an important aspect of policy. Once the trade was established, each year about five to eight junks came, carrying Chinese commodities destined for the Java market including silk fabrics, sugar, porcelain, iron pans, nails, needles and coarse textiles. Later on tea became a valuable commodity. The return cargo was initially pepper.[14]

The first merchant we know of to have collaborated closely with the early East India Company Governors-General is So Bing Kong, who was already trading successfully at Batavia when Coen arrived and who became Coen's confidante and adviser. He was probably born in about 1580 in Fujian and it is likely that he originally traded at Banten and acquired enough Malay or Portuguese to do business with both Europeans and Indonesians. Once in Batavia, Bing Kong's commercial activities continued to centre on the pepper trade which he carried on together with members of his family, including a brother who had remained in China. The family had a network of partners not only at Batavia but also at Banten, where the Chinese community remained powerful, in Sumatra where the pepper was bought, and in Taiwan, where Bing Kong owned land. His junks also visited Annam, and he seemed to have a 'regional' commercial vision which included Japan and Siam. In 1636, in fact, he left Batavia for Taiwan probably hoping to bring about direct trade between that island and Batavia. He also planned to promote the cultivation of rice and other crops among the Chinese immigrants there, and perhaps found his own trading house. As part of this endeavour, he made efforts to bring in poor Chinese from Fujian for the cultivation of sugar in addition to rice, and he opened up a trading link with Annam. None of these endeavours was very successful, and he returned to Batavia in 1639. Once returned, he continued to play an invaluable role to successive Governors-General, especially in ensuring that the Dutch retained some of the benefits of the Banten trade. He lived in a superb house just south of the Dutch castle, gave great feasts for his Dutch friends and possessed, in addition, other houses, jewels and slaves.[15]

From the beginning the Dutch at Batavia followed the archipelago entrepôt tradition of appointing headmen to take responsibility for their compatriots. On 11 October 1619 Coen wrote that the 400 Chinese in Batavia required someone over them to answer for their good order and to perform police functions.[16] So Bing Kong was appointed to this position, which in 1625 was officially entitled 'captain'.[17] So arose the Chinese officer system – gradually the titles of lieutenant and major were added as numbers grew – the members of which represented the elite of the Chinese mercantile community, first in Batavia and later in other major cities such as Semarang and Surabaya where the Dutch took up formal rule. In the early days at Batavia, recognizing the importance of the captain as an intermediary with the China fleet, the major traders with the junks were involved in the choice of a captain and sometimes even the arriving junk captains had their say. All the officers were apparently from the Hokkien-speaking area of Fujian, the region around Amoy and, by the end of the seventeenth century, the Chinese mercantile elite of Batavia had gained a permanent lien on these offices so that in some cases they were even inherited.[18]

For this Chinese elite to consolidate its position it was recognized that the junk trade was not altogether a secure proposition. From the very beginning the Dutch followed an existing local tradition of involving the Chinese in their city's finances, by farming out different government monopolies or rights to them under the 'monopoly lease-system'. So Bing Kong from the outset began to acquire Dutch revenue farms, starting with the gambling farm in 1620. Bing Kong's friend, Jan Con, joined with him to fulfil the requirements of the gambling farm. He too was born in China, had come from Banten to Batavia where he had been supplying the East India Company with pepper, and had made the decision to expand his interests in the cause of financial security. In 1622 he won new tax farms on incoming and outgoing local products such as Sumatran camphor.[19]

Their position as revenue farmers gave the Chinese elite a certain influence with the Dutch. The government was always required to be conciliatory towards the farmers and, indeed, so many items were farmed that the existing farmers had to be consulted about new ones. The Chinese were agreeable to the Company in this function as they were prepared to bid high sums at farm auctions. By the end of the seventeenth century there was a bewildering variety of revenue farms, not all continuous, such as incoming duties on rice, outgoing duties on sugar and pepper, farms for the distilling and sale of arak, the market tax, salt manufacture and sale, road tolls and river crossings. These tax farms followed the Dutch penetration of Java. The lease for buying up all local produce in a certain district, the lease of particular villages, and the market lease led to associates of the main tax farmers gradually commanding much of the intermediate trade of all Java.[20]

The third economic interest of Batavia's Chinese elite was the one in which they most showed their entrepreneurial spirit. This was the cultivation of sugar cane, the manufacture of sugar and the distilling of arak. Denys Lombard calls Chinese ventures in this field, 'industrial agriculture'.[21] The Chinese sugar and arak industries already existed at Batavia prior to 1619 and the Dutch very early on proved keen to assist their Chinese collaborators in this enterprise. Jan Con was given a lease of land outside the city in 1638 on the condition that he planted nothing but sugar cane and the second captain of the Chinese in the city, Bingam, possessed extensive sugar fields. Succeeding Chinese officers right up to 1740 held numerous sugar estates. Captain Limkeenqua was given a licence in 1699 to erect two sugar mills on his land outside Batavia, and his successor was given land to erect mills. Ni Hoe Kong, appointed captain in 1736, had about fourteen mills on his estates, which he had inherited from his father. Chinese lieutenants, too, possessed sugar estates and these and the mills were also associated with arak distilleries.[22]

Although junks came to Batavia from Guangdong, by far the largest number were from south Fujian, and it is with the evolving Hokkien community in Java that we shall be dealing. The pioneers of the sugar industry certainly seem to have been from south Fujian. The cultivation of sugar and the management of sugar mills were mostly undertaken by poor Chinese with credit from rich Chinese merchants at Batavia, from whom they hired the mills. About 200 workmen per factory were required, of whom about sixty were usually Chinese, so that in 1710 when 131 mills were operating in the rural districts surrounding Batavia no fewer than 7,000 Chinese found work. The busiest time of the year was March to May, as the sugar was required to be ready for the departure of the China junks at the end of June or early July. The success of this industry was another example of the cooperation between the Company and the Chinese mercantile elite, as sugar cultivation was sedulously fostered on orders from the Netherlands and equally adopted by the Chinese for their own customers.[23]

Considerable capital was required for the buildings and equipment on the sugar estates. The mill itself was very simple, consisting as it did of two cylinders of wood which ground on one another by being turned by two buffaloes. The cane was pressed between these cylinders to obtain the maximum amount of juice. On a sizeable estate fourteen carts, each drawn by one buffalo, took the cane twice a day to the mill to be pressed. In a period of twenty-four hours, a further thirty-two buffaloes were required to turn the mill. Finally, payment had to be made to the sugar refineries in the Chinese areas of Batavia where the crystallized brown sugar was brought.[24] Further capital was required for the exclusively Chinese arak distilleries, the industry being closely associated with sugar cultivation because molasses was the main raw material for the preparation of this alcoholic drink, which also contained fermented rice. In 1712 there were twelve arak distilleries in the environs of Batavia.[25]

The 1740 rebellion took place largely on the sugar lands and in 1750 only sixty-six sugar mills were still left in the area surrounding Batavia. However, both sugar and arak remained strong pillars of Batavia's trade,[26] and we shall return to sugar's role in Chinese commercial life after addressing the question of changing Chinese identity which we also looked at in relation to the Chinese of Manila.

The Formation of a Peranakan Identity

In 1698 Governor-General van Outhoorn wrote from Batavia with pride: 'Nowhere in Asia has the Honourable Company proceeded to hinder men from the free practice of the religion they profess or are accustomed to.'[27] Dutch religious policy could not have been more different from that of the Spaniards at Manila, and yet a similar result arose in the sense that a Chinese community with a unique identity evolved even where no policy to alter their identity existed. This community, comprising individuals who were originally Hokkien Chinese together with their families arising from intermarriage with local women and from internal marriage within the community, came to be called peranakan (literally, child of the country). Conversion to Islam continued, but the peranakan community was not usually thought of as a Muslim one; it adhered rather to versions of south China folk religion together with local pre-Islamic beliefs. By the nineteenth century it was the peranakans who dominated the Chinese community in Java and, while by then they had become more consolidated as a group, it is important to trace their origins back to the earliest Chinese interactions with the Dutch.

It is among the Chinese officers of Batavia that it is possible to see the early origins of this peranakan community because we know that many of their wives were not Chinese. The children born of these unions were markedly useful to the Dutch because of their knowledge of languages. The officers themselves, however, continued to retain strong ties with China. Even by the mid-eighteenth century individuals who were born in China reached the rank of captain and others returned to China late in life or had children or brothers living there.[28] By 1740, however, there was a recognized peranakan community living in Batavia with new Hokkien immigrants regularly absorbed into it.[29]

The characteristics of this community can only be observed by piecing together a variety of sources, some of them of a later date. However, as with the Philippines, it is necessary to complement the research available with material from two other ports and adjacent areas, in this case Semarang and Surabaya. In 1678 Semarang and the surrounding lands and villages were made over to the Dutch East India Company by the Sultan of Mataram in Central Java. Hitherto the Company had maintained a number of fortified trading posts in the main north-coast towns such as Pekalongan, Japara and Semarang, but from this time it extended its political and military power over an ever-widening area of Central Java and along the northeast coast. A study of Cirebon, between Semarang and Batavia, between 1680 and 1710, indicates an important distinction between the peranakan and Chinese inhabitants. While the Chinese were marked by their entrepreneurial activities, including sugar-milling and commerce in general, the peranakan were active in the administration, serving various branches of the royal family as ministers, and marked by their appointment to key administrative posts.[30]

This distinction between *totok* (full-blood) Chinese and peranakan Chinese is not valid all along the north coast. In the Semarang region, for example, the growing peranakan community was overwhelmed by the large-scale Chinese immigration of the late eighteenth century and there the Chinese elite was *totok*,[31] although related to the Batavia officer class by intermarriage.[32] They too mixed commerce with proto-industrial activity. The Company, unsuited to small-scale trade in local markets such as obtained on Java's north coast, and anxious to import their most important product, Indian textiles, made use of the burgeoning class of Chinese traders of all ranks after 1680 in order to reach their customers. In addition to the Chinese trade network which grew up in this area, Chinese with capital were very active in the sugar industry, which was particularly concentrated in the hands of the Chinese officers of Semarang and certain other towns and which reached a considerable level of development by the early eighteenth century.[33]

But peranakan entrepreneurial dynasties were also developing a little later in this period. Claudine Salmon has investigated the history of the Han family which was involved in sugar production in East Java.[34] About 1700 Han Siong Kong left Zhangzhou prefecture in Fujian, settled in Lasem and married a non-Chinese wife. Of his five sons, one became a Muslim and married a Javanese, while others married peranakan wives. One son became captain of Surabaya and also a leaseholder of land in East Java, delivering rice and money to the Company in the 1760s and 1770s. These leases descended to the next generation and in 1796 the Dutch granted one of Han Siong Kong's grandsons, Han Chan Piet, exclusive rights to certain districts in Besuki Residency for life. Subsequently in 1810 the districts were sold to him. These land grants led to considerable entrepreneurial activities on the part of members of the Han family. From 1799 Han Kik Ko, the brother of Han Chan Piet, was one of the pioneers of the sugar industry in East Java, particularly after the Dutch, in 1810, sold the district of Probolinggo in Pasuruan Residency to him. Other members of the family owned estates in East Java on which they grew, in addition to sugar-cane, rice, indigo, maize, coconut palms and other crops. They also developed tracts of land rented on long-lease contracts entered into with the government, which hoped to promote the production of sugar and, to a lesser extent, coffee and indigo. In the nineteenth century the Han family members also expanded to other towns in East Java near where plantations were being developed. Their main achievements resulted from ability to respond to the economic policies of their colonial rulers and, as a result, they produced an extraordinary number of officers in Surabaya, Gresik, Pasuruan, Kediri, Probolinggo and elsewhere and, marrying their daughters into other economically successful families in East Java, to some extent created a new elite based on economic assets.

As the eighteenth century passed, however, the peranakan elite became associated in particular with revenue farming and with one revenue farm in particular, that of opium, the largest and most lucrative of Java's farms. In these farms both the *cabang atas* (literally 'upper branch') peranakan elite could be accommodated, together with hordes of poorer clients who fanned out over Java as the requirements of revenue-raising dictated. The development of the *cabang atas* elite has been carefully documented by James Rush. The Dutch opium monopoly in Java began in 1688 as an outcome of a political settlement with the Javanese kingdoms. The main features changed over time, but in essence leading merchants would compete at public auction for opium farm leases that gave them a monopoly for the manufacture and sale of opium in a territory defined by the government. Huge sums were bid for this privilege and the returns to government were therefore also considerable. Ties between the elite were strengthened because it was generally necessary for a bidder to pool capital with others in a *kongsi* or Chinese commercial society. Sometimes the *kongsi* was confined to members of an extended family, although trusted associates could also be included; the idea being to maximize the use of joint capital, generally on a short-term basis. Each member of the *kongsi* would then have a particular share in the financial responsibilities and profits of the farm. *Kongsis* formed the basic principle of Chinese commercial life.[35] Writing in another context at the beginning of the nineteenth century, Raffles noted:

> If a cargo arrives too extensive for the finances of one individual, several Chinese club together, and purchase goods, each dividing according to his capital. In this manner a ready market is always open at Java, without the assistance of European merchants, and strangers are enabled to transact their business with little trouble or risk.[36]

The *cabang atas* peranakan elite who successfully bid for the most lucrative farms acquired the patronage and prestige that went with them. They were usually also involved in other enterprises, and the most prominent from the latter part of the eighteenth century were also appointed by the government as Chinese officers, thus cementing their ties with the colonial state. By the nineteenth century they were a clearly recognizable class, tied together by marriage alliances but porous enough to admit newcomers, who could often advance with amazing rapidity. Their wealth was exhibited to the public; in Semarang, for example, they lived in adjacent family compounds with luxurious houses surrounded by elaborate Chinese-style gardens. Feasts and parties were common, but the endowment of charitable institutions and temples was not forgotten. The basis of the system rested on huge Chinese commercial networks that dominated practically all non-European economic activity in Java. This peranakan diaspora funnelled Asian and European goods, money and credit into the villages, whilst extracting from them rice and other agricultural crops. Opium farms were central to these networks, and the leaseholders of the farms could virtually control commercial activity in a broad arena; competition for an opium farm, therefore, meant competition for access to Java's retail trade and agricultural markets.[37]

Rush has explained how the *cabang atas* was made up of what he calls a network of peranakan constellations. The Be-

Tan family group, for example, comprised the two most powerful families in Central Java in the nineteenth century; they were
based on Semarang, where now peranakans had replaced full-
blood Chinese both economically and as political allies of the
Dutch through the officer system. Using figures a little beyond
our period, in the farm term of 1887–89 three such groups
controlled, at the outset, thirteen of Java's twenty opium farms.
The Be-Tan group held four farms, whilst the so-called Kediri
kongsi held another four. Each of these constellations had one,
and usually more, Chinese officer members. The constellations
represented only the apex of extensive social and economic
networks, where numerous personal investments and business
activities intertwined in the struggle for dominance of commercial life in as wide a region as might be available.[38]

The wealth of these peranakan constellations financed the
enterprise of many. In addition to their opium farms, the constellations controlled other government revenue farms, commercial agricultural ventures and proto-industrial endeavours.
Each of these gave employment both to long-settled peranakan
and to newly arriving Chinese. The farms – particularly those
for opium and the market tax – permitted clients of the constellations to penetrate the countryside without defiance of
government regulations. As employees of a revenue farmer,
Chinese lived and moved freely outside of the officially
designated neighbourhoods. In 1850 it was estimated that
some 14,000 Chinese lived in Java's interior due to the market
farm – abolished in 1851 – and another 10,656 manned opium
shops. Their presence enabled them to buy up surplus produce
and to import desired items into the villages. As the client
traders penetrated to the heart of rural Java, their networks
strengthened the constellation as a whole and also its dominant
patrons.[39] From their initial collaboration with the Dutch
monopoly lease system in 1619, Chinese – and particularly
peranakan Chinese – came to dominate the entire economy of
Java. Raffles noted at the turn of the nineteenth century:

> Almost all the inland commerce is under the direction of the
> Chinese, who possessing considerable capital, and frequently
> speculating on a very extensive scale, engross the greater part

of the wholesale trade, buy up the principal articles of export
from the native grower, convey them to the maritime capitals,
and in return supply the interior with salt, and with the principal articles imported from the neighbouring islands, or from
foreign countries. The industry of the Javans being directed
almost exclusively to the cultivation of the soil, they are satisfied if they can find an immediate market for their surplus produce; and the Chinese, from their superior wealth and
enterprize, offering them this advantage without interfering
with their habits, have obtained almost a monopoly of their
produce, and an uncontrolled command of their market for
foreign commodities.[40]

But the peranakan in the countryside generally owed his
commercial success to the entrepreneurial abilities of particular
families whose economic advancement continued for several
generations. The Han of East Java, with their agricultural
innovations, were not atypical. The Tan dynasty of Semarang
was founded by Tan Bing, who migrated there with very little
in the late 1700s. After engaging in petty trade he amassed
enough capital to start his own shop and, when this venture
was successful, he leased the teak-cutting concession and,
later, the lucrative salt monopoly. Like many entrepreneurial
Chinese in Java he then moved into sugar-milling, sold his
refined sugar to markets throughout Central Java and,
eventually, created shipping connections with Batavia, Cirebon
and Surabaya. His son, Tan Tiang Tjhing, later took over his
various enterprises and ultimately expanded to hold the three
most lucrative revenue farms in Java: opium, salt and markets.
This first-generation peranakan was politically allied to the
Dutch by accepting the position of Chinese lieutenant in 1809.
Subsequently, in 1829, he became the first major of Semarang,
whilst ultimately his three sons were all appointed lieutenants
and one of them rose to the position of major. Three sons of
the latter and his two sons-in-law became lieutenants, making
nine officers in three generations of one family. Tan Tiang
Tjhing's business interests eventually included sugar, warehousing and shipping in addition to the market and opium
farms. His son Tan Hong Yan succeeded his father as opium
farmer for all of Central Java, as well as to official positions.[41]

While peranakan economic activities are transparent in many cases, the nature of peranakan identity – at least before the twentieth century – is more obscure. In Batavia and Semarang at least, we know that they maintained their connection with South China folk religion, and this will be discussed more extensively. The activities of the Tan family of Semarang show considerable patronage of religion. In 1837 Tan Hong Yan had a special structure built next to the major temple of the community, the Tay Kak Sie. This new building was given the name Tjie Lam Tjay, meaning 'guidance office', its purpose being to supervise temples and religious affairs, including graveyards. In 1845 Tan, together with other peranakan *cabang atas*, took the initiative in building the Kong Tik Soe next to the main Tay Kak Sie temple. The temple had the double purpose of permitting worship of the ancestor tablets of the major contributors, whilst at the same time performing certain charitable works on behalf of the disadvantaged in the community. In 1814 the Tan family had built its own temple as a shrine for the family ancestor tablets, and this was the largest temple in Semarang.[42]

This maintenance of a temple culture by the peranakan was rare outside the main north coast cities.[43] But nevertheless the peranakans – particularly those in urban areas – remained Chinese in their social identification, retaining their Chinese names and interlocking their own desire to succeed in business with the business abilities of the Javanese women they married. Elements of local culture which they did adopt included language, which was the Malay of the north-coast cities of Java, long used for trade.[44] They were assisted in maintaining their unique identity by the establishment of a 'quota' system for the Chinese in the interior after the 1740 uprising, whereby they had officially approved centres in which to live when carrying on commercial activities in even the most remote parts of Java.[45] Furthermore, peranakan culture was highly absorptive. Because of the patronage networks centring on the *cabang atas* constellations, many new Hokkien immigrants were quickly able to find humble tasks and possibly to rise rapidly based on recognized trustworthiness. Talent and enterprise found its best outlet by assimilating to peranakan culture and achieving social and economic mobility within it.[46] The culture accepted and indeed collaborated with Dutch authority and its status system recognized the commercially successful as standing at its apex.

G.W. Skinner argues that the formative stage of peranakan culture in the major cities of Java's north coast ended in the 1780s. During the century following, 'traditional' peranakan culture changed little, maintaining itself as a distinctive integrated whole in no sense resembling 'Indonesianization', to which newcomers rapidly assimilated.[47] But much of this culture remains unknown to us and we are left with Dutch accounts which distinguish the rural peranakans quite distinctly, and unfavourably, from all other Chinese on Java:

> The *pranakans*, or children of Chinese fathers and native mothers born in Java, are generally of an inferior nature to those born in China, and among them one encounters many individuals of a second-rate type. They do not buy up lands and establish themselves in the interior, because they possess a much lesser degree of energy than their progenitors; if one does encounter affluent individuals among them, they have usually their property by inheritance, as they are not capable of raising themselves above the middle classes by their own efforts.[48]

Business Confidence: Preadaptation and the Role of Religion

Much of the economic success of the Chinese on Java can of course be attributed to their relationship with the Dutch. But in many ways they were also preadapted to this success. Since most of the Hokkien Chinese on Java came from the same Quanzhou-Zhangzhou region near Amoy in Fujian province as did their compatriots in Luzon, much of what is said here is also applicable to the Manila situation.

The inhabitants of south Fujian lived on a series of rather infertile coastal plains intersected by fast-flowing rivers and cut off from the hinterland by mountains. Occupationally, they were obliged to turn to exports to survive, their most prominent products being agricultural crops like sugar and tea and industrial exports such as textiles, iron goods and porcelain. In return they imported rice. The period from the sixteenth to the eighteenth centuries saw a growing trend to commercialization and, at the same time, an increasing stress on the organization of lineages. These were common patrilineal descent groups of people bearing the same surname, although families of the same surname did not necessarily belong to the same lineage.

These lineages, which were frequently organized for maritime trade, developed fierce rivalry. Using capital derived originally from land, they needed an ample supply of 'trade assistants', which gave rise to a new custom in Fujian, that of adopting foster children. Adoption could be from any suitable source, including non-kin, and these adopted sons would be sent abroad at their maturity on commercial enterprises. If successful, they would marry into the family that had originally adopted them. The porous nature of the lineage is reminiscent of the porous nature of the *cabang atas* constellations on Java. The lineage was flexible in another way. To strengthen a lineage's bargaining position in a locality, the fiction of a pseudo-lineage was established so that people belonging to the same surname were usually regarded as members of the same lineage. There were struggles within the lineage for scarce resources and also competition for prestige among several lineages in one locality.[49] As these developments apply to Java, what is remarkable is the flexibility of the system, and this must be partly responsible at least for the way in which peranakan society was easily able to absorb Hokkien newcomers.

Another commercial advantage which the south Fujianese possessed in their new homelands was their readiness to integrate into a new society. At the turn of the eighteenth century the Fujianese had already become the major operators of the Amoy coastal trading network. By the early eighteenth century they were well established at Ningbo and gradually also in Shanghai and Tianjin, and here they were characterized by a strong tendency to local involvement. They were prepared to merge with the social and economic networks of the host city and in Shanghai, for example, many Fujianese were regarded as having 'become native people', enabling them to penetrate local networks in most business circles.[50]

Finally, Fujianese were preadapted to economic development in Java in particular because of the part they were playing in the opening up of the Taiwan sugar frontier. Massive migrations from the Quanzhou-Zhangzou area to Taiwan had already begun in the early seventeenth century and, by about 1700, some 20 per cent of this region's population was residing in Taiwan. Due to scarcity of land Fujian's agricultural exports, primarily sugar, were not able to satisfy the demands of the coastal shipping trade. From the 1660s sugar became a major Taiwan export; in addition to Chinese junks, the Dutch East India Company was involved, selling sugar to India, Persia and even Europe.

Various forms of credit developed in Taiwan, and we have later accounts of similar financial institutions in Java. Settlers of low socioeconomic status developed rotating credit pools to which each member contributed a fixed amount of money at a certain time. The pooled total was then available for bidding among members, and small economic ventures could thus be started. The practice developed in the 1660s when new settlers were very much in need of capital to grasp new opportunities.[51] Information and institutions from the Taiwan sugar frontier, which expanded enormously in the early eighteenth century, undoubtedly passed to Java.

In addition to their preadaptation to economic success in Java, Hokkien migrants possessed much in the way of what we would now call business confidence. Industry, frugality and hard work can be taken for granted; but business confidence requires the ability to sum up a situation, interpret it in terms of business success, and adapt behaviour to the situation to turn it to a business advantage.[52] Business decisions are about future consequences of present actions and, of necessity, deal in uncertainty, action being therefore based on interpretation rather than precision, with limited relevant information and precise calculation made difficult. The root of investment action is therefore not rational calculation but uncertainty mediated by a feeling of confidence.[53]

While the Chinese mestizos of Luzon acquired much of their business confidence from the knowledge that they had access to credit mediated through the Church, the Hokkien Chinese of Java gained theirs from the possibility of a common action based on a collective life centring on associations which were social, economic and religious. Denys Lombard speaks, in this connection, of *homo associativus*, the Chinese in Java being organized at varying times in clan associations, regional associations, professional associations, associations for social security, associations to assist new immigrants and so on.[54] Each of these associations made provision for ritual worship, and from this worship concrete rewards were believed to be obtainable. Confidence, then, comes not from the individual but, as Durkheim expressed it, from the 'collective consciousness'. At ritual worship carried out in periodic reunions, members of a community unify their common faith by manifesting it in common.[55] The individual, being 'in mutual harmony with his comrades ... has more confidence, courage and boldness in action'.[56] He leads a 'collective life'[57] and it is rites, rather than ideas, which make an individual act; action which validates the preponderating role of the cult in all religions.[58] The individual learns 'at the school of collective life'.[59]

This collective life based on temple cults was apparent from the earliest days of Chinese settlement in Batavia. The aim of much of this collective life in the religious sphere was acquisition of material reward. A study of the Batavia temples from the seventeenth century by Claudine Salmon and Denys Lombard shows that the deities worshipped were mostly Taoist, fairly evenly divided between those worshipped more or less everywhere in China and those deities peculiar to Fujian and Guangdong. Particularly prominent among temple deities was the god of earth and riches, his being the second temple established in Batavia about 1650, and Guandi, the god of trustworthiness and loyalty in war and trade, who was enshrined in the first temple built there.[60] The Guandi cult was very popular among all classes of the population in Amoy,[61] the starting point of most immigrants to Java, and indeed the wealth gods brought with the Chinese to Java have been described as forming the very bedrock of Chinese popular religion, distinguished by materialism and 'wealth mania'.[62] Guandi from the late Ming period became particularly popular with traders, for whom travel and sojourning had become a way of life and who saw the god's own history of loyalty to a friend as creating an ethic of trust in business transactions, leading to the acquisition of wealth.[63]

In addition to the numerous Guandi images in temples honouring a variety of deities, a number of temples specifically dedicated to Guandi were established from the beginning of the nineteenth century. In the early nineteenth century at Batavia a Hokkien immigrant from Nanjing district, Zhangzhou prefecture, who had succeeded in trade, established a temple to perpetuate in Batavia the cult of Guandi, who in his native place had been given the title 'The God of Nanjing'. He also intended to create an association based on common place of origin where immigrants from Nanjing would be provided with help after their arrival in Batavia. The oldest panel dedicated to Guandi is dated 1824 and reads 'The Han Kin Praises his Loyalty'. The temple was used as the headquarters of the Association of Nanjing Merchants, indicating the closeness of the tie between collective life and religious ritual. The other four Guandi temples in Java appear to have been established by peranakan, the merchants who founded them being undifferentiated by ethno-linguistic origin.[64]

Guandi, however, represented moral dimensions for the worshipper deeper than mere materialism. Chris Bayly has looked at 'the moral community of the merchant'[65] in late eighteenth-century North India, where the communities of trust in which the merchants participated were reinforced by sanctions from religious precepts and where playing an active and steady part in the temple was as important as the role played in the market.[66] Guandi in fact symbolized particular moral virtues. He was the apotheosized hero of the period of the Three Kingdoms who remained loyal to his friend from the royal house of the later Han and through loyalty he was killed. The inscriptions in the Guandi temples overwhelmingly contained compounds of the word *yi*, meaning righteousness, showing that the worshippers were familiar with the Romance of the Three Kingdoms, the author of which was concerned to explore the meaning of righteousness.[67] Guandi, therefore, represented a person who shouldered his responsibilities at a fateful historical epoch and was regarded as manifesting honour, faithfulness, devotion, generosity, courage, justice and valour, combining moral virtues and human qualities rarely united in a single individual. His painted image is intended to represent fidelity.[68]

In addition to temples dedicated to Guandi or containing images of him, there was from the seventeenth century a full range of South China temple life in Batavia and in other north-coast cities such as Semarang. Some temples were intended only for certain groups of settlers, such as sugar planters or the Chinese officers; others for people coming from particular districts; still others for individuals of a particular craft or trade; while a certain number which were ancestral temples were built by members of particular large clans.[69] The worship of ancestors – not the Confucian version – complemented the worship of the gods of wealth as the main form of popular Fujian religion brought to Java. Like the worship of Guandi there was an essentially moral side to the ancestor cult, implying as it did the need to defend and uphold the good name and reputation of the entire family, to maintain family customs and traditions, and to increase family fortunes as much as possible. In the cult morality and ritual were mutually enforcing. All temples nevertheless also stressed the community dimension of worship, with important annual community festivals such as New Year and the Feast of the Dead. Their function was to reinforce communal consciousness and their effect was to increase individual confidence. The temples never accumulated great wealth[70] and their purpose in commerce was not therefore to provide financial support for business ventures but rather promote the communal ties which made these endeavours successful.

Chinese Business in a New Era

By the turn of the nineteenth century the Chinese and the Dutch were firmly linked in the exploitation of Java. The Chinese dominated the monopoly-lease system, which gave them entry into villages right throughout the island. Besides the opium lease and the market lease, the major leases included the pawnshop lease, tobacco lease, fisheries lease, slaughter-house lease, the viaduct and bridge lease, the lease for the sale of alcoholic liquors, the poll-tax lease, the fish-sales lease, the gaming lease and the *wayang* lease. Entire districts were also leased to the Chinese.[71]

The basic unit of Chinese economic endeavours in the countryside was the shop or *toko*, which was managed and extended by using poorer individuals as agents.[72] Chinese dominated the marketplaces of Java. Late eighteenth-century and early nineteenth-century accounts reported public markets in every part of Java, often bringing together thousands of people from one area every five days. According to Raffles, the Chinese market-lease holders 'contrived, by means of the influence which their office conferred, to create a monopoly in their own favour, not only of the articles of trade but of many of the necessaries of life'.[73] In particular, the Chinese imposed monopolies on all kinds of products, especially rice, thus securing the trade in these items for themselves.[74] The introduction of land rent in the second decade of the nineteenth century consolidated this Chinese hold on harvests: as middlemen they advanced cash payments on behalf of villagers, in return for disposition over a quarter of their harvests.[75] Raffles, once again, summed up: 'Throughout the whole of Java, trade is usually conducted by the Chinese: many of them are very rich, and their means are increased by their knowledge of business, their spirit of enterprize, and their mutual confidence.'[76]

The Chinese also continued with their proto-industrial activities in the production of sugar. Sugar in the Batavia area did not continue to flourish after the 1740 upheaval. Of the sixty-six sugar mills still left in the area surrounding Batavia in 1750, only thirty-one remained by 1815 due to the 1740 troubles, unfavourable government pricing policies, and problems with finding enough wood to fuel the mills.[77] However, the sugar frontier moved east and East Java was turned into an important area of sugar production to meet the new demands of the government's Cultivation System, introduced in 1830 as a system of forced deliveries of export crops intended to make Java more profitable. As we have seen, Pasuruan Residency had already been the site of some Chinese experiments with sugar production in the late eighteenth century, and the new system gave this enterprise a new lease of life, both here and in the other eastern residencies of Surabaya and Besuki. In Pasuruan there was a group of experienced millers and growers who could be brought into the new scheme by means of official contracts for the delivery of specified quantities of sugar to the government; early contracts were made with nine manufacturers of whom six were Chinese.[78]

Unlike some of the other crops grown under the Cultivation System, sugar required processing and the need to produce large quantities regularly and cheaply led government officials to advance interest-free loans to Chinese and European private entrepreneurs to build a number of large modern sugar factories to replace the simple mills of the period. These new factories were technologically advanced, being built of stone and provided with horizontal iron crushing cylinders driven by waterwheels which could mill as much cane in nine or ten days as a contemporary Chinese mill with cylinders drawn by buffaloes could do in thirty. With official direction, but also with Chinese collaboration, the Pasuruan area was transformed into the leading sugar-producing region of Java.[79] In Java as a whole, of the 175–180 sugar contracts granted by the end of 1833, about three-quarters were in the names of Chinese.[80] Although the history of the Chinese in this period remains to be written,[81] it seems that by the 1850s many Chinese, other than in Pasuruan, had been pushed out due to European interest in the sugar contracts.[82] Nevertheless, sugar was the basis of the first great peranakan industrial enterprise in Java, and the continuous connection between this and the early days of toil in the Batavia surroundings must not be forgotten.

Reprise

In their dual identity the peranakan Chinese of Java show characteristics similar to those of the Chinese mestizos of the Philippines. But the 'spirit of capitalism' which they possessed has been shown again to rest on spiritual sources that are particular to them. Most importantly, of all the communities dealt with here none could be farther from exhibiting Weber's 'unprecedented loneliness of the single individual'.[83] Peranakan business confidence existed in a quite different emotional climate; it was acquired through the possibility of common action mediated through a collective life, and the core of this collective life was the temple cult, particularly those cults worshipping gods of wealth.

This is an interesting finding in the light of so much work that has gone into postulating a Confucian 'puritanical' spirit – cognate to Weber's Protestant spirit – as the motor force of East Asian economic development.[84] Peter Berger has already raised the question whether, in the case of Sinitic civilization, we might seek the roots of this-worldliness and activism not in the 'great tradition' of Confucianism but in 'a substratum of unsophisticated, deeply rooted attitudes to the world'.[85] While awaiting further research, we must look at Weber in a manner that does not seek a 'puritan ethos' behind every successful economic venture.

For our argument here, more important if less known is Weber's work on the diaspora[86] and commerce, and this will be taken up in the final chapter of the present volume.

Notes

1. S. Abeyasekere, *Jakarta. A History*, Singapore, Oxford University Press, 1989, pp. 8–9.
2. *Opkomst* 4, p. 215; H.T. Colenbrander (ed.), *Jan Pietersz. Coen. Bescheiden Omtrent Zijn Bedrijf in Indië*, vol. 1, The Hague, Martinus Nijhoff, 1919, pp. 163, 184; *Ibid.* vol. 4, The Hague, Martinus Nijhoff, 1922, p. 641.
3. *Opkomst* 4, pp. 197, 207–208.

4. D. Lombard, *Le Carrefour Javanais. Essai d'histoire globale*, vol. 2. *Les réseaux asiatiques*, Paris, Éditions de l'École des Hautes Études en Sciences Sociales, 1990, p. 210; D. Lombard and C. Salmon, 'Islam et sinité', *Archipel* 30 (1985), p. 74; A.L. Kumar, 'Islam, the Chinese, and Indonesian Historiography – A Review Article', *Journal of Asian Studies* 46, no. 3 (1987), pp. 603–604; P. Carey, 'Changing Javanese Perceptions of the Chinese Communities in Central Java, 1755–1825', *Indonesia* 37 (1984), p. 3.

5. W.J. Cator, *The Economic Position of the Chinese in the Netherlands Indies*, Oxford, Basil Blackwell, 1936, pp. 7, 10–11; L. Blussé, *Strange Company. Chinese Settlers, Mestizo Women and the Dutch in VOC Batavia*, Dordrecht/ Riverton, Foris Publications, 1986, p. 74; J.T. Vermeulen, *De Chineezen te Batavia en de Troebelen van 1740*, Leiden, Eduard Ijdo, 1938, pp. 11, 31; B. Hoetink, 'So Bing Kong. Het Eerste Hoofd der Chineezen te Batavia (1619–1636)', *Bijdragen tot de Taal-, Land- en Volkenkunde van Nederlandsch Indië* 73 (1917), p. 350 (hereafter *BKI*).

6. Vermeulen, *De Chineezen*, pp. 14–19, 20–21.

7. *Ibid.*, pp. 23, 36–37, 69, 79–81, 109–111, 115–117, 123.

8. *Ibid.*, p. 133.

9. *Ibid.*, pp. 134, 137, 139; C. Salmon and D. Lombard, *Les Chinois de Jakarta. Temples et vie collective*, Paris, Éditions de la Maison des Sciences de l'Homme, 1977, p. xxlii.

10. F. Valentijn, *Oud en Nieuw Oost-Indien*, vol. 3, The Hague, H.C. Susan, 1858, p. 533.

11. B. Hoetink, 'Ni Hoekong. Kapitein der Chineezen te Batavia in 1740', *BKI* 74 (1918), p. 454, fn. 1.

12. Vermeulen, *De Chineezen*, pp. 26–27.

13. Blussé, *Strange Company*, pp. 53, 71; Colenbrander, *Jan Pietersz. Coen* 3, p. 946.

14. Vermeulen, *De Chineezen*, pp 3–4, 8, 21, 126; Blussé, *Strange Company*, pp. 87, 115–116, 121–124; Valentijn, *Oost-Indien* 3, p. 534.

15. Hoetink, 'So Bing Kong', pp. 362–363, 370, 373–375, 379–380, 383; Lombard, *Carrefour Javanais* 2, pp. 239–240.

16. Colenbrander, *Jan Pietersz. Coen* 3, p. 541.

17. Hoetink, 'So Bing Kong', p. 355.

18. *Ibid.*, p. 355; B. Hoetink, 'Chineesche Officieren te Batavia Onder de Compagnie', *BKI* 78 (1922), p. 1; Vermeulen, *De Chineezen*, p. 30; Blussé, *Strange Company*, pp. 87–88.

19. Hoetink, 'So Bing Kong', p. 361; Lombard, *Carrefour Javanais* 2, pp. 240–241; Blussé, *Strange Company*, pp. 52–54.

20. Vermeulen, *De Chineezen*, pp. 27–30; Cator, *Economic Position*, pp. 19–20; J.R. Rush, *Opium to Java. Revenue Farming and Chinese Enterprise in Colonial Indonesia, 1860–1910*, Ithaca/London, Cornell University Press, 1990, pp. 2, 24.

21. Lombard, *Carrefour Javanais* 2, p. 223.

22. J. Hooyman, 'Verhandeling over den Tegenwoordigen Staat van den Land-Bouw in de Ommelanden van Batavia', *Verhandelingen van het Bataviaasch Genootschap der Kunsten en Wetenschappen* 1 (1779), p. 182; Hoetink, 'So Bing Kong', p. 361; Hoetink, 'Ni Hoekong', pp. 447–448; Hoetink, 'Chineesche Officieren', pp. 22, 50–51, 97–105, 109; Lombard, *Carrefour Javanais* 2, p. 242.

23. Hooyman, 'Land-Bouw in de Ommelanden', pp. 210, 214, 237–238; Cator, *Economic Position*, pp. 11–12; Salmon and Lombard, *Chinois de Jakarta*, p. 133.

24. Hooyman, 'Land-Bouw in de Ommelanden', pp. 202–204, 217.

25. Cator, *Economic Position*, p. 12.

26. *Ibid.*, p. 12; Hooyman, 'Land-Bouw in de Ommelanden', p. 246.

27. Quoted in Cator, *Economic Position*, p. 22.

28. Hoetink, 'Chineesche Officieren', pp. 21–22, 25, 27, 62–63, 98, 100–102, 112; Hoetink, 'Ni Hoekong', p. 449, fn. 2.

29. Vermeulen, *De Chineezen*, pp. 104–105.

30. M.C. Hoadley, 'Javanese, Peranakan, and Chinese Elites in Cirebon: Changing Ethnic Boundaries', *Journal of Asian Studies* 47, no. 3 (1988), pp. 508–510.

31. L. Nagtegaal, 'Rijden op een Hollandse Tijger. De noordkust van Java en de V.O.C. 1680–1740', Ph.D., Utrecht University, 1988, pp. 110–113. Nagtegaal states the top three families were *totok*.

32. Hoetink, 'Ni Hoekong', pp. 448–449; Lombard, *Carrefour Javanais* 2, p. 242.

33. Nagtegaal, 'Hollandse Tijger', pp. 122–129, 134–137.

34. C. Salmon, 'The Han Family of East Java. Entrepreneurship and Politics (18th–19th Centuries)', *Archipel* 4 (1991), pp. 61–63, 74, 77–79; R.E. Elson, *Javanese Peasants and the Colonial Sugar Industry. Impact and Change in an East Java Residency 1830–1940*, Singapore, Oxford University Press, 1984, pp. 20–22.

35. Rush, *Opium to Java*, pp. 1, 24–26, 46; Lombard, *Carrefour Javanais* 2, pp. 240, 259.

36. T.S. Raffles, *The History of Java*, vol. 1, London, 1817 (Kuala Lumpur, Oxford in Asia Historical Reprints, 1965), p. 204.

37. Rush, *Opium to Java*, pp. 44, 52, 63, 83, 89, 94–95.

38. *Ibid.*, pp. 95–96.

39. *Ibid.*, pp. 87, 98–100.

40. Raffles, *History of Java* 1, pp. 199–200.

41. Rush, *Opium to Java*, pp. 92–93; D.E. Willmott, *The Chinese of Semarang: A Changing Minority Community in Indonesia*, Ithaca, Cornell University Press, 1960, p. 150.

42. Willmott, *Chinese of Semarang*, pp. 135, 210–212.

43. Lombard, *Carrefour Javanais* 2, p. 211.

44. C. Salmon, *Literature in Malay by the Chinese of Indonesia*, Paris, Éditions de la Maison des Sciences de l'Homme, 1981, pp. 15, 121–122; W.F. Wertheim, *East–West Parallels. Sociological Approaches to Modern Asia*, The Hague, W. van Hoeve, 1964, pp. 47–48; The Siauw Giap, 'Religion and Overseas Chinese Assimilation in Southeast Asian Countries', *Revue du Sud-Est Asiatique* (1965), pp. 69, 76; C. Poensen, 'Naar en op de Pasar', *Mededeelingen van wege het Nederlandsche Zendelinggenootschap* 26 (1882), pp. 4–5, 7, 23.

45. Cator, *Economic Position*, p. 35.

46. Rush, *Opium to Java*, p. 97.

47. G.W. Skinner, 'Java's Chinese Minority: Continuity and Change', *Journal of Asian Studies* 20 (1960–61), pp. 356–357; G.W. Skinner, 'The Chinese Minority' in R.T. McVey (ed.), *Indonesia*, New Haven, Yale University Press, 1963, p. 104.

48. J.F. van Nes, 'De Chinezen op Java', *Tijdschrift voor Nederlandsch Indië* 13, no. 1 (1851), p. 305.

49. Ng Chin-Keong, *Trade and Society: The Amoy Network on the China Coast 1683–1735*, Singapore, Singapore University Press, 1983, pp. 20–22, 25–32, 36–37; Blussé, *Strange Company*, p. 104.

50. Ng, *Trade and Society*, pp. 96–98, 178, 182–183. For earlier commercial development in Fujian, see Wang Gungwu, 'Merchants Without Empire: The Hokkien Sojourning Communities', in J.D. Tracy (ed.), *The Rise of Merchant Empires. Long-Distance Trade in the Early Modern World, 1350–1750*, Cambridge, Cambridge University Press, 1990, pp. 401–408.

51. *Ibid.*, pp. 38–40, 96–103; J.E. Wills, 'De VOC en de Chinezen in China, Taiwan en Batavia in de 17de en de 18de eeuw', in M.A.P. Meilink-Roelofsz (ed.), *Die VOC in Azië*, Bussum, Fibula-Van Dishoeck, 1976, p. 169; compare C. Geertz, 'The Rotating Credit Association: A "Middle Rung" in Development', *Economic Development and Cultural Change* 10, no. 3 (1962), pp. 241–263; S. Ardener, 'The Comparative Study of Rotating Credit Associations', *Journal of the Royal Anthropological Institute of Great Britain* 94 (1964), pp. 201–229.

52. D.R. de Glopper, 'Doing Business in Lukang' in A.P. Wolf (ed.), *Studies in Chinese Society*, Stanford, Stanford University Press, 1978, p. 318.

53. J.M. Barbalet, 'Confidence: Time and Emotion in the Sociology of Action', *Journal for the Theory of Social Behaviour* 23, no. 3 (1993), pp. 237–238.

54. Lombard, *Carrefour Javanais* 2, pp. 258–259.

55. E. Durkheim, *The Elementary Forms of Religious Life*, New York, The Free Press, 1965, p. 240.

56. *Ibid.*, p. 242.

57. *Ibid.*, p. 251.

58. *Ibid.*, pp. 463–465.

59. *Ibid.*, p. 470.

60. Salmon and Lombard, *Chinois de Jakarta*, pp. xviii, xlviii, 124, 145–150, 173–174.

61. Ng, *Trade and Society*, p. 91.

62. B.M. Alexeiev, *The Chinese Gods of Wealth*, London, School of Oriental Studies, 1928, p. 9.

63. C. Salmon, 'The Three Kingdoms in the Malay World – Religion and Literature', *Asian Culture* 16 (1992), p. 16; P. Duara, 'Superscribing Symbols: The Myth of Guandi, Chinese God of War', *Journal of Asian Studies* 47, no. 4 (1988), p. 782.

64. Salmon, 'The Three Kingdoms', pp. 16–18.

65. C.A. Bayly, *Rulers, Townsmen and Bazaars. North Indian Society in the Age of British Expansionism, 1770–1870*, Cambridge, Cambridge University Press, 1983, p. 371.

66. *Ibid.*, pp. 31, 373.

67. Salmon, 'The Three Kingdoms', p. 19.

68. Tsai Mauw-Kuey, *Les Chinois au Sud-Vietnam*, Paris, Bibliothèque Nationale, 1968, p. 226.

69. Salmon and Lombard, *Chinois de Jakarta*, pp. xviii, xix–xxi, xxii–xxiv, xxv, lxvii, lxix–lx, 100ff., 134–136, 141–144; Willmott, *Chinese of Semarang*, pp. 209, 212.

70. Salmon and Lombard, *Chinois de Jakarta*, pp. lvii–lix, lxiv; Willmott, *Chinese of Semarang*, p. 204.

71. Cator, *Economic Position*, pp. 21, 97–98.

72. Vermeulen, *De Chineezen*, p. 133; Lombard, *Carrefour Javanais* 2, p. 255; R.E. Elson, *Village Java under the Cultivation System 1830–1870*, Sydney, Allen and Unwin, 1994, p. 255.

73. Raffles, *History of Java* 1, p. 199.

74. *Ibid.*

75. Rush, *Opium to Java*, pp. 20–21.

76. Raffles, *History of Java 1*, p. 203.

77. Cator, *Economic Position*, p. 12; Abeyasekere, *Jakarta*, p. 38.

78. Elson, *Javanese Peasants*, p. 33; C. Fasseur, *The Politics of Colonial Exploitation. Java, the Dutch, and the Cultivation System*, Ithaca, Cornell University Studies on Southeast Asia, 1992, p. 34.

79. Elson, *Javanese Peasants*, p. 39; Fasseur, *Colonial Exploitation*, pp. 88–89. Some enterprises continued to operate independently of the government system.

80. Fasseur, *Colonial Exploitation*, pp. 88–89.

81. For a favourable view of Chinese economic development, see The Siauw Giap, 'Socio-Economic Role of the Chinese in Indonesia, 1820–1940', in A. Maddison and G. Prince (eds), *Economic Growth in Indonesia, 1820–1940*, Dordrecht/Providence, Foris, 1989, p. 161.

82. Fasseur, *Colonial Exploitation*, p. 94.

83. Weber, *Protestant Ethic*, p. 104.

84. Yeu-Farn Wang, *Chinese Entrepreneurs*, pp. 7–11. Also interesting in this regard is R.N. Bellah, *Tokugawa Religion. The Values of Pre-Industrial Japan*, Glencoe, The Free Press, 1957. Bellah finds a form of 'Buddhist puritanism' motivating a leading group of merchants, the Omi merchants, in pre-modern Japan; see pp. 117–122.

85. Berger, 'East Asian Model', p. 9.

86. In the *Protestant Ethic* Weber says another author 'rightly calls the Calvinistic diaspora the seed-bed of capitalistic economy' (p. 43).

4

Bombay: The Parsi-British Affinity 1661–1940

Quite some time before Bombay was ceded to them in 1661, the British in Western India had been indebted to the Parsis in their commercial endeavours. At the time of the East India Company's arrival in Western India, Surat was the most important seaport on the west coast and the centre of trade for both the Moghul Empire and the European trading companies. The Parsis, a community descended from Iranian Zoroastrians who emigrated to India after the Islamization of Iran, were attractive to European merchants as 'brokers' who could conduct business in the hinterland with the necessary knowledge of land and language, but whose minority position in Indian society gave them an understanding of foreigners' needs. The Portuguese, French, Dutch and English factories at Surat all employed Parsis as their chief brokers and to some Parsis at Surat the Moghul Empire granted the right to collect customs duties.[1]

Brokers carried out a highly specialized function in the Indian Ocean port cities. As well as dealing with foreign merchants, the Parsi brokers also played other roles, servicing certain traders who were not foreigners and also engaging in commerce on their own account. Shippers and merchants engaged in importing and exporting relied on commodity brokers for specific goods, and these brokers would be tied to a network of middlemen who enabled them to supply the principal range of commodities desired for export and to help to sell the variety of goods imported.[2] The Dutch in Malabar used Jews for a similar purpose, and noted in 1743 of their chief broker:

> He has never yet left the Company in an embarrassing situation, and it is alone due to him that the Company's goods have never rotted in the warehouses, or been sold under the Company's prices ... The merchant ... is also the chief supplier of whatever the Company may need, nothing excepted.[3]

Brokers therefore served a crucial role. Indeed, Michael Pearson states, to the extent that the Indian Ocean world was an integrated world-economy, this was achieved by the work of these brokers.[4]

Parsi brokers were, of course, at the apex of Parsi society, and to supply the commodities desired by Europeans they were required to maintain firm links with their villages and towns of origin in the Gujarat hinterland. Gujarati textiles were the Europeans' desired article of export and the Parsi brokers of Surat were readily supplied from Navsari, the Parsis' main town, which was famous for sending its cotton cloth to the seaport.[5] Other Parsi villages were celebrated for their woven cloth.[6] The English were particularly dependent on the Parsi weavers, a 1689 account stating: 'They are the Principal men at the Loom in all the Country, and most of the silks and stuffs at Surat are made by their Hands.'[7] In addition, Parsis in Surat and its vicinity carried on a variety of occupations, such as general trade and shopkeeping, crafts, agriculture and shipbuilding.[8]

This Parsi success at Surat must, as in the case of the Hokkien Chinese, be looked at in terms of preadaptation. André Wink has questioned the traditional view that a group of Zoroastrians, fleeing Muslim persecution in Iran and seeking refuge on the coast of Gujarat in about AD 785, were the progenitors of the Parsi community in India. Rather he sees the Parsis' forebears as long associated with trade in India, Zoroastrian and Christian Persians in the centuries preceding Islam having dominated commerce in the Western Indian

Ocean. It therefore seems more likely that the migration of Parsis to the west coast of India was not so much a flight as a readjustment of commercial patterns which had arisen long before Islam and a response to new opportunities in the transit trade between the Islamic world and India.[9] In the ninth and tenth centuries unconverted Parsis are observed participating in the India trade from areas within the Abbasid Caliphate, and a possible explanation of the rise of more permanent settlements of Parsis on India's west coast is that Arab competition in the Persian Gulf obliged them to move the centre of their activities eastwards. Thus the Parsis should not be seen as a refugee community settling down in India as agriculturalists and weavers, woken to commercial life by the European East India Companies, but rather as having much earlier developed a new trading diaspora between the Arab-dominated Middle East and Hindu India. Trade was their pursuit from the time of their arrival, and early accounts of Sanjan, their major place of settlement for about 600 years, notes its extensive import and export trade.[10]

Sanjan, about 140 kilometres from Bombay, is important in Parsi history as the major Parsi centre in a Hindu environment until the Muslim intrusion in about 1315. It was the site where the newly arrived Zoroastrians agreed to modify their customs in order to make themselves acceptable to local authority, an ability which was again ready to hand in the European era. The Raja of Sanjan was only prepared to permit settlement if the Parsis would agree to five conditions, including that Parsi women should start to wear local dress, that the Parsis would give up their native language and adopt Gujarati, and that they would hold their wedding ceremonies only at night in conformity with Hindu practice. These were agreed to, while in the schedule that the Parsis prepared on their own religion they emphasized customs which they knew to be similar to those of the Hindus and maintained silence on the doctrines on which the religion was really based. This tactic was successful, and within five years of their arrival in Sanjan they were permitted to build a fire-temple. When similar situations arose later, the Parsis were prepared.[11]

Towards the end of the tenth century Parsis began to settle in other parts of Gujarat, particularly Broach, Cambay and Navsari. The earliest emigration seems to have been to Cambay in 942–997, where they were very successful in commerce. In Navsari from the fifteenth century they became prominent as revenue farmers.[12] The evidence seems to raise no doubt that the Parsis had for centuries been occupied with commerce, whatever might have been the economic activities of their lesser ranks, and their flourishing in Surat was their final preadaptation before their great economic success in Bombay.

Early Parsi Commerce in Bombay and China

The British settlement at Bombay from its earliest days required a regular supply of cloth to add to the Company's Surat shipments. The early Governors' policy was to attract weavers into the new town, many of whom were Parsis.[13] Parsi brokers assisted them. Those Parsi brokers who left Surat for Bombay were generally those whose livelihood depended on trade with the European companies, whilst those dependent on inland trade stayed behind.[14] One of the most influential Parsi brokers in Surat was Rastamji Manakji, born in the city in 1635. In 1691 he appears as an interpreter and shortly thereafter he was appointed a broker, first for the Portuguese and later for the Dutch and the English. He became an acknowledged leader of the Parsi community in Surat and acquired wealth and status through long-distance trade and through dealings in currencies, as well as through his activities as a broker. His son was in 1723 the first Parsi to go to England to present a petition to the East India Company's Court of Directors. But very soon after the death of the founder the family built up its base in Bombay. In Surat they were part of a small community with no differing entrepreneurial qualities from the Hindu Banias and Muslim Bohras; indeed, they could never hope to compete with the Banias, one family of which became the Rastamjis' deadly enemies. This might have been one factor in their removal to Bombay, where they could build up a partnership with the British. After Rastamji Manakji's grandson came to Bombay in

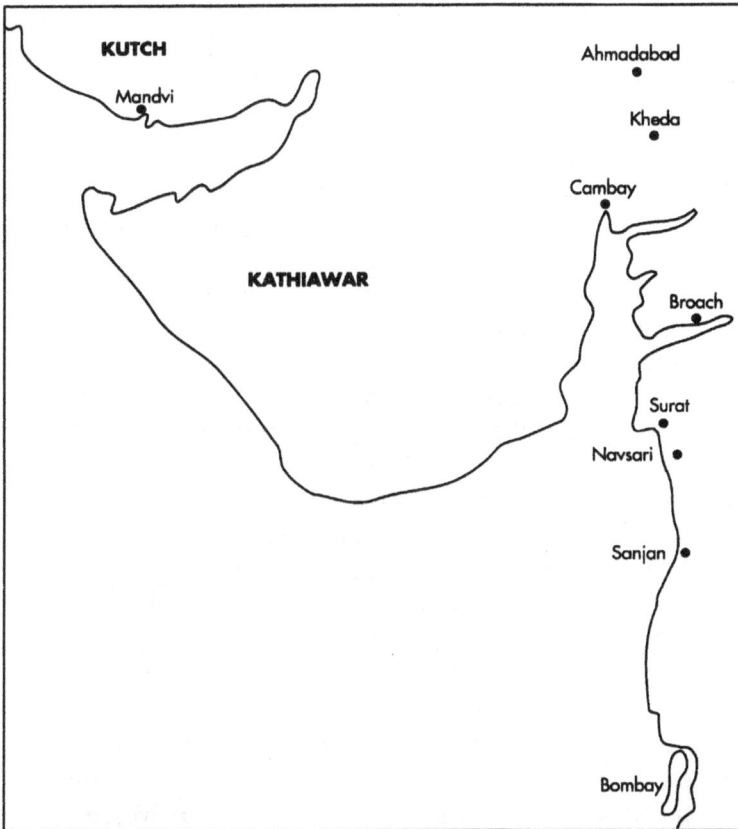

Map 4: Kutch, Gujarat and Bombay c. 1900

1730, the family engaged in extensive mercantile operations and also opened a branch firm in Mysore.[15]

Other early settler families in Bombay are not known to us in such detail, but the development of Parsi settlement there can be understood. There were already Parsis in Bombay in the Portuguese period, procuring workers and construction materials for a fortress.[16] But the Parsis' great patron was the English Governor Gerald Aungier, who aimed to make the Bombay cotton cloth sent to Surat for export equal in quality to that of Navsari, the leading centre of Parsi weavers. The chief weaver in Bombay in Aungier's time was a Parsi called Manak, and Aungier was concerned to bring Parsi weavers down to

Bombay under his patronage. By 1676 the policy of getting Parsi weavers to settle in Bombay was well established, and brokers were overseeing the work as well as acquiring textiles from areas which weavers refused to leave.[17] It was proclaimed that the 'cloth investment' on the island was one of the Company's 'principal concerns',[18] and from the very beginning Parsis acted in conjunction with the English to make this a success.

Other services traditionally provided by minorities to European trading concerns were offered by the Parsis. Kharshedji Ponchaji Pandey, the founder of a distinguished family, on his arrival from Broach in the 1660s obtained a contract to assist in the completion of the fort, supplying labour and materials such as baskets.[19] By 1716, in addition to weaving and brokerage, Parsis in Bombay were carrying out a variety of trades, were renowned as carpenters and shipbuilders, fulfilled contracts to supply the garrison, and profited from distilling spirits.[20] By 1780 Bombay had 33,444 inhabitants, of whom 3,087 or 9.2 per cent were Parsis. The European population was not more than 1,000.[21]

A symbiotic relationship grew up between the Parsis and the British which had no comparison in any relationship which existed with the Hindu or Muslim commercial communities. The greatest obstacle to European expansion in Western India was the shortage of capital in the Indian merchant community. But this difficulty was overcome in a way that is not quite clear, but which certainly included Parsi participation in the amassing of capital. By the 1780s there emerged in Bombay several powerful English trading firms or agency houses which played a vital role in the expansion of English power in Western India. Pamela Nightingale's study of the period shows mutual lending between the Company's servants and the Parsis. One officer's private account books running from 1746 to 1751 indicate a partnership with a Parsi in buying up a quantity of red lead, the Parsi being lent money at interest; other Parsi merchants were also involved in his commercial ventures. Parsis likewise lent money, and their English partners seized any opportunity which offered a profit.[22]

Initially English private traders acquired most of their money at Surat, where money was lent out at interest due to hazardous political conditions rather than being employed in commercial enterprise. As the security of Bombay became manifest, Parsis joined the English in business enterprises with long-term prospects, extracting capital from Surat and putting it to productive use.[23] It was reported in 1813 that each European house or agency had one of the principal Parsi merchants concerned with it in most of its foreign speculations.[24] The major families concerned had been established in the mid-eighteenth century, when their founders had made their fortunes in association with the Company, providing boats for the transport of troops, drinking water for officers, uniforms for coolies, provisions for Europeans, and ships for international trade.[25]

By the 1780s the East India Company in India was in considerable debt. The traditional trade in woven textiles which the Company had shipped from India to Europe was not expanding, and there was little prospect of selling British goods in India. But the Company was able to avoid bankruptcy by the fortunate growth of the fashion for drinking China tea in Europe. This new demand stimulated the enterprise of British private traders, many of whom were based in Bombay and, though prevented by the Company's monopoly from trading with Europe, they were allowed to export Indian produce to China. The major difficulty at the port of Canton was to avoid paying for tea with bullion and to find suitable products to sell to China. This niche was filled by the so-called 'country trade', run by private individuals licensed by the East India Company in India and remaining under its control in the Far East. Bombay was destined to be extremely successful in this trade because the port could ship an item desired in China, namely raw cotton from the Gujarat hinterland. Until 1823 raw cotton from India was the largest staple import at Canton.[26]

The trade was organized at the Bombay end by the agency houses, whose growing power has led one writer to speak of a 'commercial revolution' in Western India from the 1780s.[27] It was the agency houses in Bombay and not the East India

Company which built the ships and invested capital for the trade on which Bombay flourished. These private traders now had a key role in Britain's important China trade, for they transferred the funds realized by this trade in sales at Canton to the East India Company's treasury there in return for bills of exchange on London or the Indian government revenue. Without this the China trade could not have been financed, and it was on this basis that the Bombay agency houses built their prosperity.[28]

With this prosperity Parsi merchants were associated. Nearly all the European agency houses, particularly after 1813, had Parsi guarantee-brokers who guaranteed the solvency of the constituents and advanced considerable sums of money to enable them to continue to trade. Parsis were in such demand as guarantee-brokers because they themselves had started to trade on their own account and even to establish their own firms. Most of the great Parsi families by the 1840s had scions of the family acting as brokers, whilst the family heads carried on their own independent importing and exporting business, mainly with China and Britain. The first Parsi private trader, Hirji Jivanji Readymoney, appeared on the China coast as early as 1756. In 1809 there was only one private English trader in Canton compared to several Parsis residing there and, of the approximately twenty-four firms operating there, Parsis formed a significant element. In 1831 there were 32 Englishmen and 41 Parsis in China; in 1833, the figures were 35 and 52 respectively.[29]

Raw cotton was gradually superseded by opium as India's chief export to China. Parsis from the beginning joined British private traders in taking it to Canton, some beginning as intermediaries supplying opium from the growing districts. From about 1800 the production of opium steadily increased in India, as did its importance in Indian revenue, making the Company dependent on sales in China. Experimental trade along the South China coast began at the turn of the century, culminating in the opening of the treaty ports in the 1840s. With the development of firms in Canton at that period, Parsis formed a considerable element of the British community. By the early 1850s foreigners in China ran some 200 business concerns engaged in trade or connected with it; of this number half were British and one-quarter Parsi or Indian. Parsi houses maintained not only their British contacts to handle the opium, but also American ones. By about 1850 Parsi opium merchants had penetrated the lower Yangtze.[30]

Parsis, then, were the key mediating community between the British and the products of India they desired to export. All the prominent Parsi families had extensive interests in China and acquired enormous wealth. A prime example was the Readymoney family, founded by three brothers all born in the Parsi centre of Navsari, who came to Bombay in the early eighteenth century for trade. The second brother opened a business house in China and, although the three started out with small capital, they acquired considerable substance from their trade with China, built up their own fleet of several trading ships, and became guarantee-brokers to British firms.[31]

Other distinguished families too owed their origin to the China trade; these included the Kamas, the Wadias and the Dadiseths. Two members of the Kama family were the first Indians to establish a mercantile firm in London, accomplishing this in the mid-1850s.[32] The most famous Parsi China merchant was Jamshedji Jijibhai, born in 1783 in Navsari. He came to Bombay in his youth to assist his father-in-law in business and, when barely 16, he made his first voyage to China in the service of another relative. On his second voyage he started to trade on his own account and he made several subsequent voyages. These gave him an insight into the chief traders at that time in China, which assisted him in his later business. His huge profits were made by exporting cotton during the Napoleonic War and, by the 1820s, his firm dominated all others exporting to China. His connections were not only with the British; he had commercial dealings with an American firm importing opium directly to China from India. Jamshedji Jijibhai also had seven ships of his own and several others on hire at any one time, the ships being serviced in his own private docks.[33]

Most Parsi ventures were in fact carried out in Parsi-owned ships. During the period 1810 to 1815 it appears that the Wadias had eighteen ships (10,000 tons or so), the Dadiseths six (5,000 tons) and the Readymoneys and the Banajis four each (3,000 tons); this was before the Kama family and Jamshedji Jijibhai had started their shipping careers. It has been estimated that some 25,000 to 30,000 tons of shipping – or 8 to 10 per cent of the country's total tonnage for those years – belonged to Parsis. By the decade 1835–45 the Parsi community was at the zenith of its ship-owning career; the number of vessels owned by the Banaji family, to cite one example, had risen from four to forty.[34]

More important for later developments, the amount of capital sunk into the shipbuilding industry seems to have paved the way for subsequent Parsi industrial ventures. Amalendu Guha has written extensively on Parsi shipbuilding as a proto-industrial endeavour that was not allowed to reach its natural conclusion but which was distorted and then overtaken by Parsi investment in the cotton textile industry.[35] Parsis were known as expert shipbuilders from the seventeenth century and built ships for the European Companies. In 1735 the English East India Company persuaded a native Surat shipwright, Lavji Nasarvanji Wadia, to come to Bombay with ten other shipwrights to commence shipbuilding at the Company dockyard. He became the yard's master-builder and, on his death, was succeeded by his son Manakji, management continuing in the hands of the Wadia family in uninterrupted succession for 150 years. During this time more than 300 sea-going vessels were built for the British Navy, European agency houses and Indian – mainly Parsi – firms, the China trade in particular requiring vessels capable of making a long voyage and of carrying bulky cargo.[36]

Guha argues that the Bombay dockyards assisted the transition of the Parsi mentality from mercantile to industrial by way of technological innovation. In 1829 the contemporary master-builder Navroji Jamshedji Wadia assembled a 411-ton steam sloop for the East India Company. Encouraged, Ardeshir Kharshedji Wadia, on becoming a dockyard apprentice, began to study privately the theory and practice of steam engines, in 1833 launching a small 60-ton steamboat with the help of a local blacksmith and an imported piece of steam-engine. The following year he lit his house with improvised gas and introduced steam pumps for watering his gardens. In 1840 he was elected the first Indian Fellow of the Royal Society, and he and two other Wadias subsequently qualified in Britain as marine engineers. It was the Bombay dockyards which helped to produce a nucleus of Parsi engineers before the first graduating group of civil engineers from the government's Elphinstone Institution in 1847. Guha argues, however, that this incipient development of an indigenous navigation and ship-building industry was prevented by British policy, which up to 1849 spoilt the prospects of this industry by excluding Indian-built ships from European waters and putting other constraints on them. Thus the Indian shipping industry was unable to make what should have been a ready transition to iron steamships. The final act came when the British Navy stopped acquiring Indian-built ships and the Indian Marine Service was closed down in 1863.[37]

Parsis as Industrialists

So far what we have seen in the two Chinese groups we have discussed has been the clear development of activities which qualify as proto-industrialization, coupled with a question mark hanging over the future of this development. The Parsis, however, made a clear and rapid transition into the industrial civilization of the nineteenth century, partly due to their previous industrial activities and partly as a result of the Opium War in China and the opening of the treaty ports. The new arrangement on the South China coast led to the entry of other Bombay communities into the China trade, especially the Ismailis and the Bombay Jews, challenging the Parsi monopoly with new lines of business. In addition, the extension of steam communication between India and China proved strong competition for the Parsi families' sailing vessels.[38] But a new outlet for Parsi capital was ready to hand.

Cotton was exported in large quantities from India to England and then reimported into India as cotton textiles.

Members of certain Parsi families realized that there was no reason why cotton mills could not be established in Bombay as there was an ample supply of raw cotton, there existed a large market for cotton yarn in both their old trading partner China and in the Bombay hinterland, there was an abundant supply of low-cost labour and, of course, a vast accumulation of capital from the trading sector available. British official collaboration could not be expected where Lancashire's interests were threatened, but independent collaborators were found from within the British textile machine industry which was interested in establishing an Indian textile industry, whether in British or Indian hands.39 The final seal was set on the enterprise by the acceptance of the joint-stock principle, permitting a number of investors to contribute varying amounts. The starting capital of these early industrial ventures was raised exclusively by the families and relatives of the founders, but ultimately numerous Parsis outside the great families proved willing to buy shares in Parsi firms.[40]

Parsi capital was first directed into cotton mills by Kavasji Nanabhai Davar, who in 1854 established as a joint-stock company the first cotton-spinning factory worked by steam in Bombay. Davar's father was an important merchant who was connected to some of the chief British houses in Bombay and, as a young man, Kavasji had worked with him as a broker to some of these firms. With a purely commercial education, he was active in the 1840s in the establishment of a number of banks in the city where the joint-stock principle was first used to pool the community's capital resources. Aware that the necessary capital was available, he sent to England for mill plans and machinery, the outcome being the floating of the Bombay Spinning and Weaving Company by a shareholders' agreement. The Company's capital was divided into one hundred shares, the majority being taken up by Parsi merchants, although a group of twenty Gujarati – Hindu and Muslim – businessmen took nearly one-third. Later, in 1854, Manakji Nasarvanji Petit, a successful broker and China trader, arranged with a few business associates, many non-Parsi, to promote the Oriental Spinning and Weaving Company and this mill was formally floated in 1855. M.N. Petit's entry into the mill industry marks the easy transition from leading merchant to leading industrialist which was made by many merchants then and subsequently. Jijibhai Dadabhai, the father of Byramji Jijibhai who started a weaving mill in one of the Bombay suburbs, was a broker, director of banks, shipowner and trader with Europe, Egypt and China. Mancherji Naoroji Banaji, founder of the City of Bombay mill in 1885, was the descendant of a merchant who migrated to Bombay in 1690 and was himself engaged in trade shipping, real estate and company promotion. The Wadias too joined the industry.[41]

Parsis were, of course, not the only cotton mill entrepreneurs, but they certainly dominated the industry of which they were the pioneers. All machinery had to be imported in sailing vessels via the Cape and the workers had to be thoroughly trained. Of the thirteen cotton mills established in Bombay in the period 1854–70, nine owed their existence to Parsi entrepreneurs and it was the cotton industry that 'stimulated the formulation of a modern Indian entrepreneurial class'.[42] In 1895, out of seventy cotton mill owners in Bombay, twenty-two were Parsis, and the same number of Parsi owners was registered out of a total of eighty-one in 1925. It must be borne in mind that the Parsi population was extremely small. The 1864 census enumerated 49,201 Parsis, making them 6.03 per cent of the total Bombay population; in 1881, out of a Bombay total of 723,196, they represented only 48,597; whilst the Indian census of 1920–21 enumerated a Parsi population of 102,000 persons or 0.03 per cent of the total population of India. The mills provided opportunities not just for Parsi investment but for Parsis to contribute to the management as secretaries, managing agents or mill managers. Of a total of 175 directors in Bombay's textile industry in 1925, forty-nine were Parsis.[43]

Parsis were obliged to diversify in this period for other reasons. Not only did their China trade and shipbuilding interests decline, but Parsi merchants also suffered from some of the new inventions of the period. For decades they had acted as middlemen in multifarious commercial transactions.

But the railway, the electric telegraph and the steamship opened up the interior to more direct trade, and the gradual advance of education in Gujarat enabled the Hindus of those areas to deal directly with Europeans. Parsi diversified interests were wide. Mention has already been made of banking in connection with the establishment of the first cotton mills. When the European-dominated Bank of Bombay was established in 1840, one-third of its 333 shareholders were Parsis, contributing 23.6 per cent of the Bank's share capital. Dadabhai Pestanji Wadia, head of perhaps the leading house of the 1830s and 1840s and a great landlord, was the only Indian to be appointed to the committee to establish the bank; two of the leading China traders of the period, Framji Kavasji Banaji and Jamshedji Jijibhai, were soon appointed directors of the bank. The Bank of Western India, established in 1842 as a joint British-Parsi initiative and renamed the Oriental Bank in 1845, had at one time three-eighths of its share capital in the hands of Dadabhai Pestanji Wadia. By 1850 there were four such banks in the city, all attracting the heads of those Parsi firms who had for some time combined trade, banking and brokerage in one organization.[44]

Other new spheres of commercial endeavour included the raw cotton trade to Britain, which after the onset of the American Civil War in 1861 became particularly lucrative. Many leading Parsi merchants were diverted to the trade and a large number, such as Rastamji Jamshedji, the second son of Jamshedji Jijibhai, amassed fortunes. With the commencement of the construction of railways in India, several Parsis became contractors. The first to win a contract after 1850 had been a shipwright, cooper and housebuilder and succeeded in gaining a tender to carry out difficult and novel operations. Not all Parsi capital and know-how, however, was used for entrepreneurial ends. In 1855 it was estimated Parsis literally owned about half of the island of Bombay, due to the fact that in the previous decade some three or four Parsi families had acquired large portions of the island's landed property. Anyone who was prepared to buy or build even the most modest house could obtain exorbitant rents in a city which was already by

1850 taking on a chronically overcrowded appearance. One of the largest investors in landed property was Dadabhai Pestanji Wadia; before his crash he was estimated to own about one-quarter of the island.[45]

It should be clearly understood that Parsis did not work alone in these endeavours. Originally the cotton and opium trade business was organized as a family affair. But by the early nineteenth century enterprises were no longer confined to the family; first Europeans and then Hindus and Muslims were taken on as partners. When a son came of age, he was taken into the family business as a working partner but he was also free to start new firms in partnership with others. In the transition to the joint-stock enterprise, from family firms to corporate firms, the response of Parsi and other Gujarati capitalists was more or less identical. But Parsis espoused a specific form of training their young men for business leadership, placing them not in their own family firm but as apprentices in a European firm. In this way training in European business methods could be obtained, to be made use of later. Despite this difference in training, Parsis and other Gujarati merchants cooperated closely. Until the 1860s the great families of the city lived in close proximity in the Fort area, the centre of all banking and mercantile activity.[46]

The most important of all Parsi entrepreneurs, and the founder of the Indian iron and steel industry, Jamshedji Nasarvanji Tata, was the product of many of these earlier developments. His father, Nasarvanji Tata, was born in Navsari in 1822 of a priestly family. As a boy the father received business training from a country banker in Navsari and subsequently he migrated to Bombay with his father. Here he was apprenticed to a Hindu banker and general merchant, where he learned to deal with the weights and measures used in business, which varied from district to district, and also to understand which were the most suitable localities in which to acquire particular commodities. With some business successes to his credit, he established the firm of Nasarvanji and Kaliandas with a Hindu partner, built a large house in the Fort district, and became one of the first foreigners to set foot in

Japan. With the increasing price of Indian cotton as a result of the American Civil War, the firm of Nasarvanji and Kaliandas established their agents in the various cotton-growing districts and ran an extremely successful business, acquiring an interest in several smaller houses. In 1867 Nasarvanji Tata obtained the contract to furnish supplies for the troops taking part in the Bombay expedition against the ruler of Abyssinia; from the profits he was able to retire.[47]

Nasarvanji's only son and India's greatest industrial pioneer, Jamshedji Nasarvanji Tata, was born at Navsari in 1839 when his father was only 17. He was sent to Bombay at the age of 13, given a Western education at the government's Elphinstone College and, in 1859, entered his father's business with the task of promoting the China trade for the family firm. J.N. Tata was sent to Hong Kong and subsequently Shanghai, where branches of the firm were established. The business dealt chiefly in cotton and opium imports and with return consignments of tea, silks, camphor, cinnamon, copper, brass and Chinese gold. In connection with the cotton trade, Tata visited England in 1864 and stayed on for four years. He was fascinated by the industrial success of Manchester and developed the desire to replicate this in India. On his return to Bombay, he bought an old mill and in 1869 he converted it into a cotton mill. Within two years he had disposed of this, working out a new plan whereby he would locate a mill away from Bombay, well within reach of the cotton supplies, close to a profitable market, with the most modern machinery and in an area where supplies of both coal and water were available. In 1874 he journeyed through the cotton-growing districts looking for a suitable site and, after some setbacks, settled on Nagpur in the Central Provinces, some 800 kilometres from Bombay. The town was the chief market for many kilometres around and was also the terminus of the Great India Peninsula Railway. The Empress Mills were opened in 1877, innovative not only in their locality but also in J.N. Tata's intention to create a concern which would be a model for other mill-owners. In England again to buy a large amount of new plant, he determined to introduce an invention which would revolutionize the entire mill industry. This was the ring spindle, and with its installation ring spinning nearly doubled the output of the mills. New machinery was his passion, as was the education of his workforce to high standards of performance.[48]

The Empress Mills made considerable profits under the control of a company, Tata and Sons, which included several family members. This encouraged further innovation. So far Bombay mills had specialized in weaving coarse cloth for home consumption, or spinning the lower counts of yarn suitable for the Chinese market. Superior woven cloth was nearly all imported. Tata decided to compete with British manufacturers by spinning a finer yarn and weaving finer materials from local cotton. The pioneering force in this venture was the Swadeshi Mills, the yarns from which had considerable success in the China market and also as far afield as Java and Smyrna.[49]

Tata's entrepreneurship did not stop here. As a comparatively young man he had thought of building an Indian iron and steel industry, producing electric energy for economic purposes and promoting technical education for Indians. His initial plans did not receive adequate support but later he did receive encouragement from both the India Office and the Viceroy of India, Lord Curzon. At the turn of the century, after visiting American steel plants, he funded research in various parts of India to discover the best location for a plant. He died in 1903 during the planning phase but his sons pursued his vision, and the steel works were finally built with American financial and technical collaboration in Jamshedpur in Bihar, an enterprise of the Tata Iron and Steel Company (TISCO) founded in 1907.[50]

The establishment of superior types of mills and of an iron and steel industry could be said to usher in a period where Parsi economic collaboration with the British became more complicated. In the middle of the nineteenth century British officialdom was forging an alliance with the leading representatives of commerce in Bombay city similar to the economic alliance between private traders and local merchants in agency houses several decades earlier. The leading merchants of the city were given the respectful designation *shet*, and at the pinnacle of these *shets* stood the richest merchant princes of the city, the great *shetia*s, among whom there were many Parsis.

The Bombay *shetia*s were important to the British Raj in Western India. Writing of the leading Baghdadi Jews in November 1862, Governor Sir Bartle Frere noted: 'They are, like the Parsees, a most valuable link between us and the natives – oriental in origin and appreciation – but English in their objects and associations, and, almost of necessity, loyal.'[51] Frere was most concerned to carry the rich mercantile community with him in all his projects – educational, building, or beautifying the city. Close association with the Parsis in particular was, however, possible because they had no taboos on mixing with Europeans. The hospitality and spectacular entertainments of the Jijibhais, the Wadias, the Banajis and the Readymoneys attracted all important members of the official community from the Governor down. Officialdom came to rely on those *shetia*s which it knew to be well disposed to the Raj. Jamshedji Jijibhai became a confidential adviser to several Governors of Bombay and, of the first thirteen Indians to be appointed Justices of the Peace in 1834, nine were Parsis.[52]

This symbiosis continued into the twentieth century, under somewhat differing circumstances. The cotton textile industry and the cotton trade continued to be the two mainstays of Bombay's economy. By 1920 Bombay's industrialists dominated extremely broad economic power bases, with approximately fifty individuals controlling the whole Indian-owned mill industry together with most of the other secondary industries and the Indian-owned modern financial institutions. Five great family-based managing agencies, including the Parsi Naoroji Wadia and Sons, Tata and Sons and D.M. Petit Sons and Co., controlled over half the spindles and looms in the city, yet in 1921 there were only 84,868 Parsis in Bombay. In 1924 Parsis comprised 18.3 per cent of the paid-up capital of the Bombay textile industry, controlled 28.1 per cent of the total spindles and 34.9 per cent of the total looms and held 26.4 per cent of the directors' positions. Some of these houses also controlled their own joint-stock banks and gave their children a technical education.[53]

Nevertheless the 1920s and 1930s were a frustrating period for Parsi mill-owners. The cotton textile industry increased its production by almost 50 per cent during the 1920s, but Japanese success in the Indian market was becoming more and more apparent. The Bombay mills were particularly affected by Japanese inroads and the Bombay cotton industry practically ceased to expand after 1922. Families such as the Petits began to move out of mill-owning, investing their capital in property and other assets. Nevertheless the managing agency system, which allowed a single firm to control a considerable number of companies with minimal investment in each of them, continued and this favoured the concentration of economic power in a few hands. The Tatas attained the position of the biggest indigenous group, with in 1931 Rs 26 crores invested in companies controlled by the group.[54]

In this period of the florescence of the Bombay textile industry, with its huge Parsi involvement, the close relationship of the Parsi industrialists to the British was subject to varying changes in fortune. J.N. Tata, more than any other Parsi entrepreneur, had been an economic nationalist pursuing various courses which would encourage India's economic self-sufficiency. But, generally speaking, Bombay industrialists were only moderately inclined towards the Indian National Congress's doctrine of economic nationalism and they were by and large opposed to the nationalist movement.[55] The Parsis among them in particular had already become enmeshed in European culture and attitudes and their economic position gave them common interest with government policies in relation to infrastructure and markets. There was much mixing on a business and political level. Many Indian-owned mills placed Europeans on their boards, and the reverse also occurred. In 1925 three Europeans sat on the boards of three Parsi-owned mills, and eight Parsis sat on the boards of European-owned firms. Parsi industrialists continued their nineteenth-century tradition of acting as agents for European firms. The Wadias, for example, held the European agency of

Platts, British mill machinery suppliers, as well as of other European firms.[56]

Gradually the official view of empire, particularly after the war, came to be one that regarded Indian industrial enterprise as beneficial to British Indian interests. For the Tatas, for example, their symbiotic relationship to the colonial state was structurally induced by the nature of their major business interests. The state was directly or indirectly the biggest buyer of some of their products – rails – while they were the only Indian suppliers of steel and rails to government railways and arsenals. Victory in Mesopotamia had only been possible due to the rails supplied by the Tatas. From 1918 a situation of mutual interdependence evolved between the imperial government and India's leading industrial group. In addition to this economic interdependence, the British were required to cement certain alliances in the face of the rising nationalist movement. The result was a measure of protection granted to certain industries, particularly in 1924 to the iron and steel industry. This policy was successful in moving the Parsi industrial elite of Bombay city away from any possibility of collaborating with the Indian National Congress. The early 1930s were a period of contraction in world trade; the Tatas and other groups wanted to gain as much benefit as possible from the imperial connection, in particular easy access to the British market and some protection against non-British competitors in the Indian market. Only towards the close of the 1930s was there some rapprochement with Congress, but by then it was too late to seriously influence Congress economic policies.[57]

The Parsi Moral Community

Chris Bayly has placed considerable emphasis on the notion of the moral community of the merchant in his study of the North Indian mercantile elite in the hundred years after 1770. To be part of these communities of trust, the merchant was required to play an active and steady part in the temple as well as the bazaar. Reverence for religious values was required. 'Moral peril and economic unreliability', says Bayly, 'were seen to be closely connected.'[58] Not surprisingly, considering their minority status, Parsis participated in a moral community of shared religious values which were unique in Western India and which appear both to have given them economic motivation and to have attracted the British to them.

Parsis are followers of the Iranian prophet Zoroaster. The core of Zoroastrian belief is that the world is in no sense perfect but rather the scene of confrontation between God, Ahura Mazda, the creator of every good thing, and an opposing spirit, Angra Mainyu, the source of evil and death. Man has the free will to stand up for the good principle, but to do this he must not involve himself in the renunciation of worldly life or turn to ascetic values. Traditional Zoroastrian teachings are found in the holy book, the Avesta, and in Pahlavi (Middle Persian) literature. The teachings emphasize that good deeds done in support of the good principle are done in the material world and that material work is intrinsically good. Man possesses free will and conscience so that he can commit himself to good or evil through his own responsibility. Important for our purpose is the emphasis in Zoroastrian teachings on the achievement of the victory of good by working, coupled with self-reliance and self-help. Such teachings, Zoroastrian scholars have argued, were favourable to the development of individual effort and human energy. The goal of work in the material world being the establishment of the Kingdom of Perfect Order, to be created in the mundane world with material goods, a high worth was placed on these goods.[59]

Scholars further argue that the increasing material wealth of Zoroastrian believers is regarded as glorifying Ahura Mazda. A verse testifying to this is repeated sixty times throughout the Gathas (seventeen hymns contained in the Avesta), bearing witness to the central importance of a believer addressing his efforts towards ever-increasing prosperity. In this way the Parsi joins a moral community. He must keep the wealth he has won through hard work and so he establishes his certain religiosity. Certain aspects of the Zoroastrian marriage and initiation ceremonies echo Zoroaster's teaching that it is good not only to acquire but also to maintain wealth. The Parsi learns from his religion to affirm life, to be active in shaping the world, and to see his material reward as proof of his espousal of good principles.[60] It was these values, argues Robert Kennedy, that shaped the commercial bent of the Bombay Parsi's mind in the nineteenth century and even before. Of course, Parsis also required opportunity to pursue their inclinations, but the value system of the moral community cannot be overlooked in explaining their enormous commercial successes under British rule.[61]

This account of the Parsi value system has not been and cannot be anchored to the biography of any particular individual acquiring wealth at any particular period. There are however certain insights we can gain from the historical material available. One concerns the Parsi priesthood, which was a hereditary occupation but which did not exclude members of priestly families from taking up secular occupations. It is interesting to note that some of the greatest Parsi commercial magnates, beginning with Rastamji Manakji and continuing on to both Jamshedji Jijibhai and J.N. Tata, came from priestly families.[62] Their understanding and absorption of the Parsi scriptures can be assumed to have been more thorough than that of other members of the community. In fact Rastamji Manakji passed through the ceremony of initiation into the priesthood at the age of 40; his biographer celebrates him as a person of deep faith, and barely mentions his success in business, reflecting perhaps Rastamji's own priorities.[63]

It appears that from the beginning of the Parsis' economic success that there were movements among successful businessmen to purify the religion and query the authority of the priesthood, leading to the latter addressing themselves to their fellow priests in Iran. As early as the fifteenth century, Parsi priests of the sacerdotal centre of Navsari sent an Indian Parsi to Iran to obtain guidance on certain religious and social questions relating to Parsis. This consultation continued, and from the same period the first of a series of letters or *Rivayets* was sent by Iranian co-religionists to answer Parsi questions relating to religious practice. These letters continued until the eighteenth century. Although it has been noted that the letters show clearly that the spirit of the Zoroastrian religion was alive in India, they have been interpreted as implying an increased reluctance on the part of the laity to comply with priestly teachings and decisions. The priests, on their part, were looking to a higher authority which could pronounce on ritual duties rather than on philosophical or canonical themes.[64] Certain leading Parsi commercial families, joined by the Kamas, the Dadiseths and the Patels, led a split in the community in 1746, ostensibly over the dating of the Zoroastrian calendar. The Dadiseth fire-temple was the centre of an 'Iranizing' movement, migrant Zoroastrian priests bringing ancient texts and traditional knowledge; attempts were made to inculcate a strong consciousness of the Zoroastrian heritage.[65]

This tradition of Parsi *shetia*s taking over the role of purifying religion from a weakened and ill-educated priesthood continued in the nineteenth century. English policy in Bombay had been from the beginning to encourage various communities to form *panchayat*s (councils to arbitrate internal or group disputes), and the Parsi *panchayat* of Bombay had been established between 1673 and 1728. The five founding members included the three sons of Rastamji Manakji from Surat, and the positions on the *panchayat* became hereditary in certain merchant families. In addition to all its duties in relation to migratory Parsis from Gujarat, from the early nineteenth century it concerned itself more and more with purifying Parsi customs from Hindu and Muslim influences. Parsi priests played a relatively subordinate role in what was largely a *shetia*s movement.[66] These *shetia*s attempts to purify the Zoroastrian faith became more earnest when, by the 1850s, they were joined by young Parsi graduates from the newly founded Bombay University.

In 1851 K.N. Kama financed the establishment of the Rahnumai Mazdayasnan Sabha, led by a young graduate, with the aim of purging contemporary Zoroastrianism of ceremonies and beliefs which made it ridiculous in the eyes of Western rationalism – in particular the extravagant ceremonies associated with funerals, betrothals and marriages; the custom of infant marriage; and the belief in astrology. In fact the lectures and pamphlets of the Parsi intelligentsia initially outran the views of the original *shetia* reformers, but in time the desire to reconstruct the Parsi past and to research into its literature animated *shetias* and intelligentsia alike, resulting in publications from both sides on current Iranian glories, Iranian literature, and an investigation into the community's history, customs and religion. It was realized, however, that real knowledge could come only by applying contemporary philological techniques to the Zoroastrian sacred texts and languages, by means of which the Parsi priesthood would be reformed. The leader in this enterprise was Kharshedji Rastamji Kama, a second cousin of K.N. Kama. Returning to India from England in the late 1850s, he stopped for some time at Paris and Erlangen to study Iranian languages with some of the leading European scholars. On his return to Bombay he opened an informal class in 1861 to instruct a small group of priests in the new scientific approach to their sacred books, and in 1864 he established a society to further this work. The aim of the society was to enlist the sympathy of traditional scholars for the new research, in the hope that an authoritative version of Parsi religious belief could be placed before the Parsi public. A number of sacred works were translated due to Kama's patronage, and he himself produced works based on original sources.

Other *shetias* assisted. In 1854 K.N. Kama set up a priestly school to teach Zend, Pahlavi and Persian to the priesthood. In the 1850s, too, Jamshedji Jijibhai set up a translation fund to enable the fruits of modern research to be presented to the community. In 1863 he followed with the founding of a priestly college to which other *shetias* contributed funds. Advances in religious education continued for the rest of the nineteenth century.[67] The Parsi moral community benefited greatly from the religious motivations of its business leaders, and these motivations undoubtedly assisted them in their commercial life.

The Parsi moral community was enhanced by the establishment of a comprehensive welfare system under *shetia* control, based again on the religiously motivated attitude that the possession of wealth is a fundamentally positive attribute. Parsi charities were remarked on even from the days of Rastamji Manakji in Surat, when the broker constructed roads and bridges, assisted the poor, and paid for religious ceremonies and some of the clergy's needs.[68] Subsequently in Bombay the Parsi *panchayat* administered benevolent funds and, even after its technical demise after 1830, it continued to administer charitable foundations and public welfare activities. Some of the largest merchants in the China trade in the early nineteenth century, such as S.M. Readymoney and P.B. Wadia, were immensely charitable and fed thousands during the Gujarat famine.[69] On the announcement of his knighthood in 1842, Sir Jamshedji Jijibhai established a fund which evolved into the Sir Jamshedji Jijibhai Parsi Benevolent Institution, to educate the poor of the community in Bombay and Gujarat. Aware that the trade of the Parsi weavers in Gujarat had been entirely destroyed, he understood that education would provide them with alternative employment.[70] Other *shetia*s of the Petit, Readymoney and Tata families endowed hospitals, schools, libraries and university buildings.[71] It has been argued that involvement in this philanthropy was consistent with the cautious, risk-averse character of the merchant mentality, a way of establishing one's credibility as a trustworthy businessman. Forms of giving changed under the imperial power, but merchants continued to show their desire to maintain their reputations within their community by strong charitable involvement with schools, libraries and hospitals.[72] In accommodating to the influence of Victorian values, Parsi merchants were able to gain considerable respect in imperial circles and at times even to act in solidarity with British officials.[73]

The final metamorphosis of the Parsi community, just as it was undertaking the reform of its religious practices, was its increasing Anglicization. It has been argued that, long before the introduction of English education in Bombay in the early nineteenth century, there was a religious affinity between the two communities. Governor Aungier in the seventeenth century drew attention to the parallels between Zoroastrianism and the Protestant faith: judgement was based on morality and ethics and early travellers commented favourably on the Parsis' monotheism, their lack of idols and their high moral standards.[74] The high regard of the British for the Parsis, and the latter's ready response in adjusting some of their social customs to British tastes, fostered the Parsi commercial rise and the advancement of the entire community.[75]

The initial Parsi response to opportunities for English education in Bombay came not from the major families but from those below them who saw an opportunity for their sons to rise. A far higher than average number of Parsis acquired the language and educational qualifications necessary for access to new types of occupation in administration, law, education and health as well as in the commercial and technical branches. In 1898 forty out of seventy-three Indian lawyers in Bombay were Parsis; similarly, four out of the twelve higher Indian civil servants were Parsis. Journeys to England for education became more and more common. A survey of Indians in 1884 indicated that Parsis formed 70 per cent of the student body. By the end of the nineteenth century there were three Parsi members of Parliament in Westminster. The British also raised leading Parsis to the nobility. By 1908 three Parsis had been made hereditary baronets, and a total of sixty-three Parsis received knighthoods up to 1946. Gujarati, although still spoken within the family, had been replaced by English as the cultural and educational language of the Parsis.[76] A Parsi author, writing in 1884, stated: 'The Parsi mode of life may be described to be an eclectic *ensemble*, half-European and half-Hindu. As they advance every year in civilisation and enlightenment, they copy more closely English manners and modes of living.'[77]

This final stage in the development of the Parsi moral community, in which the community became Anglicized while taking care to reform its own customs and religion, constitutes only part of a long process which Eckehart Kulke calls 'selective assimilation'.[78] And Parsis selected to their advantage. The Parsi intelligentsia, unlike the Parsi *shetias*, added much to the economic philosophy of the Indian National Congress. Their English education and upbringing did not prevent them confronting their English rulers with theories such as Dadabhai Naoroji's 'drain of wealth' argument. But even in this they were true to the hopes of the statesman who had introduced English education into India. 'We must', said T.B. Macaulay in 1835, 'at present do our best to form a class who may be interpreters between us and the millions whom we govern – a class of persons, Indian in blood and colour, but English in taste, in opinions, in morals and in intellect.'[79]

Reprise

Max Weber was concerned with the characteristics of the entrepreneur, and particularly with his 'spirit'. He saw him possessed of 'clarity and vision and ability to act' and characterized by 'very definite and highly developed ethical qualities'.[80] Later writers on the sociology of entrepreneurship, such as Schumpeter, stressed creativity and the ability to undertake 'deviating conduct'.[81] Turning to India, Weber failed to find the entrepreneurial personality:

> The conception that through simple behavior addressed to the 'demands of the day', one may achieve salvation which lies at the basis of all the specifically occidental significance of 'personality' is alien to Asia ... They were, indeed, protected by the rigid ceremonial and hierarchic stylization of their life conduct from the modern Occidental search, for the individual self in contrast to all others, the attempt to take the self by the forelock and pull it out of the mud, forming it into a 'personality'.[82]

Yet of all the stranger communities dealt with here, it was an India-based diaspora, the Parsis, who were most congruent in their personality type with their European partners. They made a decisive and rapid transition to the industrial civilization of the nineteenth century, the first Parsi steam sloop being assembled in 1829. Just as sixteenth-century Seville had implications for Manila, nineteenth-century Manchester had consequences for Bombay, and, in the case of Bombay, conjoining was voluntary rather than imposed.

It has been argued by Everett Hagen that differences in personality, rather than differential circumstances, were the major reasons for Britain's primacy in the Industrial Revolution.[83] Britain's diverse and long-continued superiority in technical innovation during the early modern era and the eighteenth century, Hagen claims, was the result of an innovational mentality in all spheres of life, including government. The British personality was marked by trust in an individual's own capacity,

> a resultant willingness to approach the world around oneself and operate on it. Further, this personality was characterised by objectivity, an ability to understand the attitudes and reactions of other persons and thereby adapt social institutions to new situations.[84]

For at least a century after its founding Bombay was isolated and remote from other British settlements in India; its existence was precarious and its growth difficult. In the Parsis the British found a community which 'could do the things the English most valued better than the English themselves'.[85] They were consummate shipbuilders and at length they had in service many British ships and captains. The two stranger communities discovered an affinity. The cross-fertilization of these two communities is remarkable, and nowhere more so than in the field of industrial endeavour, where a series of Parsi personalities achieved enormous technical and organizational successes. Both communities were marked, in Schumpeter's words, by 'creative response', by the ability to 'do something else, something that is outside the range of existing practice'.[86]

Notes

1. D.F. Karaka, *History of the Parsis including their Manners, Customs, Religion, and Present Position*, vol. 2, London, Macmillan, 1884, pp. 8, 22–23; Kulke, *The Parsees*, p. 32.

2. M.N. Pearson, 'Brokers in Western Indian Port Cities. Their Role in Servicing Foreign Merchants', *Modern Asian Studies* 22, no. 3 (1988), pp. 457–459.

3. Quoted in A. Das Gupta, *Malabar in Asian Trade 1740–1800*, Cambridge, Cambridge University Press, 1967, p. 104.

4. Pearson, 'Brokers', p. 472.

5. Imperial Gazetteer of India, *Baroda*, Calcutta, Superintendent of Government Printing, 1908, p. 102.

6. A. Das Gupta, 'The Merchants of Surat, c.1700–50', in E. Leach and S.N. Mukherjee (eds), *Elites in South Asia*, Cambridge, Cambridge University Press, 1970, p. 220.

7. Quoted in R.B. Paymaster, *Early History of the Parsees in India from their Landing in Sanjan to 1700 A.D.*, Bombay, Zartoshti Mandli, 1954, p. 50.

8. *Ibid.*, pp. 42-43, 45, 51.

9. A. Wink, *Al-Hind. The Making of the Indo-Islamic World*, vol. 1: *Early Medieval India and the Expansion of Islam, 7th–11th Centuries*, Leiden, E.J. Brill, 1991, p. 105; A. Wink, 'The Jewish Diaspora in India: Eighth to Thirteenth Centuries', *Indian Economic and Social History Review* 24, no. 4 (1987), pp. 350–351.

10. Wink, *Al-Hind*, pp. 105–106; Paymaster, *History of the Parsees*, pp. 35–36.

11. Karaka, *History of the Parsis*, vol. 1, pp. 31–34; Paymaster, *History of the Parsees*, pp. 13–14; Kulke, *The Parsees*, pp. 28–29.

12. Karaka, *History of the Parsis*, vol. 1, pp. 35–36; 2, p. 4; Paymaster, *History of the Parsees*, cf. pp. 17, 23; A.V. Desai, 'The Origins of Parsi Enterprise', *Indian Economic and Social History Review* 5, no. 4 (1968), p. 309.

13. Forrest, *Selections from Letters, Despatches* 1, p. 110; C. Fawcett, *The English Factories in India*, vol. 1 (New Series) *1670–1671*, Oxford, Clarendon Press, 1936, p. 56.

14. Desai, 'Parsi Enterprise', pp. 314–317.

15. T. Raychaudhuri, 'The Commercial Entrepreneur in Pre-Colonial India: Aspirations and Expectations. A Note' in R. Ptak and D. Rothermund (eds), *Emporia, Commodities and Entrepreneurs in Asian Maritime Trade, c.1400–1700*, Stuttgart, Franz Steiner Verlag, 1991, pp. 345–346; Das Gupta, 'Merchants of Surat', pp. 210–214, 222; Karaka, *History of the Parsis*, vol. 2, pp. 12–13, 16–17; Kulke, *The Parsees*, pp. 32–33.

16. Kulke, *The Parsees*, pp. 33–35.

17. Fawcett, *English Factories* 1, pp. 44, 56, 165; Forrest, *Selections from Letters, Despatches* 1, pp. 121, 130.

18. Bombay to London, 3 Apr. 1677, Forrest, *Selections from Letters, Despatches* 1, p. 130.

19. Paymaster, *History of the Parsees*, p. 89.

20. J.R. Hinnells, 'Anglo-Parsi Commercial Relations in Bombay Prior to 1847', *Journal of the K.R. Cama Oriental Institute* 46 (1978), pp. 8–9; Karaka, *History of the Parsis*, vol. 2, pp. 55-56.

21. Kulke, *The Parsees*, pp. 33–35; P. Nightingale, *Trade and Empire in Western India 1784–1806*, Cambridge, Cambridge University Press, 1970, pp. 13–14.

22. Nightingale, *Trade and Empire*, pp. 17–20.

23. *Ibid.*, pp. 20–22.

24. Hinnells, 'Anglo-Parsi Commercial Relations', p. 15.

25. C. Dobbin, *Urban Leadership in Western India. Politics and Communities in Bombay City 1840–1885*, London, Oxford University Press, 1972, p. 9.

26. Nightingale, *Trade and Empire*, pp. 6–7; J.K. Fairbank, *Trade and Diplomacy on the China Coast. The Opening of the Treaty Ports, 1842–1854*, Stanford, Stanford University Press, 1964, pp. 59–60.

27. Nightingale, *Trade and Empire*, p. 23.

28. *Ibid.*, pp. 23–24; Fairbank, *Trade and Diplomacy*, pp. 59–60.

29. Nightingale, *Trade and Empire*, pp. 128, 134, 188; Fairbank, *Trade and Diplomacy,* pp. 59–60; Dobbin, *Urban Leadership*, pp. 9–10; A. Guha, 'Parsi Seths as Entrepreneurs, 1750–1850', *Economic and Political Weekly* 5 (1970), pp. m-107, m-111.

30. Fairbank, *Trade and Diplomacy*, pp. 63–67, 155, 160, 173; Karaka, *History of the Parsis*, vol. 2, pp. 43–44; Hao Yen-p'ing, *The Commercial Revolution in Nineteenth-Century China. The Rise of Sino-Western Mercantile Capital*, Berkeley/Los Angeles, University of California Press, 1986, p. 191.

31. Karaka, *History of the Parsis*, vol. 2, pp. 54, 57–58; Dobbin, *Urban Leadership*, pp. 9–10.

32. Karaka, *History of the Parsis*, vol. 2, pp. 59–60, 71–72, 76–77; Dobbin, *Urban Leadership*, p. 11.

33. Karaka, *History of the Parsis*, vol. 2, pp. 78–79, 88; Dobbin, *Urban Leadership*, p. 12; Hao, *Commercial Revolution*, p. 126; Guha, 'Parsi Seths', p. m-111.

34. Guha, 'Parsi Seths', pp. m-104, m-111.

35. *Ibid.*, pp. m-111–m-115.

36. Desai, 'Parsi Enterprise', p. 308; Kulke, *The Parsees*, p. 122; Nightingale, *Trade and Empire*, p. 22.

37. Guha, 'Parsi Seths', pp. m-111, m-113, m-115.

38. Karaka, *History of the Parsis*, vol. 2, pp. 257–259.

39. C. Markovits, *Indian Business and Nationalist Politics 1931–39. The Indigenous Capitalist Class and the Rise of the Congress Party*, Cambridge, Cambridge University Press, 1985, p. 8; Kulke, *The Parsees*, pp. 122–123.

40. Dobbin, *Urban Leadership*, p. 19; Kulke, *The Parsees*, p. 125.

41. Dobbin, *Urban Leadership*, pp. 18–20; Desai, 'Parsi Enterprise', p. 312.

42. Kulke, *The Parsees*, p. 123; see also pp. 56–57 and Karaka, *History of the Parsis*, vol. 2, p. 248.

43. Kulke, *The Parsees*, pp. 56–57, 123, 125–126; Dobbin, *Urban Leadership*, p. 8; Karaka, *History of the Parsis*, vol. 1, p. 91; R.E. Kennedy, 'The Protestant Ethic and the Parsis', *American Journal of Sociology* 68 (1962–63), p. 19.

44. Dobbin, *Urban Leadership*, pp. 16, 18; Guha, 'Parsi Seths', pp. m-113, m-114.

45. Dobbin, *Urban Leadership*, pp. 12, 17; Karaka, *History of the Parsis*, vol. 2, pp. 253–257.

46. A. Guha, 'The Comprador Role of Parsi Seths, 1750–1850', *Economic and Political Weekly* 5 (1970), pp. 1935–1936; Dobbin, *Urban Leadership*, p. 21.

47. F.R. Harris, *Jamsetji Nusserwanji Tata*, Bombay, Blackie and Son, 1958, pp. 2–3, 5–7, 10–11.

48. *Ibid.*, pp. 2–6, 9, 13, 21, 24–33; S.D. Mehta, *The Cotton Mills of India 1854 to 1954*, Bombay, The Textile Association, 1954, pp. 57–62.

49. Harris, *Jamsetji Nusserwanji Tata*, pp. 41, 47, 52–59.

50. *Ibid.*, pp. 146, 154–155, 159, 165–168, 170; Kulke, *The Parsees*, pp. 127, 130–132.

51. Quoted in Dobbin, *Urban Leadership*, p. 23.

52. *Ibid.*, pp. 23–24.

53. A.D.D. Gordon, *Businessmen and Politics. Rising Nationalism and a Modernising Economy in Bombay, 1918–1933*, New Delhi, Manohar, 1978, pp. 49, 62–63, 65–66, 109.

54. *Ibid.*, p. 66; Markovits, *Indian Business*, pp. 12, 14–15.

55. Gordon, *Businessmen and Politics*, pp. 1, 7; Kulke, *The Parsees*, pp. 130–132.

56. Gordon, *Businessmen and Politics*, pp. 5, 59–62.

57. Markovits, *Indian Business*, pp. 11–12, 27, 179–181.

58. Bayly, *Rulers, Townsmen and Bazaars*, p. 385; see also pp. 31, 371, 373.

59. R.E. Kennedy, 'The Protestant Ethic', pp. 13–15; Kulke, *The Parsees*, pp. 253–256; J.R. Hinnells, 'Zoroastrianism', in J.R. Hinnells (ed.), *The Penguin Dictionary of Religions*, Harmondsworth, Penguin Books, 1984, pp. 361–362.

60. Kulke, *The Parsees*, pp. 253–256; Kennedy, 'The Protestant Ethic', p. 16.

61. Kennedy, 'The Protestant Ethic', pp. 17–18, 20.

62. Raychaudhuri, 'The Commercial Entrepreneur', p. 346; Kulke, *The Parsees*, pp. 48–49.

63. Raychaudhuri, 'The Commercial Entrepreneur', pp. 347, 351.

64. Karaka, *History of the Parsis*, vol. 2, pp. 5–6; Paymaster, *History of the Parsees*, pp. 66–83; Desai, 'Parsi Enterprise', p. 308; J.R. Hinnells, 'British Accounts of Parsi Religion, 1619–1843', *Journal of the K.R. Cama Oriental Institute* 46 (1978), p. 26.

65. Karaka, *History of the Parsis*, vol. 1, pp. 105–117; J.R. Hinnells, 'Bombay, Persian Communities of', *Encyclopaedia Iranica* 4, no. 4, London, Routledge and Kegan Paul, 1993, p. 344.

66. C. Dobbin, 'The Parsi Panchayat in Bombay City in the Nineteenth Century', *Modern Asian Studies* 4, no. 2 (1970), p. 150; Kulke, *The Parsees*, pp. 61–66, 77–78; Karaka, *History of the Parsis*, vol. 1, pp. 230–233.

67. Dobbin, *Urban Leadership*, pp. 59–64, 247.

68. Raychaudhuri, 'The Commercial Entrepreneur', pp. 346–347.

69. Karaka, *History of the Parsis*, vol. 2, pp. 58, 71–72.

70. Dobbin, 'Parsi Panchayat', p. 157.

71. Kulke, *The Parsees*, pp. 73–75.

72. D.E. Haynes, 'From Tribute to Philanthropy: The Politics of Gift Giving in a Western Indian City', *Journal of Asian Studies* 46, no. 2 (1987), pp. 340–341.

73. Dobbin, *Urban Leadership*, pp. 23–24.

74. Hinnells, 'British Accounts', pp. 20–31, 35; Kulke, *The Parsees*, p. 240.

75. Hinnells, 'Anglo-Parsi Commercial Relations', pp. 11–12.

76. J.R. Hinnells, 'Parsis and British Education, 1820–1880', *Journal of the K.R. Cama Oriental Institute* 46 (1978), pp. 53, 56–57; Kulke, *The Parsees*, pp. 55, 78–83, 85, 138–139.

77. Karaka, *History of the Parsis*, vol. 1, p. 123.

78. Kulke, *The Parsees*, pp. 78–79.

79. C. Dobbin, *Basic Documents in the Development of Modern India and Pakistan, 1835–1947*, London, Van Nostrand Reinhold, 1970, p. 18.

80. Weber, *Protestant Ethic*, p. 69.

81. Schumpeter, *The Theory*, p. 86.

82. Weber, *Religion of India*, p. 342.

83. E.E. Hagen, 'British Personality and the Industrial Revolution: The Historical Evidence', in T. Burns and S.B. Saul (eds), *Social Theory and Economic Change*, London, Tavistock Publications, 1967, p. 37.

84. *Ibid.*, pp. 41–42.

85. P. Spear, *The Nabobs. A Study of the Social Life of the English in Eighteenth Century India*, London, Oxford University Press, 1963, p. 74.

86. Schumpeter, 'Creative Response', p. 150.

5

From Gujarat to Zanzibar: the Ismaili Partnership in East Africa 1841–1939

The British experiment in opening up East Africa to economic development after 1886 would have been a difficult enterprise without the willing participation of certain communities from Western India. From the earliest decades the official view was that East Africa was 'the natural outlet for Indian emigration',[1] accepting at the same time that a certain area might be reserved for white settlement. Of the Indian Muslim communities which took up these new opportunities, one of the most prominent was that of the Ismailis from Kutch in Gujarat, commonly called the Khojas. It is intended to argue here that the Ismailis succeeded economically in East Africa not merely because they entered the region under British patronage, but because they had earlier adapted themselves in a variety of ways to success in a new and challenging venture.

The Ismailis possessed a unique and many-textured identity. Their homeland, Kutch, to the north-west of Gujarat and adjacent to Sind, was a treeless, barren and rocky region surrounded by water and waste land. The region was known for its frequent recurrence of scarcity and famine, while more than 50 per cent of its total area consisted of the uninhabitable Rann of Kutch. Outmigration was a way of life in Kutch, which also possessed a coastline bordering on the Indian Ocean, giving the area the double advantage of established trade routes both by land and by sea. The main port of Mandvi traded with the Persian Gulf, Zanzibar, the Malabar coast and Bombay, and from here the main trading castes, both Hindus and Muslims, established a tradition of leaving their homeland for outside gain.[2]

Kutch had long had a high percentage of Muslim conversions. In 1821 it was estimated that more than one-third of the population was Muslim.[3] The form of Islam brought to Kutch was highly suited to local beliefs, where there was a tradition of worshipping local saints and a belief in divinely reincarnated human teachers according to the spiritual needs of the time. Of the three main Muslim commercial groups which eventuated from these missionary activities, the Bohras, Memons and Ismailis, the Ismailis were by far the most complex. The Ismaili missionaries of the fourteenth and fifteenth centuries represented a Shia sect, the Shia Imami Ismailis, which believed in a divinely inspired and infallible *imam* (spiritual and temporal leader).[4] They gained their first success among the commercial caste of the Lohanas, followers of the Hindu god Vishnu. But this caste had itself already evolved from an Afghan trading group, probably non-Muslim, which used the great trade routes from Kabul and Kandahar to descend regularly on the Hindustan plains and return with cloth, sugar and aromatic roots.[5]

Conversion of the Lohanas probably first took place in Sind and the religious writings of the Ismailis were in the Sindhi language. The Lohanas, who must have already been highly syncretic in their religious beliefs, found Ismaili teachings extremely congenial. The concept of the *imam* and the doctrines surrounding him were readily accepted, as the Lohanas' Vaishnavism already incorporated the concept that divinity could be reincarnated in human teachers according to the needs of the time.[6] The Shia practice of *taqiya,* or permissible dissimulation of real belief in difficult situations, meant that Hindu beliefs and practices could be retained by converts. Periodical additions of new converts maintained the strength of Hindu ways and thought, while correspondence was maintained with the Ismailis' divinely inspired *imam* in Iran, who in the late sixteenth century wrote for his Indian followers a book entitled *The Maxims of Fortitude* which became part of the scriptures of the Ismailis.[7] In this way the Ismailis developed a dual identity which served them well in adapting to new commercial situations.

The Ismailis, however, also possessed a unifying religious institution by means of which they conducted their affairs as a community. From the beginning the missionaries established Ismaili religious lodges, the so-called *jamatkhana*,[8] where prayer and community administration were conducted. A mixture of Hindu and Muslim religious beliefs prevailed in the *jamatkhana*, but administrative techniques gradually evolved which gave the community its unique administrative solidarity. From the very earliest days Ismailis were exhorted to save their money in order to pay a tithe and also certain minor contributions to their revealed *imam* living in Iran. The tithe was paid every month, while there were also occasionally extraordinary levies on Ismailis' possessions. Although these funds were often spent on improvements for the Ismaili community in the place of collection, they were regarded as the personal property of the *imam* and were controlled by his agents. These agents also advised on the *jamatkhana*'s election of a *mukhi* (treasurer) and *kamaria* (accountant). The *jamatkhana* also served as a council hall, where members voted on issues placed before them and were theoretically equal and at liberty to speak on any issue. The *jamatkhana* provided for a highly institutionalized form of religious life which gave shape to the varying, imperfectly defined religious beliefs of the community.[9] Ismaili identity, therefore, mingled flexibility of religious views together with strict rules for the administrative maintenance of the community. When they came, Ismailis were ready to seize new opportunities.

The Zanzibar Preadaptation

Long before the Ismailis became one of the major Indian communities to assist the British in the penetration of East Africa, they had adapted themselves to the commercial life of the East African coast, particularly as it came to centre on

Zanzibar. Kutchi vessels brought a range of goods to the coast, including salt, opium and cotton cloth.[10] But Kutchi merchants were particularly involved in the rise of the Sultanate of Oman, based from the late eighteenth century on Muscat, to a position of commercial predominance in the Western Indian Ocean. As Oman became an expansionist commercial power, more Indians from Kutch settled in Muscat, assisting the Omani merchant class to exchange slaves and African ivory for Indian cloth, and transporting Indian and British manufactured goods to the Persian Gulf. By 1744 the Omanis had installed their own governor on Zanzibar and attempts were being made to secure the routes into the East African hinterland. These attempts became more urgent when the ivory trade received a great boost in the late eighteenth century from demand by the newly affluent in the industrializing West.[11]

By the turn of the nineteenth century Indian merchants from Kutch were well represented in Muscat. They included a considerable settlement of Ismailis. But they were also beginning to make Zanzibar their chief port of call as gradually the island developed into an entrepôt and came to control the flow of imported cloth and beads used in the interior trade.[12] As the Omani state expanded, so did Indian enterprise. More produce was imported into Zanzibar, including British iron. Gradually Ismailis settled on the island itself, generally as agents of commercial firms established in Kutch, Surat or Bombay. In 1841 the ruler of Muscat, Said bin Sultan, moved his capital to Zanzibar, bringing as a result many Indians from Kutch and Surat who had been commercially active in Muscat. Zanzibar developed in the nineteenth century as the centre of a large trading empire acting as a commercial intermediary between the interior of Africa and the newly industrializing West. With the huge trade expansion in the hinterland, the Omani state attempted to centralize the whole foreign trade of Africa from Eastern Zaire to the Indian Ocean on their entrepôt, sustained by the Sultan's monopoly over the coastal termini of trade routes from the interior.[13]

Indian mercantile success in Zanzibar was initially associated with the rising demand for ivory, which in turn brought with it the need to exploit the resources of the interior. By 1819 the Indian settlement on the island was 214, some of whom were offshoots of the Indian mercantile class in Muscat. They were described as wealthy and as dominating trade. Their dominance over imports related to the demand for 'Surat cloths' from Kutch and Gujarat; in 1811 it was estimated that nearly 50 per cent of the imports at Zanzibar consisted of these cloths, which were known to be of good quality and durable and yet to cost only half as much as the Manchester product. Kutch, the home of the Ismailis, dominated the trade. Kutch imported twice as much ivory as the ports of Bombay and Surat and as late as 1839 she was still supplying three times as many cotton goods. This Zanzibar trade, linked with the East African coast, came to dominate the foreign trade of Kutch. In 1839 as many as twenty vessels from the main Kutchi port of Mandvi were involved.[14]

It has been argued that Zanzibar's Indian traders gradually became an indigenous force in East Africa owing to the weakening of their ties with India when ivory, their main export, came to be rerouted from Bombay to London. Cloth supplies, too, became unreliable after the famines of 1803, 1813, 1823–25 and 1833–34 in Gujarat. The Omani authorities also facilitated this process by trying to integrate Indian merchants into the commercial existence of the port, granting control over customs to an Indian firm in 1819.[15] Although the number of Ismailis is not known at this period, in 1870 it was reported that, of a total Indian population of 3,620 – the vast majority of whom were Muslims – 2,558 were Ismailis. The Ismaili community was so large because there was a tradition of bringing wives from India.[16] In any case, the size of the Ismaili community must be borne in mind when dealing with sources which only refer to the Indian community without further subdivision. The notion of indigenization too must be viewed critically. While the Indian firms on Zanzibar were not merely branches of Bombay firms (indeed, apparently none originated from that city), a number did move their head-quarters to Bombay during the second half of the nineteenth century.[17]

Family tradition in many cases represented poverty as the cause of emigration to Zanzibar.[18] It seems likely that early capital was acquired on a credit basis from Western traders at the port, initial short-term credits having been granted by American Salem vessels arriving in the 1830s. Gradually a substantial amount of merchant capital came to reside in the hands of Indian merchants and, as early as the mid-1840s, there began to be a reversal in the flow of credit. Initially Indian credit was provided by Jairam Sewji, the customs master, but by the 1860s and early 1870s many foreign firms seem to have been working substantially with loans from Indian financiers.[19] The main port of Zanzibar became a huge emporium for all the trade of the east coast of Africa, and Indians were involved in every conceivable business undertaking. A report on Zanzibar in 1860 referred to the extensive trade with Bombay, Kutch and Arabia in which Indian traders played a vital part, and in fact nearly all of Zanzibar's foreign trade passed through their hands. Ivory was sent down to them at the coast, as was gum copal, whilst the entire cargoes of American and Hamburg vessels were purchased by them. They also carried on the entire retail trade of the port. By the 1870s trade continued to be based largely on its traditional pattern of exchanging Indian goods – cloth, metalware, grain and beads – for African produce such as ivory, cloves, gum copal, hides, horns and copra.[20]

The success of these Ismaili and other Indian merchants in Zanzibar was looked upon indulgently by the British authorities in Western India. Their success validated British policy, which had chosen the island Sultanate as the instrument to ensure British control over the East African coast towns and their hinterlands and so reinforce British dominance in the Indian Ocean. British officials had encouraged the Sultan to move his capital from Muscat and in 1841 they established a consulate there. A prime interest of the Consul, up to the partition of East Africa in the late 1880s, was to foster the use of Indian merchants for the so-called 'legitimate commerce', which was to be expanded to the extent that it drove out the slave trade, still functioning on Zanzibar for clove production in the 1840s and 1850s. By 'legitimate commerce' it was hoped that not only would the slave trade be suppressed but that the interior of tropical Africa would be civilized and developed. Indians were beginning to assist in this latter goal too, Indian business firms acting as bankers and suppliers for the mainland expeditions of British explorers.[21] In this way, before the coming of the scramble for Africa, Ismaili traders were an important part of the British system of informal control on the East African coast, and were preadapted to success in the interior.

The final phase of the preadaptation process came with Ismaili and other Indian involvement with the caravan trade to the interior. The core of Zanzibar's commercial empire was the central region of East Africa directly facing Zanzibar. It was crossed by two sets of long-distance trade routes entering right into the African heartland as far as Uganda in the north-east, eastern Zaire in the west, and northern Zambia in the south-west. With the increased demand for ivory from the beginning of the nineteenth century, coastal traders were pushed far into the interior; the route to Buganda had been pioneered by coastal traders, largely Arab and Swahili, by the mid-nineteenth century. By 1873 eastern Zaire was yielding ivory. In this trade Indian merchant capital found a profitable outlet. Indians themselves did not venture to the interior, but their capital was used in trading enterprises from the middle of the nineteenth century. Goods were advanced to Arab and Swahili traders at a price which was usually 50 per cent above their real value, many of the traders being individuals of limited capital who became agents of the Indian financiers. Long-term credit was vital, and so large amounts of Indian capital came to be tied up in the caravan trade.[22]

As the volume of trade coming down from East Africa increased by the 1870s, a growing number of Indian merchants settled along the coast in towns such as Kilwa, Bagamoyo, Mombasa and Malindi, largely acting as agents for firms headquartered in Zanzibar. Much Indian financing of the local caravan traders was in the form of loans and advances, on various kinds of security, of a spectrum of goods which were

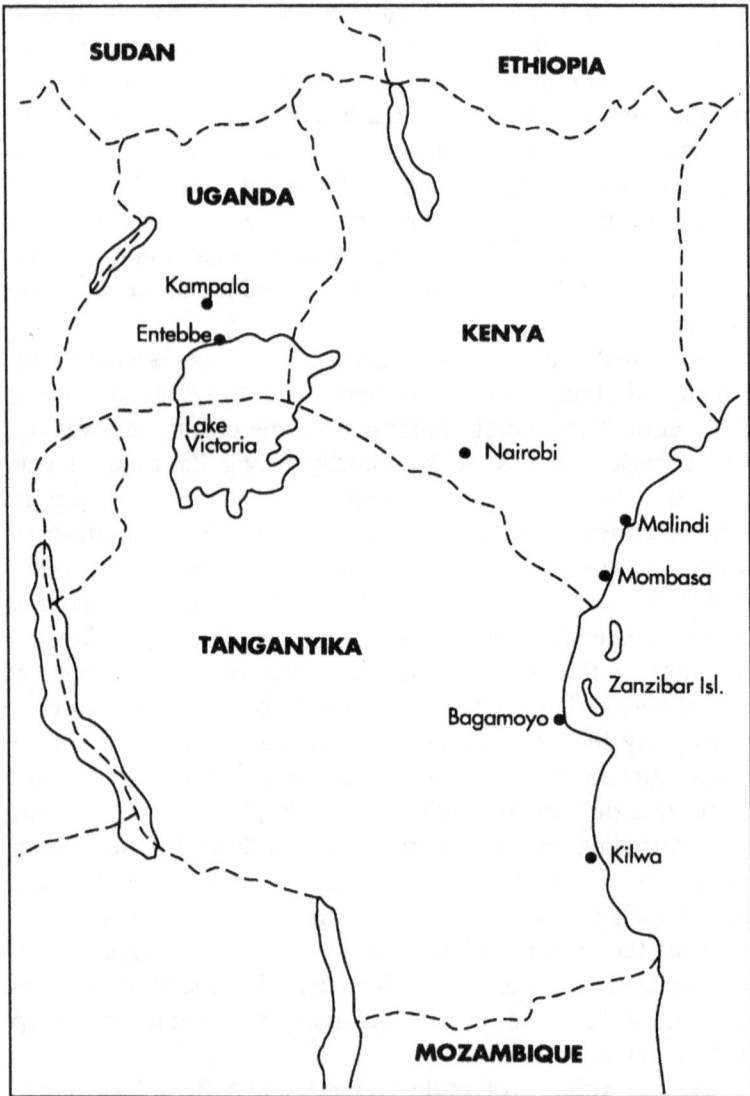

Map 5: East Africa c. 1914 (based on Mangat: *Asians in East Africa*)

to be bartered in the interior for local products, particularly ivory. Indian merchants were also able to extend valuable services to the European explorers by acting as their local bankers, helping to equip their expeditions and forwarding additional supplies up-country. Some did themselves penetrate the interior. Ismailis are reported to have been the first Indians in the interior, one reaching Lake Victoria in 1872.[23] Certain Ismailis acquired considerable fortunes in this financing of the caravan trade. Taria Topan arrived in Zanzibar to join his father and, from 1851, became the principal intermediary of certain American traders, buying up whole cargoes of their imports. Once established in business, in the late 1860s he began a new enterprise by giving an advance in goods to a caravan leader going to Lake Tanganyika. After this was successful he financed other Arab-Swahili merchants and also Europeans.[24] By 1871 he was described as the only merchant able to compete with the leading Hindu firm in Zanzibar.[25] H.M. Stanley reported at the time of his 1874 expedition:

> One of the richest merchants in town is Tarya Topan – a self-made man of Hindustan, singularly honest and just; a devout Muslim, yet liberal in his ideas; a sharp businessman, yet charitable. I made Tarya's acquaintance in 1871, and the righteous manner in which he then dealt by me caused me now to proceed to him again for the same purpose as formerly, viz. to sell me cloth, cottons, and kanikis at reasonable prices, and accept my bills on Mr Joseph M. Levy, of the *Daily Telegraph*.[26]

The total weight of this expedition when fitted out required 300 men to carry it.[27]

Taria Topan went on to become the Customs Master of Zanzibar and, as leader of the majority Indian community, he played an important role in Zanzibar affairs in the 1870s and 1880s. His success gave an impetus to Ismaili enterprise in East Africa generally. His activities were all those which might gain British approval. He financially supported schools and hospitals and, for his assistance to British anti-slavery efforts, he was knighted in 1890. By then he had already left Zanzibar, moving his headquarters to Bombay from where, in the 1860s, he entered the lucrative China trade with three large vessels. He also made efforts to develop commercial ventures in Europe; in his 'London business' he had a considerable sum invested.[28]

The Crystallization of Religious Identity

On the eve of the scramble for Africa, Ismailis had evolved institutionally in a way that gave them even greater advantage over other communities in African enterprise. Zanzibar was not the only place of emigration for Kutchi Ismailis. A considerable number had been migrating to Bombay since the late eighteenth century. Like the Parsis, by the 1840s so many Ismailis had migrated from Kutch and Kathiawar that Bombay had become their headquarters in Western India, containing as it did about 2,000 of them. The local produce of Kutch, such as pulses, cloth, cotton-seed and garlic, were purchased by Ismaili merchants from cultivators and sold in Bombay.[29]

But certain members of the Ismaili community rose to considerable economic heights and, by the 1850s, had even reached the position of *shetias*. One Ismaili *shetia*, Habib Ibrahim, was by 1859 a shareholder in Bombay's first cotton mill. These *shetias* wanted to reform Ismaili religion and steer the community in the direction of Sunni forms and observances. As early as 1822 the Ismaili *shetias* erected a Sunni mosque in the community's burial ground, to which they attempted to wean the rest of the community largely without success. There was, of course, considerable personal advantage for the richer members of the community in declaring their allegiance to the Sunni form of Islam. They wished to be rid of their contributions to their *imam* in Iran and of his interference in the workings of the community. In 1829 Habib Ibrahim and the other leading *shetias* refused to pay the customary tithe and set on foot a programme of educational reform in the community.[30]

The reform movement received a setback when the Ismaili *imam*, having received the title of Aga Khan from the Shah of Iran in 1834, arrived in Bombay in 1845 as a result of certain intrigue in his homeland. He soon became popular in British circles. The reformers pushed ahead with their efforts to make the community Sunni, so that by 1866 it was estimated about 700–800 adult male Ismailis belonged to the reform party compared to 3,000 who retained allegiance to the Aga Khan. For the latter, given the prestige of their leader in the eyes of the British government, there was now no need to conceal Shia usage, and the stage was set for a clash between the two groupings. In October 1861 the Aga Khan openly published a short paper stating that the time had come for all Ismailis to adopt uncompromisingly Shia Imami Ismaili customs in all social matters such as marriages, ablutions and funeral ceremonies. The outcome was the great Aga Khan judicial case of 1866, which reached the verdict that the community was Shia Imami Ismaili, that it was bound by ties of spiritual allegiance to the hereditary *imams* of the Ismailis, and that the Aga Khan had absolute legal ownership of communal property. Those who did not agree, usually the wealthiest members of the community in both Bombay and East Africa, seceded.[31]

The community which remained with the Aga Khan obtained great advantages from the family's closeness to the British. The Aga Khan died in 1881 and was followed by his son who died in 1885. The latter was succeeded by his 8-year-old son, who in later life lived a European lifestyle, set on foot a programme of reform for the community, and was able to reap numerous advantages for his followers in East Africa.

Ismailis and the Opening up of East Africa

Spheres of influence had been demarcated in East Africa by 1886, and the British proclaimed their East African Protectorate in 1895. The first major undertaking was to construct a railway from the coast to Uganda and, in association with this and with the encouragement of British officials, Indians from the coast began to move inland. The first Indians arrived in Nairobi as contractors, to build official government residences, and they were followed by railway workers specially recruited from India. The British government was particularly keen on attracting settlers to cover the cost of the railway, although it was presumed Europeans and Indians would go to different areas. Successive government enquiries concluded that Indians were essential to the making of East Africa – their presence as subordinate staff alone making government possible – while economic development would not have been possible without their trading activities.[32]

Ismaili traders were among the first to penetrate East Africa. One of the earliest Ismailis in Zanzibar to launch such expansion into the interior was Sewa Haji Paroo, who first managed the Zanzibar branch of his father's business, Haji Kanji and Co., with its headquarters at Bagamoyo. The business specialized in making advances in merchandise to caravans going to the interior, the caravans in return depositing at the entrepôts of the company cargoes of ivory and other goods from the interior. S.H. Paroo took charge of Bagamoyo at the age of 18 in 1869. However, he evolved his business considerably from the type of business carried out by Taria Topan. He opened up stores or agencies of his firm as far as the Lake region, provisioning advance posts and transporting merchandise by his own caravans. By the 1890s he had agents throughout Tanganyika and Uganda. In 1891 his shop at Station Ukumbi on Lake Victoria held large stores of imported articles such as guns, gunpowder, gun caps and cotton cloths. With the accumulation of large sums of money from this trade, investments could be diversified.[33]

Sewa Haji Paroo was murdered in 1897, but his work of penetrating the interior was brought to fruition by a fellow Ismaili, Allidina Visram. From the late 1870s Allidina was employed as an assistant to Haji Paroo in Bagamoyo, and from the 1890s he created his own business at Bagamoyo. He established stapling posts in the interior where imported goods could be sold for ivory and skins. But the opening up of the Uganda railway in 1901 diverted his attention from the old caravan routes towards Uganda and Kenya, where he acted in partnership with the advancing British by establishing *duka* or shops which also offered banking facilities. To these shops he encouraged the sale of local produce such as hides, ground-nuts, chillies, sesame and cotton. By the early twentieth century he had established 'a veritable commercial empire'.[34]

The result was the stimulation of East African economic development. The marketing services for local produce pro-vided by the early *duka*s encouraged greater local production

in various parts of East Africa and the consequent transition
from a barter to a money-based economy. In Uganda Allidina
Visram opened a shop at nearly every government station and
subsequently built a chain of stores in Kenya on the pattern
used in Uganda. By the first decade of the century his firm
employed over 500 Indian and many more African assistants,
apart from the traders who acted as his agents.[35] By the time
he died in 1916, Allidina Visram had 240 shops in East Africa
and Zaire. Originally they were staffed by his poor relations
from India but later, with prosperity, other Ismailis were
invited. Allidina Visram, as a wholesaler, also supplied and
bought from small but semi-independent *dukawallahs*
(shopkeepers) who acted as his agents. He supplied them with
a variety of imports which they sold in return for local produce
which he could then market internationally. The agent was tied
to the wholesaler not as an employee but by chains of credit
and by communal ties. Once an agent had saved up a
sufficient amount, he would establish his own *duka* with a
licence and supplies, encouraging family members to come
from India.[36] This system was extremely advantageous to the
British. The Chief Secretary's Office in Uganda commented
concerning Allidina Visram in 1925:

> He opened a store at nearly every government station, and in
> the early days was of the greatest assistance to the government
> in many ways, such as transport, purchase of local produce,
> etc. Officers in out-stations were dependent, in those days,
> upon Allidina's agencies for the necessaries of life.[37]

Stimulation of local crop production was only the
beginning of development efforts in East Africa. In 1909
Allidina Visram commenced a series of small industries. He
invested part of his trade profits in soda factories and furniture-
making shops at Kampala and Entebbe, and then in factories
using local products such as sesame seed, copra and logs. His
crowning achievement, brought to fruition before he died in
1916, was the establishment of two small cotton-ginning
establishments at Mombasa and Entebbe. To these was added a
cotton ginnery at Kampala between 1912 and 1914, which
represented a substantial capital investment and provided the

foundations, together with another cotton ginnery established by a Bombay firm in 1914, for the subsequent Asian role in the cotton industry of Uganda.[38]

Ismailis were associated with the Uganda cotton industry from the beginning. The introduction of cotton cultivation into Uganda around 1903 provided an impetus to the enterprise of small Indian traders. Already adept at acquiring local produce, they continued this function with the purchase and collection of the cotton crop. From 1907, until it was overtaken by coffee, cotton furnished the largest single item in the export trade of Uganda. The beginning of the First World War and the break in shipping between Uganda and Liverpool provided the Indian ginner with considerable opportunities, as capital flowed into Uganda from Bombay textile interests and Indian ginners from Bombay came across to set themselves up in business. Flowing up-country, they were financed from India. The pattern set by the wholesale trader's assistant or agent was repeated again in another section of the economy. In 1925, out of a total of 114 ginneries of all sizes, 100 were owned by Indians.[39] By the same period about 50 per cent of the crop was imported by Bombay mills, and Ismailis continued to be important in the Bombay cotton mill industry.[40] The tie with India remained strong. Prior to the 1920s Indian capitalist interests in Bombay wanted to transform Kenya into an Indian sub-colony, but the battle was lost to European interests. In the 1920s and 1930s Kenya was replaced by Uganda as the main hunting ground for Indian capitalists in East Africa.[41]

Ismaili economic success was based on community solidarity – despite individual commercial rivalries – which evolved together with the role of the Aga Khan after the great law case of 1866. The third Aga Khan, who succeeded in 1885, had a British upbringing and a talent for organization. His *firmans* (decrees) advised Ismailis to migrate to Africa, to escape Indian misery. These migrants set up not only individual *jamatkhanas* but also a pyramid of councils to oversee territorial concerns. The councils were dominated by a small group of wealthy families; the competition for prestige among these families ensured that those who maintained themselves in the system were generally the shrewdest and therefore able to offer advantages to lesser members of the community. They faced the critical eyes of the community and therefore could never relax their efforts to promote community endeavours.[42] Embedded deeply within this system was the Aga Khan. He took pride in what he called the community's 'fluidity', which was coupled with the inassailability of his own position.[43] His success was to adapt a traditional organization to Western political and economic conditions. Visiting East Africa for the first time in 1899, he explained the economic benefits of his reforms:

> In Africa, where I have been able to give active help as well as advice, we have put the finances of individuals and of the various communities on a thoroughly safe basis. We established an insurance company – the Jubilee Insurance, whose shares have greatly increased in value. We also set up what we called an investment trust, which is really a vast association for receiving money and then putting it on loan, at a low rate of interest, to Ismaili traders and to people who want to buy or build their own houses.[44]

'Fluidity' was indeed the key word. The Aga Khan was confronted with a peculiarly difficult task, in attempting to alter a whole traditional system of statuses and what was regarded as appropriate behaviour without disturbing his own position at the apex.[45] He succeeded because, living the life of a European aristocrat, he was at home in the world to which he was leading his followers. His *firmans* were read in the *jamatkhana*; they often directed Ismailis to channel their efforts to effective action such as migration, education and adoption of Western dress.[46] A study of Ismaili family firms in East Africa at a somewhat later date found there were considerable economic advantages in belonging to the Ismaili community: a series of financial institutions which lent money to members; an advisory service which investigated business prospects for new ventures; various sorts of cooperatives; an excellent education system; and a scheme which enabled every Ismaili in East Africa to own his own home.[47] By the 1930s the Aga Khan's private fortune had long since made him more or less independent of the revenue produced by his followers and he could therefore act as a kind of clearing house in redistributing most of the annual revenue or money collected on special occasions.[48]

The Aga Khan was a modern intellectual, a humanist and a cosmopolitan. He stated his views thus:

> Ismailism has survived because it has always been fluid. Rigidity is contrary to our whole way of life and outlook. There have really been no cut-and-dried rules, even the set of regulations known as the Holy Laws are directions as to the method and procedure and not detailed orders about results to be obtained.[49]

Concerning his followers:

> So far as their way of life is concerned I have tried to vary the advice which I have given to my followers, in accordance with the country or state in which they live. Thus in the British colony of East Africa I strongly urge them to make English their first language, to found their family and domestic lives along English lines and in general to adopt British and European customs – except in the matter of alcohol and slavery to tobacco. I am convinced that living as they must in a multiracial society, the kind of social life and its organization which gives them the greatest opportunities to develop their personalities and is the most practically useful is the one to follow.[50]

Gustav Papanek has summed up the advantages possessed by Ismailis *inter alia* in East Africa and later in Pakistan. Group loyalties played an extremely important role in hiring and employment in commercial enterprises and there was a continuous supply of manpower and entrepreneurial replacements because of the strong emphasis on self-employment in business. Within the business communities there was a well-functioning information network, producing not only intensive rivalries among competitors but also diffusion of information, a system for assessing credit-worthiness, and a much better access to credit facilities than would be available to unaffiliated individuals. All these factors produced a tendency towards more innovative entrepreneurial behaviour.[51] As Ernest Gellner remarks, the Ismailis, with no good cause to welcome the modern world, produced 'a brilliant *economic* performance'.[52] And this performance was produced as a partnership.

Reprise

Although Georg Simmel alluded to the European Jew as the classical stranger, his *excursus* was largely confined to the characteristics of the individual stranger. The concept of 'stranger communities' as commercial entities has, however, been elaborated subsequently. Particularly pertinent is Edna Bonacich's 'A Theory of Middlemen Minorities', where the author states quite clearly her intention to treat middleman minorities as stranger communities.[53] So far we have not looked closely at the theoretical foundations of this collectivity, but with the Ismailis – and the Nattukottai Chettiars of the next chapter – we have reached an appropriate juncture.

It may be asked whether the creativity and dual identity Simmel has imputed to the individual stranger is replicated in a community as a whole. The response is that it has been one of the major themes of this work that there do exist creative communities, and nowhere more so than in a 'conjoint situation'. Further, these communities tend to produce certain families of exceptional economic creativity. The importance of 'family capitalism' for the rise of capitalism in Europe is now well accepted; families proved extremely significant to the success of entrepreneurs in early capitalism.[54]

For the Asian situation, the Ismailis offer a clear paradigm. Their changes in identity were always communally based, as they converted from Hinduism to varying strands of Islam and, finally, overlaid their identity with a veneer of Anglicization. Similarly it was as a community that they were gradually preadapted to their economic success in East Africa, starting as they did with the need to face the challenge of the arid wastes of Kutch and taking up yet another challenge as they began their trading activities along the shores of the eastern part of the 'dark continent'. Possessing many of the characteristics Bonacich delineates for a 'middleman minority' – and particularly a 'distinctive religion'[55] – they, as Ernest Gellner says, 'prospered famously, displaying entrepreneurial virtues and an ideology which is virtually an inverse Weberian paradigm'.[56]

Also an inverse of the Weber paradigm is the dynamic role of the family in the Ismaili enterprise. The section in Weber's *The Religion of China* entitled 'Sib Fetters of the Economy'[57] is well known, as is Weber's opinion that the family in general served to obstruct Asian capitalism. But our work has indicated so far – and the subject will be resumed – that even as the members of entrepreneurial minorities face and deal with multiple realities, individuals were given a core strength by the family-centred nature of their enterprises. Those members of middlemen minorities who triumphed as entrepreneurs based their success on a set of interlocking and interdependent relationships with the family at the core.[58] It was only certain families which triumphed. Of the communities we have looked at so far, all have been characterized by possession of only a small group of families which have truly succeeded as entrepreneurs; for example, the mestizo *ilustrado*s, the peranakan *cabang ata*s and the Parsi *shetia*s. The remainder of the community has often been the object of their betters' charity, of benevolent institutions, scholarshipship, even of food relief.

Rather than throttling capitalism, as Weber argues for India and China, the extended family provided capital, labour and trust where it was needed.[59] A pioneer study, already mentioned, on the role of the family and the family firm a little later than our period, has been made by Burton Benedict in relation to the Ismailis of East Africa. He finds that those firms were at the heart of Ismaili business life and that they possessed numerous advantages. Often based on a joint family living communally, the family firm was able to generate capital and manpower resources; it was able to keep information about the firm and its operations secret; family members had incentives for putting forth effort. The family could make the most of new commercial opportunities, the pattern of consultation between father and sons enabling the business to move quickly to profit from a favourable situation. Kinship connections meant wider sources of financing, useful business connections and a new pool of personnel. Kinship-financing also avoided the need for a reputation for creditworthiness in the early days. Later, larger amounts of credit could be given to a family than to an individual, for the family could offer more security to an outside lender. Connections advantageous to the growth of the firm could often be made by marriage, and an emotional climate conducive to business nurtured.[60] The family more than the individual could be flexible in its range of associates, and it always had a wider range of choices open to it.[61]

The stability, then, of certain constituent families, coupled with the minority's ability to confront society bearing multiple identities, is an important feature of the entrepreneurial success with which we are dealing. The key point to note here is that there are two aspects to our entrepreneurial minorities: the dual or multiple identity which produces creativity and the ability to get things done, and the family and its diaspora which gives a stable core to the whole enterprise.

Notes

1. Secretary of State of Colonies A. Lyttelton, quoted in G. Bennett, *Kenya. A Political History*, London, Oxford University Press, 1963, p. 19.

2. Government of Gujarat, *Gujarat State Gazetteers. Kutch District*, Ahmedabad, Government Printing Gujarat State, 1971, pp. 6, 116–118, 290.

3. Gujarat, *State Gazetteers. Kutch*, p. 115.

4. *Ibid.*, pp. 128–129; R.E. Enthoven, *The Tribes and Castes of Bombay*, vol. 2, Delhi, Cosmo Publications Reprint, 1975, pp. 217–200; H.S. Morris, 'The Divine Kingship of the Aga Khan: A Study of Theocracy in East Africa', *Southwestern Journal of Anthropology* 14 (1958): 458–459.

5. Enthoven, *Tribes and Castes* 2, p. 220; Wink, *Al-Hind* 1, p. 168; T. Ahmed, *Religio-Political Ferment in the N.W. Frontier During the Mughal Period. The Raushaniya Movement*, Delhi, Idarah-i Adabiyat-i Delhi, 1982, pp. 27–28; C.A. Bayly, *Indian Society and the Making of the British Empire*, Cambridge, Cambridge University Press, 1988, p. 75.

6. Gujarat, *State Gazetteers. Kutch*, pp. 128–129; A. Bharati, 'A Social Survey', in D.P. Ghai (ed.), *Portrait of a Minority: Asians in East Africa*, Nairobi, Oxford University Press, 1965, p. 25; S.R. Walji, 'A History of the Ismaili Community in Tanzania', Ph.D., University of Wisconsin, 1974, p. 140.

7. Enthoven, *Tribes and Castes* 2, p. 222; Morris, 'Divine Kingship', pp. 458–459.

8. Enthoven, *Tribes and Castes* 2, p. 221.

9. *Ibid.*, pp. 221–222, 228–230; Morris, 'Divine Kingship', p. 463; Dobbin, *Urban Leadership*, pp. 113–114.

10. Gujarat, *State Gazetteers. Kutch*, p. 290.

11. A. Sheriff, *Slaves, Spices and Ivory in Zanzibar. Integration of an East African Commercial Empire into the World Economy, 1770–1873*, London, James Currey, 1987, pp. 21–22, 26; P. Risso, *Oman and Muscat. An Early Modern History*, London/Sydney, Croom Helm, 1986, pp. xv, 22, 81–82.

12. Risso, *Oman and Muscat*, pp. 122, 128, 192; Walji, 'Ismaili Community', p. 25; J.S. Mangat, *A History of the Asians in East Africa c.1886 to 1945*, Oxford, Clarendon Press, 1969, pp. 2–3.

13. Sheriff, *Slaves, Spices and Ivory*, pp. 1–4; Mangat, *History of the Asians*, p. 2; M. Mamdani, *Politics and Class Formation in Uganda*, New York/London, Monthly Review Press, 1976, pp. 66–67; J.C. Penrad, 'La présence isma'ilienne en Afrique de l'est. Note sur l'histoire commerciale et l'organisation communautaire', in D. Lombard and J. Aubin (eds), *Marchands et hommes d'affaires asiatiques dans l'Océan Indien et la Mer de Chine 13ᵉ-20ᵉ siècles*, Paris, Editions de l'Ecole des Hautes Etudes, 1988, pp. 229, 233.

14. Sheriff, *Slaves, Spices and Ivory*, pp. 78, 84–87.

15. *Ibid.*, pp. 84–87.

16. H.S. Morris, *The Indians in Uganda*, Chicago, University of Chicago Press, 1968, p. 23.

17. Sheriff, *Slaves, Spices and Ivory*, p. 105.

18. Walji, 'Ismaili Community', pp. 21–23.

19. Sheriff, *Slaves, Spices and Ivory*, pp. 105–107.

20. Mangat, *History of the Asians*, pp. 6–9.

21. R. Robinson and J. Gallagher, *Africa and the Victorians. The Official Mind of Imperialism*, London, Macmillan, 1961, p. 45; Z. Bader, 'The Contradictions of Merchant Capital 1840–1939', in A. Sheriff and E. Ferguson (eds), *Zanzibar Under Colonial Rule*, London, James Currey, 1991, pp. 165–169.

22. Sheriff, *Slaves, Spices and Ivory*, pp. 107–108, 172–173, 184, 190.

23. Mangat, *History of the Asians*, pp. 9–11, 25–26.

24. Penrad, 'La présence isma'ilienne', p. 224.

25. Mangat, *History of the Asians*, p. 20.

26. H.M. Stanley, *Through the Dark Continent*, vol. 1, London, George Newnes, 1899, pp. 49–50.

27. *Ibid.*, p. 50.

28. Mangat, *History of the Asians*, pp. 19–21; Sheriff, *Slaves, Spices and Ivory*, p. 107; Bader, 'Contradictions of Merchant Capital', p. 169; W.G. Clarence-Smith, 'Indian Business Communities in the Western Indian Ocean in the Nineteenth Century', *Indian Ocean Review* 2, no. 4 (1989): 18–21.

29. Dobbin, *Urban Leadership*, pp. 113–114; Gujarat, *State Gazetteers. Kutch*, p. 290.

30. Dobbin, *Urban Leadership*, pp. 20, 114–115.

31. *Ibid.*, pp. 116–119; Walji, 'Ismaili Community', pp. 72–73.

32. Bennett, *Kenya*, pp. 5, 7, 19, 27, 29.

33. Penrad, 'La présence isma'ilienne', pp. 225–226; Walji, 'Ismaili Community', pp. 57–59; Mangat, *History of the Asians*, p. 51.

34. Penrad, 'La présence isma'ilienne', p. 228; see also p. 227; Mangat, *History of the Asians*, pp. 33, 51–52; Walji, 'Ismaili Community', pp. 60–61.

35. J.S. Mangat, 'Was Allidina Visram a robber baron or a skilful and benevolent commercial pioneer?', *East Africa Journal* 2 (1968): 34; Mangat, *History of the Asians*, pp. 53, 77–78.

36. Mamdani, *Politics and Class Formation*, pp. 80–81.

37. Quoted in Mangat, *History of the Asians*, p. 59.

38. Mangat, *History of the Asians*, p. 34; Penrad, 'La présence isma'ilienne', pp. 228–229.

39. Mangat, *History of the Asians*, p. 89; Mamdani, *Politics and Class Formation*, pp. 45–54, 86–88, 90–92.

40. Mangat, *History of the Asians*, pp. 89–90; A.K. Bagchi, 'European and Indian Entrepreneurship in India, 1900–30', in E. Leach and S.N. Mukherjee (eds), *Elites in South Asia*, Cambridge, Cambridge University Press, 1970, pp. 249–250; Gordon, *Businessmen and Politics*, p. 42.

41. Markovits, *Indian Business*, p. 187.

42. Penrad, 'La présence isma'ilienne', p. 230; Morris, 'Divine Kingship', pp. 465–467.

43. *The Memoirs of Aga Khan: World Enough and Time*, London, Cassell, 1954, pp. 185–187.

44. *Ibid.*, p. 188.

45. Morris, 'Divine Kingship', p. 471.

46. Walji, 'Ismaili Community', p. 100.

47. B. Benedict, 'Family Firms and Economic Development', *Southwestern Journal of Anthropology* 24, no. 1 (1968): 16–17.

48. Morris, 'Divine Kingship', p. 466.

49. *Memoirs of Aga Khan*, p. 185.

50. *Ibid.*, p. 90.

51. Papanek, 'Pakistan's Industrial Entrepreneurs', pp. 242–243, 245, 249–250.

52. E. Gellner, *Muslim Society*, Cambridge, Cambridge University Press, 1981, p. 104.

53. E. Bonacich, 'A Theory of Middleman Minorities', in N.R. Yetman and C.H. Steele (eds), *Majority and Minority: The Dynamics of Racial and Ethnic Relations*, 2nd ed, Boston, Allyn and Bacon, 1975, pp. 77–89; see p. 88.

54. Abercrombie *et al.*, *Sovereign Individuals*, pp. 115–117; see also Schumpeter, 'Creative Response', p. 158.

55. Bonacich, 'Middleman Minorities', p. 80.

56. Gellner, *Muslim Society*, p. 109.

57. Weber, *Religion of China*, pp. 95–100.

58. J.W. Cushman, *Family and State. The Formation of a Sino-Thai Tin-mining Dynasty*, Singapore, Oxford University Press, 1991, p. 123.

59. J. Goody, *The Oriental, the Ancient and the Primitive. Systems of Marriage and the Family in the Pre-industrial Societies of Eurasia*, Cambridge, Cambridge University Press, 1990, pp. 482–485.

60. Benedict, 'Family Firms', pp. 9–13.

61. Cushman, *Family and State*, pp. 123–124.

6

From Madras to Burma: the Nattukottai Chettiars and Development 1852–1939

From the time of their conquest of Lower Burma in 1852 the British were aware of the great potential of the fertile Irrawaddy Delta region as a source of foodstuffs and raw materials and a possible market outlet for British manufactured goods. So far, throughout the eighteenth century, the Delta had been poorly developed, sparsely populated and a mere backwater of the last Burmese kingdom.[1] Indian commercial ties to the region were long-standing, but they were now given substance by the British conquest. The earliest British endeavours to develop the region were based on attempts to settle Indian agriculturalists on land by a programme of land grants begun in 1874. Between 1876 and 1878 more than 15,000 Indians came to the Delta to claim government land as free cultivators, but the type of agriculture was unfamiliar to them and these efforts were generally regarded as unsuccessful. An equal failure was an attempt to make large grants to Indian capitalists on attractive conditions, and although about 9,500 Indians were brought to work on these estates, this too did not succeed.[2]

Instead, Indian settlement in Lower Burma proceeded very similarly to that of Chinese settlement in the early days of Manila and Batavia. In 1862 the four provinces of Pegu, Martaban, Arakan and Tenasserim became consolidated as the

Province of British Burma, directed from the port city of Rangoon. While Indian land settlement schemes had failed, Rangoon acted as a magnet for Indians from across the Bay of Bengal in Madras Presidency. The entire character of the city was Indian; where there were only nineteen Indians in Rangoon in 1838, by 1881 there were approximately 65,000. By 1891 the Indian population of Rangoon outnumbered the Burmese, a trend that continued until 1931. In that year Indians were 54 per cent of the population and Burmese 32 per cent.[3] The majority of the Indian immigrants were labourers coming to work on the docks, but Indians of all castes and classes made their way from Madras to the new frontier city. Among these were members of a small Tamil caste, the Nattukottai Chettiars, first recorded in Rangoon in the early 1850s, who arrived in the train of the early Indian expeditionary forces and found among them the possibility of engaging in their developing occupation of moneylending, an opportunity which expanded when they discovered they were able to collaborate with arriving British exchange banks to open up the Delta frontier.[4]

The Madras Preadaptation

The term Chettiar is etymologically allied to the Sanskrit term *sreshti*, the literal meaning of which is 'banker' or 'big merchant'. The prevalence of the term *shetia* in Bombay has already been discussed. In the nineteenth century the homes of the most important part of the caste were the districts of Ramnad and Trichinopoly in the Presidency of Madras in Southern India. The Nattukottai Chettiars had their business headquarters in an area popularly known as 'Chettinad', comprising the eastern part of Ramnad district and a part of Trichinopoly.[5] They were a tiny caste, numbering 7,851 in 1891, and divided into exogamous subdivisions or 'clans' named after nine temples in Chettinad.[6] Their homeland was in close touch across the Bay of Bengal with developments in the Delta and their long centuries of evolution as a commercial community, culminating in involvement with European commerce, prepared them to work with Western banks and

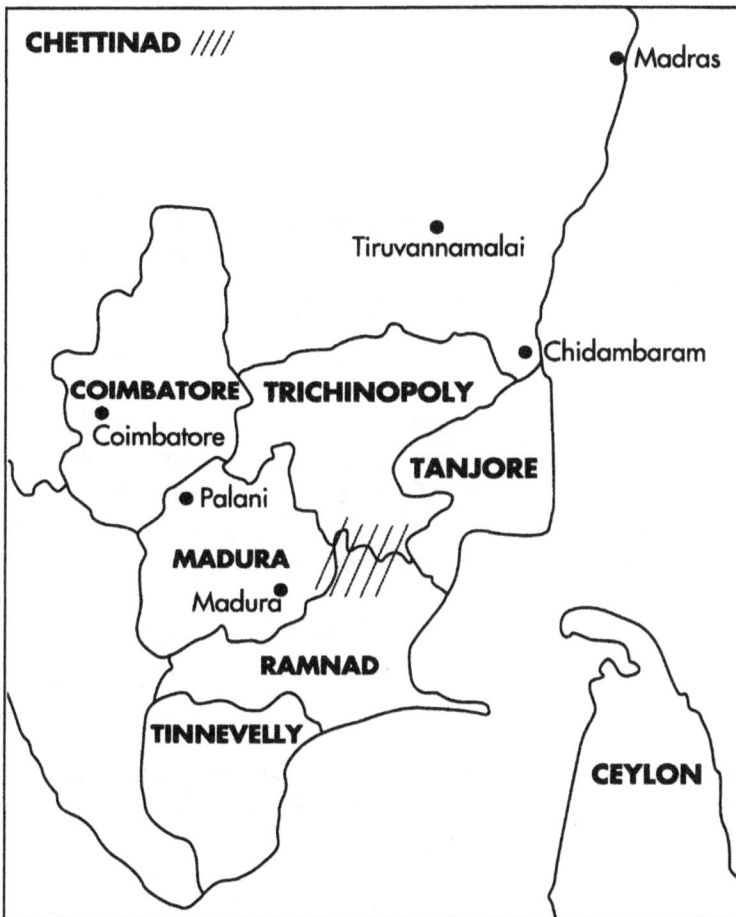

Map 6: Madras Presidency Districts c. 1900

joint-stock companies such as the Imperial Bank of India and the Indian Overseas Bank, which provided them with sources of working capital not readily available to Burmese brokers and moneylenders.[7]

Chettiars espoused a unique blend of religion and commerce dating from at least the eleventh century. The economic function of the South Indian temple is well known. Temples in the Tamil cultural area functioned as institutions of capital investment, accumulation and distribution, initially receiving endowments from local rulers and notables and from trading guilds. This income not only covered temple capital and operating expenses, but was used as loan money for irrigation, animal breeding and long-distance trade. Temple assets were generally located in regional market towns and managed by assemblies representative of the towns' chief merchants.[8] David Rudner has carefully explained the role of temples and temple-gifting in the economic development of the Nattukottai Chettiar caste, a phenomenon which led the caste from the interior of Tamilnad to economic relations with Europeans on the coast. Their gradual involvement in the economic life of the temple preadapted the caste to take advantage of the new opportunities presented by the encroaching world-economy from the seventeenth century.

Rudner focuses on the seventeenth-century commercial expansion of the Nattukottai Chettiar caste in terms of its rituals of religious gifting to temples. In that period, Nattukottai Chettiars were primarily employed as salt traders in a small area of ninety-six villages in the northern part of present-day Ramnad district. Salt in various forms was produced in coastal districts and traded inland. By this time Nattukottai Chettiar lineages had already established links with temples in their residential villages throughout their Chettinad homeland, exerting control over the markets, fairs and economic activities associated with their own temples.[9] But in order for itinerant trading activities to be successful outside their own residential limits, it was necessary for further ties to be forged by individual Nattukottai Chettiar traders by involvement in religious gifting in the locality to which they addressed their commercial endeavours.

Rudner uses the example of Nattukottai Chettiar salt traders in the pilgrimage town of Palani, about 80 kilometres west of Chettinad. A manuscript beginning in 1600 recounts the story of a Nattukottai Chettiar trader who came to Palani from Chettinad to investigate the prospects for expanding his salt business. Much more than merely selling in the market, he was required to establish a relationship with the temple deity of Palani, mediated through the deity's priest, by giving a tithe on his profit. Other salt traders gradually joined him and, at periods of pilgrimage, Nattukottai Chettiars established religious endowments at the temple. These acts of religious gifting and collective worship were 'integrative temple rituals'[10] which made it possible for new traders to enter market towns. The gifts were functional and were thought of, in part, as licence fees and financial investments. By worshipping in temples that lay outside their residential homeland, small groups of Nattukottai Chettiars established themselves over a broad geographical area, while at the same time retaining their ability to draw on the financial resources of other members of the caste.

Rudner's salt trader ultimately became Endowment Manager of the temple in Palani; he was judged by his trustworthiness and, in return for his transactions with both the deity and other members of the temple community, he received a certain share of the endowment he managed which was available for reinvestment in his business. This, in turn, led to further endowments to the temple and further Nattukottai Chettiar involvement in the Palani economy. Trustworthiness provided the moral basis of credit on which all mercantile activities were based. Rudner concludes that religious gifts performed not only religious and political functions but also important economic functions, including the acquisition and reinvestment of funds in mercantile enterprises. The Nattukottai Chettiars were able to engage in trade by worshipping the deities of their customers and, gaining positions of trust in the temple, were able to expand the market for their salt.[11]

The Nattukottai Chettiars were now ready to take advantage of new opportunities. With the coming of the European companies and the expansion of commerce the Nattukottai Chettiar caste, already specialized around activities of capital accumulation and investment, was preadapted for economic success. Their inland location initially placed them at a disadvantage compared to the coastal castes which were the Europeans' first collaborators, but their ritual techniques for entering new markets, pooling capital and transferring money enabled them to compete very rapidly.[12]

Capital was, of course, a European requirement on the coast. Francis Day chose the site of Madras city in 1639 for the English East India Company's settlement because the region was known for its superior weavers and dyers who produced cloth more cheaply than that which European rivals were buying elsewhere.[13] Within a very short time merchants of some substance were attracted to set up residence in Madras and to engage in a whole range of wholesale and retail trading in a variety of merchandise. Several Chettiar castes came, including Nattukottai Chettiars.[14] From the mid-eighteenth century an increasingly large European private trade led to additional opportunities for Indian middlemen, and a small circle of elite merchants came to exercise a dominant role in the organization and financing of Anglo-Indian trade. South Indian society became 'credit hungry', as local chiefs engaged in military forays and European trading companies depended on forward advances of credit provided by local moneylenders.[15]

The Nattukottai Chettiars were prepared to adapt their traditional practices to these new circumstances. Their chief seventeenth-century occupation, salt-trading, did not recover from a development that took place towards the end of the eighteenth century, when a severe drought reduced commerce between the inland salt-consuming and the coastal salt-producing regions. By 1805 the major salt renters had become so weak that the East India Company was able to do away with them as middlemen in the salt trade and take on something like monopolistic control over salt production. Nattukottai Chettiars responded by slowly extending their commercial operations as far south as the pearl, rice, cloth and arak trade of Ceylon and as far north as the rice and wheat trade of Calcutta. By the end of the eighteenth century they had gained control of the pearl fisheries in the Ceylon Straits, and from at least 1820 they also dominated the major coastal trade in arak and in coconut products from Ceylon to Madras. Contemporaries claimed they had cornered the Ceylon rice market, controlling all imports not only of Tanjore rice but of Bengal rice too. As early as 1820 they had also established firms in Calcutta, exchanging salt for Bengal grains.[16]

Nattukottai Chettiar financial transactions formed the heart of these commercial enterprises. In a process that is still unclear, they developed a sophisticated financial apparatus which included provisions for making forward loans, for extending short-term and long-term loans to political and military collaborators, and for transmitting bills of exchange among themselves and their clients. By obscure and not so obscure means they evolved into a long-distance, merchant-banking caste. Rudner states that there remains scope for considerable research into the precise nature of Nattukottai Chettiar credit networks and the various commodities' markets with which they were involved. What is clear is that late eighteenth-century and early nineteenth-century Nattukottai Chettiar commodities trading was tied to some kind of exchange banking system, the Chettiars combining their trade undertakings with the purely financial transactions of moneylending, remittance of funds between geographically distant locations and to government authorities, and the supply of credit to the new landlord class of Madras Presidency.[17]

The final alteration in the Madras business climate before large-scale Nattukottai Chettiar investment in the Burma rice Delta comprised a series of changes which made further profit in the Madras Presidency difficult to acquire. The credit needs of the cotton traders of Coimbatore, once a Nattukottai Chettiar preserve, were taken out of their hands. Beginning in 1843 with the founding of the Presidency Bank of Madras, Europeans established their own banks, thereby excluding Nattukottai Chettiars and other indigenous moneylenders from the market in mercantile finance and currency exchange for private European firms. An alternative was sought in investing in or converting bad debts into land ownership, and Rudner estimates that between 1850 and 1900 perhaps 200 Nattukottai Chettiars were able to obtain minor landlord titles but these, using a population basis of 10,000, could have represented at most one-fifth and more likely one-tenth or even one-twentieth of joint family units. For the remainder, the failure of opportunities for financial investment in India, coupled with caste techniques of capital penetration, provided a stimulus to search for new ways of putting money to use.[18]

The Nattukottai Chettiar Firm in Burma

Displaced from the credit markets of Madras, displaced from exchange markets throughout the greater part of British India, Nattukottai Chettiars found a new niche in servicing the credit needs of indigenous Southeast Asians who were being drawn into the production of agrarian commodities for the world market. Involved in both Ceylon and Malaya, the leading economic frontier in which they became enmeshed was the Lower Burma Delta. Their first offices were opened in Rangoon in 1852, not for agricultural lending but to advance money to contractors who brought over coolies and also to invest in the rising import-export business carried on between India and Burma. Some also invested money in businesses unconnected with agriculture, such as the sale of wholesale oil and the operation of saw mills.[19]

British policy, however, gradually opened the Delta area to a mass of Burmese peasant proprietors, sucked into the region by new opportunities for profitable rice-growing for a European market brought closer by the opening of the Suez Canal. In terms of subsequent Chettiar involvement, one of the most important British changes introduced after 1852 was the introduction of a new system of land tenure. The loose, non-contractual rights which had been common in the previous period were replaced by a land tenure system modelled on that of South India. This had as its major goal the concentration of ownership in the hands of individual cultivator-landholders. The implication of this system was that agriculturalists would be able to mortgage their holdings as security for loans granted by moneylenders and others. Further, the village system was reorganized in a new, decentralized manner whereby self-government no longer existed over any unit larger than the village; such villages were internally weakened and ripe for moneylenders' activities.[20]

As peasant contractors were drawn into the Delta, paddy acreage began to expand. Whereas in 1845 annual exports totalled only 74,000 tons, this had slowly increased to 160,000 tons by 1861. In 1864–65 exports amounted to 470,000 tons until, after some decline, the 1872–73 figure rose rapidly to 720,000 tons. After that figures were much higher. In the decade 1889–99 the annual average tonnage was about 1,370,000 and by 1911–14 that figure had increased sixfold.[21] There was a concomitant huge expansion in the area under rice cultivation, and a population increase of from approximately 1 million in 1852 to over 4 million in 1901.[22] Lower Burma was now fully integrated into the world-economy. With the disruptions of the American Civil War, Burma became a major rice supplier for London, Liverpool and continental milling centres like Hamburg and Bremen. 'The expansion of the Delta rice industry in the last half of the nineteenth century', writes Michael Adas, 'represents one of the most impressive examples of sustained economic growth under the aegis of a European colonial regime.'[23] But the British government and private British firms never had the money or the administrative apparatus to undertake so vast an enterprise as the development of the Delta. This would have been impossible without Nattukottai Chettiar capital.[24]

Migrants from Upper Burma or migrants from more populous areas of the Delta normally possessed little or no capital when they arrived on the rice frontier. They rarely succeeded in bringing waste land under cultivation without borrowing. Although there is no record in the settlement reports of the 1880s of cultivators taking loans from Nattukottai Chettiars, it is likely that agriculturalists who lived in the neighbourhood of Rangoon and other large towns did so. In some regions Chettiars financed agricultural production indirectly through loans to Burmese moneylenders, who in turn lent to cultivators at higher rates. In 1881 only 587 professional moneylenders were recorded in Lower Burma, while by 1901 nearly 3,200 bankers and moneylenders were enumerated. From the 1880s agents of Nattukottai Chettiars began to penetrate the Delta area beyond Rangoon and other urban areas. They established branches in the larger villages and also in towns along the railway line. In this way Rangoon-based millers gained control of the rice crop; once the agriculturalist began borrowing Chettiar capital, his indebtedness forced him to sell his crop at the miller's prices in order to meet his obligations. These rice-millers were largely Europeans, who developed a symbiotic relationship with the Nattukottai Chettiars' commercial activities. The opening of the Suez Canal in 1869 enabled them to supply large quantities of higher-priced husked and even white rice to European markets, leading to a considerable growth in the rice industry from which both Chettiars and European rice millers profited. Rice mills multiplied, from 52 in 1890 to 613 in 1930. Rangoon became a great modern port through which the world's largest rice exports flowed.[25]

Because there never developed any significant alternatives to Chettiar agricultural credit in either the private or public sector of Burma's economy, nor did there develop any alternative to Chettiar land alienation when debts could not be met. Large-scale transference of land out of Burmese ownership was a key aspect of Nattukottai Chettiar activities in Lower Burma, becoming noticeable as early as 1872.[26] The indications are that the Chettiars did not generally want land; in most areas they took over debtors' lands only as a last resort in order to prevent further monetary losses. By the end of the first phase of development, about 1905, the incidence of land alienation to non-agriculturalists was highest in the frontier districts of the tidal Delta and in the districts near Rangoon where rice production was particularly market-oriented and agricultural credit most readily available. Where Chettiars were forced to take over rice lands for unpaid debts, they normally tried to resell them as soon as possible; only if this was unsuccessful would they become landlords, with tenants working for them.[27]

Whatever their aims, the world-economy in which they were enmeshed disrupted totally their preferred commercial pattern. Quite some time before the Great Depression, the Delta rice frontier was experiencing serious agrarian problems. In the years after the First World War the export market upon which the Delta economy had grown dependent began to

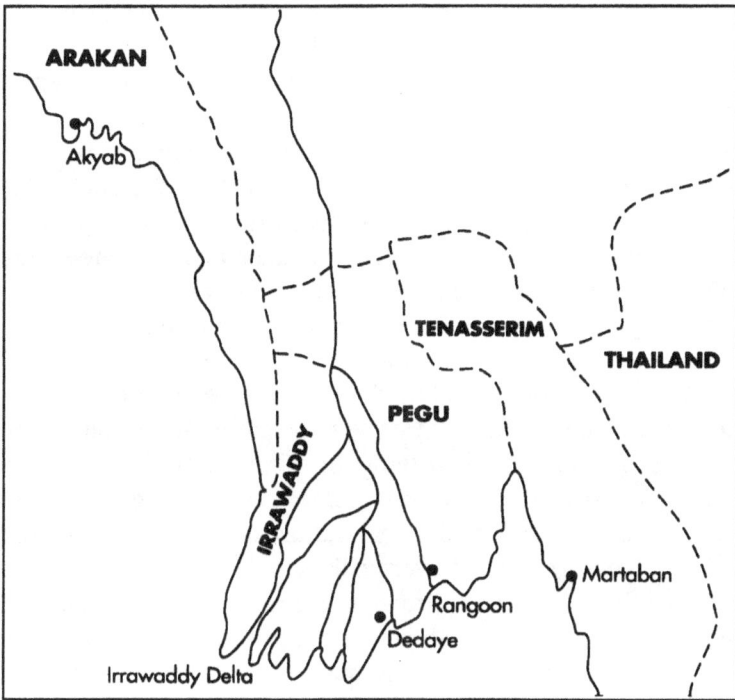

Map 7: Lower Burma Divisions c. 1930

deteriorate, with new competitors and new market demands for higher quality. Debtors became unable to repay loans and by the early 1930s there was a great acceleration of land alienation.[28] The amount of the total occupied area in Lower Burma held by non-agriculturalists rose from 31 per cent in 1929–30 to nearly 50 per cent by 1934–35. The proportion of land held by Nattukottai Chettiar moneylenders greatly increased. In 1930 they were listed as the owners of only 6 per cent of the total land occupied in the Delta and 19 per cent of the area held by non-agriculturalists; by 1937 they controlled 25 per cent of the cropped area in Lower Burma, and 50 per cent of that held by non-agriculturalists.[29] The regular functioning of Chettiar moneylending depended on the maintenance of a balance between their liquid assets and investment in immovable property. The new conditions placed a considerable strain on their moneylending system and many small Chettiar firms and a few large ones collapsed.[30]

Up to this point the history of the main Nattukottai Chettiar moneylending firms had been one of considerable economic success. The magnitude of the Chettiars' investment in Burma's rice production is indicated by the fact that by the late 1920s there were over 1,650 Chettiar firms in the main rice-growing districts of the colony. These firms advanced an estimated 450–500 million rupees a year in both crop and long-term loans to cultivators or to middlemen who lent it to cultivators. The government's role in credit provision remained marginal.[31] Of the 1,650 businesses mentioned, 360 or above one-fifth were in Rangoon while about 1,443 or seven-eighths of the total were in Lower Burma including Rangoon. Chettiar businesses were carried on in 217 towns and villages, and throughout every well-populated part of Lower Burma there was a Chettiar within a day's journey of every cultivator.[32]

Nattukottai Chettiar firms in Burma operated under an agency system very similar to that of the Ismailis in East Africa. At the age of about 18 a young man would be sent away from Chettinad for a tour of duty under older members of his clan, lasting approximately three years. Prior to this, from quite a young age the caste member would have undergone instruction in the arts of banking and moneylending. Scholars have stressed certain individualistic aspects of the young apprentice's family life as helping to provide an explanation for Nattukottai Chettiars' particular success. From at least the late nineteenth century family members, while living in the same compound, were constituted an independent unit on marriage and required to purchase, cook and eat their food separately. The married couple formed a separate unit of accounting and were obliged to exist as a discretionary and self-reliant entity.

Brought up in this system, children learned to practise thrift. Males were usually presented at birth with a small sum of money which was left to earn interest until it was needed for education or investment. Then at the age of 12 or so the boys were apprenticed to their fathers or to other members of the clan.[33] The milieu in which they lived, stressing the importance of bearing one's own financial burden, has been argued to have made young Chettiars self-reliant, ambitious and anxious to make their own fortunes. This strong emphasis on personal accountability, individual achievement, separate private consumption together with joint ownership of resources could then be the basis for successful long-distance commercial migration. The strict accountability of small units made it possible for Nattukottai Chettiars to send representatives abroad with small amounts of money which would not be rapidly exhausted in consumption.[34]

The Nattukottai Chettiar banker at home in Tamilnad began his career early. The age of 12–15 being the age of apprenticeship, about nine years were spent in this position or in a subordinate position in the banking business. At 22–25 years of age promotion occurred to a principal position. In the early years payment was generally in the form of board and lodging supplemented by bonuses. Those young Chettiars who were sent abroad could often be entrusted with sums as large as 100,000 rupees. The frugality and responsibility learnt at home were now rewarded, since each employee was normally allowed a percentage from the profits of any successful enterprise he was involved in. He was encouraged to save such allowances and use them, together with his salary, for further investments. After home leave and further training, his second tour saw him granted increased responsibility with the possibility of acting independently in ways such as lending money on his own initiative. Renewed success led to even more independence on his third tour, and increasing sums to supervise.[35]

Generally every place at which a firm carried on business had a separate agency. There were also outstations opened in villages at a reasonable distance from the main town, although usually not more than one for one business.[36] An agent, who was usually in his fifteenth or later year of employment, generally had an establishment of five to six, the main individuals being the assistant, the cashier and the accountant. The Burma Banking Inquiry noted:

> Great care is taken in selecting agents and other members of the establishment. Owing in part to this and to the family con-

nections often existing between them and the principals, there
are practically no cases of dishonesty ... in addition to the salary every employee, including the agent, receives free board
and lodging and has all his reasonable wants in other directions satisfied, so that he has no need to use any money of his
own.[37]

No member of the establishment, not even the agent, was
permitted to bring his wife with him.[38]

The individualistic manner in which the joint family treated
its members did not mean that the family was not the key
economic unit in Burma. Most Nattukottai Chettiar firms there
were owned by individual families, generally consisting of two
or more individuals in partnership, with the bulk of the capital
provided from within the family. The Banking Inquiry looked
at this closely:

> Each Chettiar business is owned by a partnership of closely
> related persons and managed by an agent. The partners are
> commonly related to each other through their wives, people
> who are related directly being more likely to set up separate
> firms because of certain rules of a Hindu joint family as to
> ownership of property. When a partner has grown-up sons
> willing and able to take part in managing a business, he usu-
> ally breaks off and sets up a new partnership consisting of
> himself and his sons; when the father dies the sons generally
> separate before long to form independent firms. Agents who
> have done well are sometimes taken into partnership. Under
> these conditions there are fairly frequent dissolutions of part-
> nerships and formations of new firms ... Another result is that
> by the relationships of partners a firm is often closely con-
> nected with other firms, which accordingly, in case it gets into
> difficulties, can have reliable knowledge of its affairs and are
> often more willing therefore to help it over its difficulty than
> other firms would be.[39]

Whatever its other activities, each Nattukottai Chettiar firm
operated as a commercial bank, taking money on deposit or
drafting bills or other financial instruments for use in the
transfer of loanable capital to branch offices and to other
banks. All firms, largely headquartered in Chettinad, were in
practice tied together to form a unified banking system
employing sophisticated accounting techniques and possessing

an efficient organization for collective decision-making. Each firm maintained contact with the 'clearing house' of Chettiar activity in Burma, the community temple in Mogul Street in Rangoon.[40] It was in this street that all Chettiar firms in Rangoon were concentrated. Six rooms in the temple were used by firms to do business with their clients. The Banking Inquiry pointed to the solidarity generated by this form of business existence:

> A few other buildings in Mogul Street, within a hundred yards from the temple up and down the street, have ground floors divided into similar rooms, making altogether (including the six-rooms) 23 such rooms. About 14 or 15 of the very largest firms have separate flats including either one or two business rooms, usually on the first floor of a building, and all situated in the same short piece of Mogul Street; most of the 14 or 15 firms have a desk also in one or other of the 23 rooms. In the 23 rooms and the flats and the temple itself all the Chettiar business is conducted. All the managers and their staff live close by, mostly in the rooms above the business-rooms; some sleep in the 23 rooms themselves to act as guardians. All meet one another frequently, not only in business and in attendance at the temple and at communal meetings, but also on the casual occasions of everyday life, such as the morning toilet, and in the casual attendances at the six-rooms in the morning to hear the gossip.[41]

In the towns and villages Nattukottai Chettiars occupied brick houses for security reasons. Anywhere between two to eight firms could occupy the same building, and where there was more than one Chettiar building in a town the other would unfailingly be close by. Disputes were settled out of court, with community elders conciliating. Apart from lending money these firms, whether in Rangoon or in the towns or villages, offered a range of financial services; they accepted deposits, honoured cheques, discounted bills of exchange, changed money, accepted documents and valuables for safe deposit and even dealt in gold.[42]

A further institution promoting caste solidarity was the *vituti* or community-supported lodging house located in the same building as or adjacent to a Nattukottai Chettiar-supported temple. These *vitutis* provided services for travelling caste members which greatly facilitated their commercial operations; they were able to obtain accommodation and meals, use mailing facilities, find assistance with travel arrangements and baggage clearance and even arrange for absentee prayers at local temples. Nattukottai Chettiars built *vitutis* whenever they had permanent business interests; commercial information could be readily exchanged and the reputations of individual houses investigated.[43]

Of course there was a wide difference between the scope of the activities of the largest and smallest firms. The largest firms belonged to *adathis* – important men – who controlled wealthy 'parent banks' and business enterprises[44] throughout South and Southeast Asia. In 1929 a new form of association appeared with the registration in Madras as a private company of the Bank of Chettinad, consisting of members of one family who had previously constituted two partnerships working in Burma, Ceylon, Malaya and Cochin China. The bank had a paid-up capital of 30 million rupees and its head office was established in the Ramnad district in Chettinad. All agencies of the two partnerships were converted into branch offices of the bank.[45] This bank, and other major Nattukottai Chettiar firms, were able to maintain excellent connections with European banks in both Madras and Rangoon; from these they occasionally borrowed money during periods of seasonal shortages. Relations were often so good that the Chettiars could acquire loans merely on promissory notes without collateral.[46] An *adathi* has been called a 'merchant-prince and banker';[47] while all Nattukottai Chettiar firms acted like commercial banks, making loans and taking deposits, *adathis* acted like reserve banks for the Nattukottai Chettiar banking system as a whole. David Rudner calculates their number in Burma in 1953 as twelve, based on the size of their landholdings; they held political office and served on boards or acted as trustees of temples and charitable institutions. Like the Parsi and Ismaili *shetias*, they were an elite group with interlocking connections,[48] and, as disparities of wealth and economic differentiation became a marked feature of the community, internal solidarity became less firm. Community concern about this development was publicly uttered in Rangoon in the early 1920s, when attempts were made to regain the cohesiveness of the community and revive a sense of unity in the face of severe internal competition for resources and government favour.[49]

The Nattukottai Chettiar Religious Identity

The Nattukottai Chettiars are Saivaite Hindus, worshippers of Siva. Siva is one of the major gods of the later Hindu pantheon, forming with Brahma and Vishnu the great triad of Hindu deities. Most of the Chettiar temples were dedicated to Siva's son, and this deity was sometimes regarded as the chairman of the temple committee.[50] The role of 'temple gifting' in the Nattukottai Chettiars' preadaptive period has already been noted. The temple's role in business in the later period in Burma has also been seen to be important; the main Chettiar temple in Mogul Street was called the 'Chettiar exchange' where regularly current interest rates were determined, business disputes settled and commercial information exchanged.[51] Hans-Dieter Evers and Jayarani Pavadarayan have shown for the Singapore Chettiar temple at a later period that religious significance was attached to borrowing from temple deposits, which were accumulated from a percentage contribution from the profits of firms. Capital drawn from temple funds and lent to traditional firms was felt to have special religious significance, as it drew the major deity of the temple into direct participation in business. The god was treated as a divine witness and dishonesty and default invoked religious sanctions.[52]

But of course there was a spiritual side to the Nattukottai Chettiars' religious existence, and Evers and Pavadarayan have pointed out that this leads to a curious dual identity in the community, where business life was conducted on principles of strict asceticism and yet much spiritual life was in the form of more popular, ecstatic religion.[53] The earliest indication of this is in the particular school of Saivaism which Nattukottai

Chettiars followed. This was the Saiva Siddhanta, which placed great emphasis on *bhakti*, 'attachment' or fervent devotion to god. *Bhakti* seems to have had its origin in the Dravidian South as part of a great medieval spiritual revival, stressing the need for a personal relationship with god and a deeply emotional worship of him. A series of Tamil saints spread the gospel that salvation could only be won by a total self-surrender to Siva and the hymns of these saints remained vital among overseas Tamils. All *bhakti* sects were characterized by self-abandonment to a personal god, carried out with considerable emotion.[54] This is not to say that emotion and religious ecstasy were ungoverned and uncontrollable. The path of devotion, as Milton Singer points out, could also be one of discipline, subject to well-understood rules in which the devotee finds a model for his attitude of devotion to the deity and disciplines his emotions and actions in accordance with the requirements of the model he wishes to follow.[55]

Nevertheless, *bhakti* is one aspect of the 'ecstasy' that has been noted in Nattukottai Chettiar religion. The other, described by Evers and Pavadarayan for contemporary Singapore but without doubt having much earlier roots, is their association with popular Tamil temple festivals and participation in the ecstatic rituals connected with these.[56] In the late nineteenth century Nattukottai Chettiars spent large sums on restoring several of the famous Saivaite shrines in the Madras Presidency, notably those at Chidambaram, Madura and Tiruvannamalai. Associated with this was extensive spending on ceremonies and festivals, some newly established after years of neglect, coupled with a particular attention to the repair and restoration of those shrines that were hymned by the great poet-saints.[57]

We do not know the details of the rituals that took place at these festivals, but Evers and Pavadarayan have described these for the Thaipusam festival in Singapore, of which the Nattukottai Chettiars were the main organizers and participants. The ecstasy involved in these religious manifestations included elements such as entering into a trance, dancing while in a trance, frantic utterances and bodily mutilation, although the ecstatic manifestations of the Nattukottai Chettiars were some-

what restrained and regulated. Further, the religious verses
sung by Nattukottai Chettiars contained references to the caste
as a separate cultural and religious entity, pledged to lead a life
of sobriety and refraining from indulgence in the ways of the
world.[58] Evers finds this a strange contrast of both asceticism
and ecstasy[59] but, looked at within the framework of the dual
nature of a minority business community, perhaps the combination is somewhat more explicable. Evers himself notes that
one might assume that tremendous internal stress and strain
arise from leading a highly inner-worldly ascetic life in which
frugality, self-discipline and self-control are emphasized. The
response might then be a restrained and controlled type of
religious ecstasy, coupled with extensive involvement in
charitable works, which often involved paying for religious
festivals.[60] In this respect there is a clear line of connection
with the medieval period, when an emphasis on *bhakti* and
the construction of temples went together.[61] There is a connection, too, with Milton Singer's group of Madras industrialists
– which included Chettiars – who, he found, downgraded
ritual observance generally and concurrently moved to
adherence to *bhakti* as a path suited to their entrepreneurial
existence.[62]

From Commerce to Industry

It is hardly surprising that the Nattukottai Chettiars followed
the pattern of all other communities dealt with so far and
responded to opportunities for industrial ventures. In Burma
they began by exporting considerable quantities of timber to
India and hence becoming involved in the saw-milling
industry. Ties between Rangoon and Madras were strong. An
important figure in the Madras timber business was P.A.
Chockalingam Chetty, who inherited a family timber concern
and came to notice about 1902 for the huge quantities of
timber he imported weekly from Burma. Among his customers
were the government of Madras and private contractors as far
afield as Hyderabad and Mysore. Other firms also imported
huge quantities of timber.[63] Not surprisingly, considering the

direction of their lending activities, Nattukottai Chettiars also either established or acquired a number of rice mills, some being set up by Burmese with Chettiar capital. Among important Chettiar rice mills by 1915 was the M.M.P.L. Palaniappa Rice Mill at Akyab, with further Burmese branches at Dedaye and Rangoon. Its registered headquarters was in Ramnad district in Madras and it also had branches spread over India and Ceylon. The Chettiars who engaged in rice-milling, many of whom had come to Burma from Calcutta, were formidable rivals for the European rice-millers, whether they milled in Rangoon or Madras. The Depression and the concomitant loan foreclosures meant that considerable sums were converted from liquid to fixed assets such as mills.[64]

It was in South India itself, however, that the change from traditional moneylending to modern enterprises took place, the pace accelerating in the period after the Depression. Here individual Nattukottai Chettiars were among the first Tamil businessmen to divert their assets from banking and trade to capital-intensive industry.[65] Their chief success was in the cotton textile industry, centred around Coimbatore in Madras Presidency. By the 1950s this was by far the most important factory industry in Madras state, dominated by Coimbatore spinning ventures but with some money also put into factories in Chettinad itself.[66] Chettiar groups such as the Raja Sir Annamalai Chettiar Group and the A.M.M. Murugappa Chettiar Group were established, the capital involved being accumulated by joint families. Collaborative arrangements with foreign capital also played their part in the rise of Nattukottai Chettiar business combines.[67]

Milton Singer collected material in 1954–64 on nineteen industrial leaders in Madras, most originating in banking and trade. Four of the nineteen were Chettiars, although it is not specified whether they were Nattukottai Chettiars.[68] One of the Chettiar industrial leaders owed the origin of his financial stability to his grandfather, who had gone into overseas banking at the age of 14 and made a vast fortune through this and the purchase of rice land in Burma and elsewhere. He brought his three sons into the business during the First World

War while they were still in their teens. Before the outbreak of the next war they anticipated difficulties ahead in Southeast Asia, transferred their banking operations to Madras City, and started a small manufacturing industry in 1938. By 1949 they were able to negotiate conjoint agreements with British and American firms to manufacture bicycle tyre tubes, cycle saddles, chains, dynamo sets, lamps and other bicycle parts. Three of the grandsons were sent to England for technical training in the collaborating British plants.[69] It was in this period, if just a little later, that the founders of the great Chinese conglomerates on Java were beginning their collaboration with foreign firms,[70] repeating a pattern originating in the days of the East India Companies. In both cases, and in others we have mentioned, the importance of the joint-family system was paramount, making individual families' unique characteristics deserving of the closest attention. It was never an entire community which developed specific areas of economic activity, but only a small number of families from within that community; no matter, as Singer says, how much members of a particular community are predisposed to enter a particular line of economic activity, only a small and localized fraction of the community may be so predisposed by special experience, abilities, opportunities and other circumstances to lead and to succeed.[71]

Reprise

The Nattukottai Chettiars' dual identity as a business community has been explained in terms of the tension between the need to carry on a strictly ascetic business life and the affinity for a spiritual life of a more populist, ecstatic kind. It is in this duality that must be sought the spirit of Nattukottai Chettier economic creativity. At the same time, as we have noted in earlier chapters, the joint family and then the community, rather than the individual, was at the centre of business existence.

As David Rudner has now shown, under the heading 'A Collectivist Spirit of Capitalism', Nattukottai Chettiars belonged to a range of social groups: joint families, lineages, village clans, business associations operating out of specific localities and the caste as a whole. Like the peranakan of Java, 'these groups were marked by common and collective forms of worship in cults of specific deities, and these collective ritual practices were central to the way business was carried out in the wider society'.[72] Their ethic was marked, 'from a Weberian viewpoint, by a paradoxical amalgam of rationality and collectivism, rather than by rational individualism'.[73]

Weber, as we have already noted, insists that he was only investigating a series of conditions necessary for the emergence of modern capitalism, not for its subsequent adoption elsewhere. However, Weber did deny the existence of collectivist or supra-individual actors, and committed himself to a distinctive ethical approach to the individual.[74] What we have seen so far in our communities, however, is that in them the spirit of capitalism rests on the spirit of business confidence and economic creativity. This emotional climate can flow from numerous spiritual sources, and in particular from the creativity brought into being by the florescence of certain types of identity. But it is economic creativity in the collective sense, with the family at the core of the collectivity. In this collectivity, 'the sacred is seen as group life and a moral individual as one who grows as a social person'.[75]

Notes

1. M. Adas, 'Immigrant Asians and the Economic Impact of European Imperialism: The Role of the South Indian Chettiars in British Burma', *Journal of Asian Studies* 33, no. 3 (1974): 387.

2. P. Siegelman, 'Colonial Development and the Chettyar: A Study in the Ecology of Modern Burma, 1850–1941', Ph.D., University of Minnesota, 1962, pp. 18, 88–90.

3. *Ibid.*, pp. 86 ftn. 13, 267.

4. D.W. Rudner, 'Caste and Commerce in Indian Society: A Case Study of Nattukottai Chettiars, 1600–1930', Ph.D. University of Pennsylvania, 1985, pp. 89–91.

5. L.C. Jain, *Indigenous Banking in India*, London, Macmillan, 1929, pp. 37–38; E. Thurston, *Castes and Tribes of Southern India*, vol. 5, Madras, Government Press, 1909, pp. 249–250; Siegelman, 'Colonial Development and the Chettyar', pp. 122–123.

6. H.D. Evers, 'Chettiar Moneylenders in Southeast Asia', in Lombard and Aubin, *Marchands et hommes d'affaires*, pp. 202–203.

7. M. Adas, *The Burma Delta. Economic Development and Social Change on an Asian Rice Frontier, 1852–1941*, Madison, The University of Wisconsin Press, 1974, p. 114.

8. For the classic formulation see B. Stein, 'The Economic Function of a Medieval South Indian Temple', *Journal of Asian Studies* 19 (1959–60): 163–170; D.W. Rudner, 'Religious Gifting and Inland Commerce in Seventeenth-Century South India', *Journal of Asian Studies* 46, no. 2 (1987): 362.

9. Rudner, 'Religious Gifting', pp. 361, 363–365.

10. *Ibid.*, p. 369; see also pp. 365–368.

11. *Ibid.*, pp. 365, 375–377.

12. *Ibid.*, p. 377.

13. M. Singer, *When a Great Tradition Modernizes. An Anthropological Approach to Indian Civilization*, London, Pall Mall Press, 1972, p. 307.

14. S. Arasaratnam, *Merchants, Companies and Commerce on the Coromandel 1650–1740*, Delhi, Oxford University Press, 1986, p. 217; S. Arasaratnam, 'Society, Power, Factionalism and Corruption in Early Madras 1640–1746', *Indica* 23 (1986): 115–116.

15. Rudner, 'Caste and Commerce', pp. 41–42, 92–95.

16. *Ibid.*, pp. 92–95, 98–101.

17. *Ibid.*, pp. 96–97, 101–106, 194–199.

18. *Ibid.*, pp. 108–110, 116–117; R. Mahadevan, 'Immigrant Entrepreneurs in Colonial Burma – An Exploratory Study of the Role of Nattukottai Chettiars of Tamil Nadu, 1880–1930', *Indian Economic and Social History Review* 15, no. 3 (1978): 331.

19. Siegelman, 'Colonial Development and the Chettyar', pp. 132–133.

20. *Ibid.*, pp. 61–63, 88, 90; Adas, *Burma Delta*, p. 28; Adas, 'Immigrant Asians', p. 387.

21. Siegelman, 'Colonial Development and the Chettyar', pp. 101–102, 106–108.

22. Adas, *Burma Delta*, p. 58.

23. *Ibid.*, p. 58; see also pp. 30–31.

24. Adas, 'Immigrant Asians', p. 390; Siegelman, 'Colonial Development and the Chettyar', p. 182.

25. Adas, *Burma Delta*, pp. 62–63, 66–67, 109–110; Adas, 'Immigrant Asians', p. 390; Siegelman, 'Development and the Chettyar', pp. 108–117.

26. Siegelman, 'Colonial Development and the Chettyar', pp. 171, 224.

27. Adas, *Burma Delta*, pp. 71, 119, 172–173.

28. *Ibid.*, pp. 128, 185–187.

29. *Ibid.*, p. 188.

30. Mahadevan, 'Immigrant Entrepreneurs', pp. 356–357.

31. Adas, *Burma Delta*, pp. 136, 138.

32. Burma. *Report of the Burma Provincial Banking Inquiry Committee, 1929-30*, vol. 1, Rangoon, Superintendent of Government Printing, 1930, p. 203.

33. Rudner, 'Caste and Commerce', pp. 173–175, 180; Jain, *Indigenous Banking*, pp. 31–32, 37; Thurston, *Castes and Tribes* 5, pp. 250, 258; Adas, *Burma Delta*, p. 115.

34. Jain, *Indigenous Banking*, p. 37; S. Ito, 'A Note on the "Business Combine" in India – with Special Reference to the Nattukottai Chettiars', *Developing Economies* 4 (1966): 370; H.D. Evers and J. Pavadarayan, *Asceticism and Ecstasy: The Chettiars of Singapore*, University of Bielefeld, Sociology of Development Research Centre Working Paper No. 79 (1986): 5.

35. *Burma Banking Inquiry* 2, pp. 135–136; Siegelman, 'Colonial Development and the Chettyar', pp. 126–127.

36. *Burma Banking Inquiry* 1, pp. 205–206.

37. *Ibid.*, p. 207.

38. *Ibid.*, p. 208.

39. *Ibid.*, p. 204.

40. Rudner, 'Caste and Commerce', pp. 159, 244ff.; Siegelman, 'Colonial Development and the Chettyar', p. 142.

41. *Burma Banking Inquiry* 1, p. 195.

42. *Ibid.*, pp. 194, 196–197; Thurston, *Castes and Tribes* 5, p. 263.

43. Rudner, 'Caste and Commerce', pp. 201–205; an institution of this type was important for commercial castes: the Marwaris had their *basa* or collective messes as described in T.A. Timberg, *The Marwaris. From Traders to Industrialists*, New Delhi, Vikas, 1978, pp. 5–6.

44. *Burma Banking Inquiry* 1, pp. 196–197; Rudner, 'Caste and Commerce', pp. 180–182.

45. *Burma Banking Inquiry* 1, p. 205.

46. *Ibid.*, 2, p. 134; Siegelman, 'Colonial Development and the Chettyar', p. 238.

47. Markovits, *Indian Business*, p. 121.

48. Rudner, 'Caste and Commerce', pp. 180–188.

49. Mahadevan, 'Immigrant Entrepreneurs', pp. 347–348.

50. Evers, 'Chettiar Moneylenders', p. 204.

51. Jain, *Indigenous Banking*, p. 37; Thurston, *Castes and Tribes* 5, pp. 262–263; Adas, *Burma Delta*, p. 117.

52. H.D. Evers and J. Pavadarayan, 'Religious Fervour and Economic Success. The Chettiars of Singapore', in K.S. Sandhu and A. Mani (eds), *Indian Communities in Southeast Asia*, Singapore, Institute of Southeast Asian Studies, 1993, p. 856; see also Rudner's view, 'Caste and Commerce', pp. 263–264.

53. Evers and Pavadarayan, *Asceticism and Ecstasy*, pp. 18–21.

54. P. Jash, *History of Saivism*, Calcutta, Roy and Chaudhury, 1974, p. 18; R.C. Zaehner, *Hinduism*, London, Oxford University Press, 1962, pp. 164–167, 171, 182; Thurston, *Castes and Tribes* 5, p. 254.

55. Singer, *A Great Tradition Modernizes*, p. 233.

56. Evers and Pavadarayan, *Asceticism and Ecstasy*, pp. 13–17; Evers and Pavadarayan, 'Religious Fervour', pp. 857–860.

57. Thurston, *Castes and Tribes* 5, pp. 251, 254; see also Rudner, 'Caste and Commerce', p. 257.

58. Evers and Pavadarayan, *Asceticism and Ecstasy*, pp. 13, 15–17.

59. *Ibid.*, p. 20; Evers and Pavadarayan, 'Religious Fervour', pp. 860–861.

60. Evers and Pavadarayan, *Asceticism and Ecstasy*, p. 20; Evers and Pavadarayan, 'Religious Fervour', p. 862.

61. Jash, *Saivism*, pp. 18–26.

62. Singer, *A Great Tradition Modernizes*, p. 336.

63. *Burma Banking Inquiry* 1, pp. 197–198; Mahadevan, 'Immigrant Entrepreneurs', p. 351.

64. Mahadevan, 'Immigrant Entrepreneurs', pp. 349–350; Siegelman, 'Colonial Development and the Chettyar', pp. 259–260.

65. Evers, 'Chettiar Moneylenders', pp. 212–213; Rudner, 'Caste and Commerce', p. 38.

66. J.J. Berna, *Industrial Entrepreneurship in Madras State*, Bombay, Asia Publishing House, 1960, pp. 22–23, 44; Singer, *A Great Tradition Modernizes*, pp. 309, 359; Lamb, 'Indian Business Communities', p. 105; Government of Tamil Nadu, *Tamil Nadu District Gazetteers. Ramanathapuram*, Madras, Director of Stationery and Printing, 1972, p. 339.

67. Ito, '"Business Combine" in India', pp. 371–372, 374; Mahadevan, 'Immigrant Entrepreneurs', p. 330; Rudner, 'Caste and Commerce', pp. 160–166.

68. Singer, *A Great Tradition Modernizes*, pp. 283–284, 301, 346.

69. *Ibid.*, p. 305.

70. Robison, *The Rise of Capital*, pp. 277–305.

71. Singer, *A Great Tradition Modernizes*, p. 310.

72. D.W. Rudner, *Caste and Capitalism in Colonial India. The Nattukottai Chettiars*, Berkeley and Los Angeles, University of California Press, 1994, p. 105.

73. *Ibid.*

74. For a discussion, see Abercrombie *et al.*, *Sovereign Individuals*, p. 16.

75. *Ibid.*, p. 129.

Changing Chinese Enterprise in the Philippines and Java 1830–1940

Mestizo Dynamism and the World Sugar Market

The period from 1820 to 1870 was one in which the Philippines moved from a subsistence economy to an export crop economy. During these fifty years Philippine raw products such as hemp and sugar started to be exported in quantity, while products of European factory industry, particularly English textiles, began to find markets in the Philippines. Non-Spanish Europeans were allowed to reside in the colony, a precondition for the development of an export crop economy. The Chinese mestizos became dynamically involved with these changes, gradually abandoning commerce and increasingly involving themselves with agriculture.[1] The new export crop economy raised the value of land and made landholding and export crop production an attractive means of livelihood. By the 1890s it was alleged that the prophecies of Zuñiga's day had been realized; the Chinese mestizos had taken over half the lands of the country.[2]

The total population of the Philippines by the mid-nineteenth century was something in excess of 4 million with the mestizo population estimated by one source to be 240,000 or some 5–6 per cent of the total.[3] But their geographic distribution was changing, as they pushed further into Luzon. Their landholding interests burgeoned and in some towns they owned industrial facilities, such as sugar mills, the evolution of which is the main theme of this section.[4] But their cultural situation places a question mark over their existence as a separate group, and indeed Wickberg speaks of this period as representing 'The Disappearance of the Mestizo Community'.[5] Unlike the peranakan in Java, the mestizos were not a special kind of Chinese but, Wickberg says, a special kind of Filipino. They had evolved a social style based on wealth, ostentation, sumptuous feasts and the disbursement of huge sums of money at fiesta time. Great prestige came to be attached to wealth in particular. These tendencies were crystallized by the Spanish government's abolition of the legal distinction between *indio* and mestizo in the 1880s; there was now officially speaking no separate mestizo culture and mestizos' only choice was to adopt fully the Filipino culture which they had played such a large part in creating.[6]

This culture itself came to be more Hispanicized. By the late nineteenth century Manila had developed a more sophisticated version of Spanish culture than that known previously, and a Filipinized Hispanic culture was part of this mosaic. Newly rich mestizos and *indios* in the provinces travelled to the capital, or sent their sons there for education, acquiring a form of culture never before available to them.[7] In provinces such as Pampanga the *indio*-mestizo upper class became more and more cosmopolitan in behaviour and outlook; some kept residences in Manila and a select few were able to send their children to Europe for education. Now at the pinnacle of native society were the *ilustrados*, not the *principalia* in general but those families which claimed education and preeminence beyond a single region. Land, wealth, Spanish higher education and broad social contacts differentiated the nineteenth-century *ilustrado* from the rest of the *principalia*.[8]

Many of the Filipino nationalist leaders came from the *principalia* or *ilustrado* class. The Filipino national hero, José Rizal, may by lineage be considered a fifth-generation Chinese mestizo. His paternal ancestor, a Catholic Chinese named Domingo Lamco, married a Chinese mestiza. Their son and grandson both married Chinese mestizas. His son and Rizal, his grandson, were considered *indio* and were landowners in Laguna province.[9] The educational opportunities of the nationalist leaders were derived from the export crop economy and, whatever their political views, their orientation was to some form of Spanish culture.[10]

Although we might speak of the decline of the Chinese mestizo, the history of the Philippine sugar industry indicates that the mestizos formed part of the Filipino entrepreneurial elite of the late nineteenth and early twentieth centuries, and some account of this entrepreneurship is necessary to end the story of the Chinese mestizo. Sugar and entrepreneurship became concomitant in the Philippines. From about 1836 there was an enormous expansion of the Philippine sugar industry, and during the period from 1836 to 1920 'sugar society' became firmly linked to the world-economy and responsive to its fluctuations. The world-economy supplied an ever-increasing demand for sugar, while outsiders played a vital role in supplying the industry with credit and technology. In 1920 the industry represented almost half of all Philippine foreign trade and it represented, too, the islands' most advanced manufacturing technology.[11] American policy was, of course, responsible for this. In 1909 the United States passed the Payne–Adrich Tariff Act and admitted 300,000 tons of sugar from the Philippines free of duty. This encouraged United States capital interested in sugar production in the Philippines, and a number of sugar companies entered. In 1913 the United States passed the Underwood–Simmons Tariff Act which freed all trade between the Philippines and the United States. This gave a tremendous advantage to the Philippines as a sugar producer and a large amount of investment was channelled into cane cultivation and milling. It was the sugar group which received favourable treatment at American colonial hands.[12]

The sugar barons of a province like Pampanga, largely of mestizo origin, had become more and more oriented towards the business dimensions of farm management even before the American period. To prosper within the burgeoning cash-crop environment of the mid-nineteenth century, the entrepreneur of Pampanga required economic acumen and managerial skills, ability to purchase and maintain new processing equipment, recruit and maintain mill workers, and keep tenants' accounts. Unlike their predecessors, they needed a talent for business, knowledge of market conditions, and comprehension of technical changes. Larkin calls Pampanga's Chinese mestizos active in sugar 'the province's most active entrepreneurs since the late eighteenth century'.[13]

Entrepreneurial abilities were particularly required in the sugar-milling industry. Originally juice was expressed from cane between two horizontal wooden rollers, boiled down in earthen vessels and crystallized. For years the Philippine processors turned out the same low-grade sugar, but the intruding demands of the world market made the requirement for a higher standard urgent. Several improved inventions were crowned finally by the invention in England in the 1840s of a centrifugal separator: a steam-driven cylinder that removed molasses from crystal sugar clearly and rapidly. Initially the Philippines could not afford centrals and ultimately their cost was met by foreign entrepreneurs, private families fearing to make big investments on their own when they knew little of financing and constructing such machines. The first central was erected in 1909 by an American syndicate; it was capable of milling some 1,500 tons of cane daily. The shortage of domestic capital caused difficulties for Filipinos, but the Roxas family and Esteban de la Rama managed to erect small centrals on their own properties and finally Miguel Ossorio was able to organize the private support necessary to construct two big centrals in Negros in 1917 and 1921. It took government intervention to make certain that Philippine interests could afford to build centrals, based on lending by the Philippine National Bank.[14] A number of the families that succeeded were of mestizo background.[15]

The advent of centrals brought a significant change to provinces such as Pampanga. Investment in the new centrals allowed investors to profit from both the farming and milling side of their operations. The period 1921–34 was a period of unprecedented prosperity in the Philippine sugar industry, with the island's crop having privileged access to the United

States market. Production increased at an amazing rate as processing facilities multiplied to accommodate overseas demand. More efficient milling, increased sugar hectarage, and guaranteed markets infused huge amounts of capital into the sugar industry and augmented the wealth, political power and prestige of the sugar barons. Society became strongly hierarchical. At the socio-economic apex stood the *centralistas*, Filipino, Spanish and American owners managing either corporate or family interests. The leading Filipino capitalists were José de León, Augusto Gonzalez and the Montillas, Aranetas and Lizareses. They were intertwined by marriage and had originated, not recently with the establishment of the sugar centrals, but from the older sugar-planting class which had accumulated money to invest in the new centrals. Later the families diversified into paint, lumber and shipping. Larkin has argued that sugar money ultimately penetrated almost every area of Philippine enterprise from agriculture and food processing to mining. The new central mills clearly represented a huge jump in technical and economic efficiency although, while improved milling facilities represented a degree of modernization to the Philippines, they also absorbed much of the private and governmental credit which would have been available to local commerce and processing.[16]

Despite Wickberg's argument that the Chinese mestizo disappeared by the turn of the twentieth century, this view is not shared by other writers on the American period. Observers wrote of them as 'capable, prosperous, and powerful'[17] and as 'the most active and enterprising class in the Islands'.[18] Typical is the career of the Cojuangco family, the family of President Corazón Aquino. José Cojuangco Sr, who owned Central Azucarera de Tarlac and Tarlac Distillery, was the grandson of an immigrant from Fujian. Soon after this immigrant arrived in Manila in 1861 he became a Catholic, received the Christian name José and married a Filipina. He began working as a carpenter and soon became a building contractor, ultimately investing his money in rice and sugar lands in Tarlac and making a large fortune. He had three children: Ysidra born 1867, Malicio born 1871, and Trinidad born 1876. Melicio married a Chinese mestiza in 1894 and his eldest son, José Cojuangco Sr, was born in 1896. Melicio entered politics using the family wealth as a base, and in this he was followed by his son in the 1930s. In the late 1920s the family established with its own funds a sugar central called Paniqui Sugar Mills. The family also diversified its interests. José Cojuangco Sr, in addition to his sugar activities, also had considerable banking interests.[19]

Development in this direction was possible because the Americans followed the Spanish model of development, which stressed that the Philippines' comparative advantage was in the export of minerals and tropical agricultural products. Industrialization remained limited to the processing of agricultural goods, thus reinforcing the concentration of wealth and political power in the hands of a landholding elite which, other than the industrial development of their estates, was not interested in developing the country's manufacturing sector.[20] Nevertheless, one of the leading writers on this subject has called them 'a powerful industrial elite'.[21]

A similar pattern developed in Cebu and Iloilo. By 1830 Cebu had become a distributive centre for a rapidly rising commercial sugar production. During the 1840s Cebu's hinterland and most of the lowland plains along the east coast were given over to sugar cultivation, simple milling devices were erected and sugar was shipped to Manila for export. By the mid-century Cebu province had become one of the Philippines' leading sugar producers. As in Luzon, Chinese mestizos were active in this new development. From the 1840s the mestizo elite of Cebu's Parian began to acquire substantial agricultural lands. The prime sugar lands closest to the city were obtained by leases purchased from the indebtedness of the cultivator, and gradually lands further afield were acquired under resold mortgages, the former owner becoming a tenant.[22] This trend was encouraged by the coming to the province of Chinese traders, who provided commercial competition for the mestizos.[23]

Most of Cebu's dominant mestizo families now became attracted to land, and several acquired considerable fortunes through commercial agriculture. During the late nineteenth century the sugar frontier on Cebu island moved to the south of the city and to the west coast. Mestizos took an active part in the commercial exploitation and elite families planted branches throughout the island. A number of brothers, cousins or in-laws of leading merchants established themselves in the municipalities and channelled business into the family's ventures in Cebu City, often obtaining loans from their rich merchant relatives. Of the original 30 or so *principalia* families of the mestizo *gremio* in the early 1850s, most had clearly established branches of their families in the provinces by the 1890s. A province- and region-wide elite was in the making, intermarried with local *indio* families and strongly tied to Spanish culture.[24]

This elite also came to be tied to the world-economy. In 1860 the Spanish government opened the port of Cebu to direct foreign trade, and by 1866 four major foreign business houses had established agencies in Cebu. Sugar and hemp, the primary export products, were now sent directly to foreign markets through the agency of the British and American commercial houses. Local entrepreneurs, largely Chinese mestizos, quickly established close ties with the foreign businesses, which acted as creditors for mestizos expanding into sugar land. Agents supervised the collection and shipment of the agricultural products to the port of Cebu, so that the sugar growers became dependent on distant foreign markets. By the end of the nineteenth century Cebu, after years of focusing its mercantile ties on Manila, had become an autonomous entrepôt dealing directly with the centres of a global economy and with a firm grip on a greatly expanded hinterland. By the second decade of the twentieth century it was the archipelago's second city.[25]

Similarly dependent on the world sugar economy were the sugar planters of Negros, who represented Iloilo families who had crossed the Guimaras Strait to Negros as the local cloth industry declined and new entrepreneurial ventures were needed.[26] In 1855 Iloilo city was opened to foreign commerce. The new British Vice-Consul, Nicholas Loney, landed the next year and, as the commercial agent for British and American firms, he devoted himself to the introduction of cheap British cottons as a replacement for Iloilo cloth and the promotion of sugar production as a return cargo.[27] Loney encouraged the clearance of the Negros frontiers for sugar *haciendas* by extending crop loans and giving the agricultural entrepreneurs access to means of production such as mills and cauldrons on easy, long-term payments without interest.[28] Loney, writing specifically of the Chinese mestizo settlers, described them as a 'remarkable commercial and speculative race' who

> invested in the large tracts of fertile and well-situated land on the coast of Negros, each taking with them several families from Molo, Jaro, Miagao and other pueblos of the province to settle in their estates and work on the usual system of proportionate share of profits. Most of these mestizos have hitherto been engaged in the piece goods trade in this province, but finding that the importation of goods at Iloilo from first hands at Manila interfered with their usual practice of obtaining them from the Manila shops for subsequent sale here, and that of the increasing number of Chinese shopkeepers rendered their retail sale of goods at the different markets much more difficult, precarious and unremunerative, they have directed their attention to agriculture in preference. The new tendency thus given to their capital and industry will by increasing the area of cultivation and amount of production, be much more beneficial than their former employment in a branch of commerce where they had become superfluous.[29]

The Negros economy became enmeshed in the London and New York sugar markets. But there was a continuity between Iloilo's pre-1865 elite and the new sugar elite, many having weathered the decline of the cloth trade by obtaining large loans from European entrepreneurs. The Negros planters remained loyal to Spain until the collapse of Spanish rule in September 1898. Very shortly thereafter they decided to seek formal protection under the United States, their main market for several decades.[30] Gradually a Negrense identity emerged on the island, springing from intermarriage between various groups of land colonists, and largely used to identify the emergent *ilustrado* class from the turn of the century. Their wealth and power were tied to business or entrepreneurial success.[31] Among this class were families with Chinese mestizo blood such as the family of Teodoro Benedicto, who began his career as a petty cloth merchant and became the founder of one of the region's major dynasties. In 1871 Benedicto purchased Hacienda San Bernadino in La Carlota, Negros Occidental; during the following five years it grew from its original 300 hectares to 1,120 hectares.[32]

As in Luzon, these families' positions were consolidated with the introduction of centrifugal mills. From 1914 to 1927, local and foreign capitalists invested sufficient funds to replace some 820 plantation steam mills with seventeen centrifugal factories. The modernization of milling facilities triggered the industrialization of cane production, with easy access to loans guaranteed to the planters. Government support was generous; the government financed some 20 million pesos for the construction of six centrifugal mills. Sugar yields increased and the government accorded preferential treatment to domestic sugar producers.[33]

Philippine Chinese Economic Activities

By the 1780s the Spaniards had finally realized their official objective of the seventeenth century to permit only those Chinese 'necessary' to maintain essential economic services to reside in the Philippines. A cautious figure of 4,000 was maintained, 90 per cent being in Tondo province, in other words Manila and areas adjacent.[34] In the 1780s the new Governor Don José Basco y Vargas sent a special commissioner to China to persuade 4,000 immigrants to come over. A list of trades in need was given to the commissioner, and this included silk-workers, porcelain-makers, dyers familiar with Philippine dyeing plants, foundrymen, blacksmiths, miners, and artisans who could paint, lacquer and varnish.[35]

However, as Philippine economic life underwent a fundamental transformation and as entrepreneurship in the export-crop economy was encouraged, Spanish immigration policy towards the Chinese moved from one of limiting numbers to widespread encouragement to come. The entire spectrum of Spanish opinion seemed ready to concede that the Chinese would be useful in achieving the goal of developing the Philippines economically and in 1839 they were granted the liberty to choose their place of residence and whatever occupation best suited them.[36] Bowring reported in 1859:

> A great majority of the shoemakers in the Philippines are Chinese. Of 784 in the capital, 633 are Chinamen, and 151 natives. Great numbers are carpenters, blacksmiths, water-carriers, cooks, and daily labourers, but a retail shopkeeping trade is the favourite pursuit. Of late, however, many are merging into the rank of wholesale dealers and merchants, exporting and importing large quantities of goods on their own account, and having their subordinate agents scattered over most of the islands.[37]

The Chinese population expanded from about 6,000 in 1847 to perhaps 90,000 in the 1880s, out of a total population of nearly 6 million. Manila was the largest centre of Chinese residence.[38] The vast majority were again from the Amoy area of Fujian province.[39]

Chinese commercial efforts assisted in tying the Philippine economy to that of the wider world. Unlike the mestizos, they carried out wholesaling and collected export crops in a systematic way. The mestizo practice of random, speculative buying up of export crops and slow disposal of imports by offering them at a series of periodic markets, could not compete effectively with the basic Chinese rural feature, the *sari-sari* store. These stores spread into many provinces where Chinese had never settled before. In 1891 over 12–15 per cent of the Chinese in the Philippines were located in abaca (Manila hemp) regions where previously there had been no significant number of Chinese. There was also some attraction to sugar and tobacco. The Chinese economy changed in character. Previously the Chinese had traded by sea, sold provisions and other items in urban settlements, and worked as artisans. Now they acted as commercial agents or middlemen, collecting produce for export and selling it at some stage or another to Europeans for shipment to world markets on European ships. They were also wholesalers of imported goods, which they then sold to a wider and wider circle of regions. By the end of the Spanish period they had become, on their own account, importers of European goods and exporters of cash crops to world markets.[40]

It appears that these Chinese intermediaries were financially dependent on European and North American merchants, although some Chinese formed their own commercial and industrial capital through tax-farming contracts and coolie brokerage. The key function of the North American and Northern European entrepreneurs in Manila was banking. Their funds – received from sources such as the Church, rich families and Manila businessmen – were loaned out, mostly in the form of crop advances. Advances were also made to Chinese wholesalers to help them sell European imports.[41] The extension of credit kept the Chinese middleman in a state of constant indebtedness; British merchants were particularly active in this manner of doing business, forming what Edgar Wickberg has called 'almost an informal Anglo-Chinese economic partnership'.[42]

The Chinese intermediary trade system was well organized around the *sari-sari* store. At the head of a firm was the *cabecilla*, approximately equivalent to the *taokeh* in the rest of the Southeast Asian world, who was usually a wholesaler of imported goods and export produce. Generally he was established in Manila, negotiating with foreign business firms, but he had several agents settled in the regions and they established *sari-sari* stores to operate as retail outlets for the imports he received from his foreign partners and to acquire products to deliver to the latter. The *cabecilla* extended credit to his agents, though this tended to be a short-term arrangement. The agent's shop, a general merchandise business, was established in market towns. Unlike the periodic markets, the *sari-sari* store was open all the time and customers were offered credit. A customer who required supplies rather than cash could be accommodated. Shops contained all household goods including grocery items, oil, soap, matches, candles, thread, needles and buttons.

The *cabecilla*-agent system offered a number of advantages to all concerned. The relationship between individuals was usually kept secret, so that agents whose businesses failed were regarded as standing alone and so the final responsibility could be concealed from the creditors as far as possible. The agent benefited because, with neither capital nor access to credit to commence his own business, he could acquire these from the *cabecilla* who basically started his shop for him, kept him supplied, and provided a steady outlet for the produce the agent bought. The foreign merchant was also sure that his goods would receive the widest possible distribution.[43]

The *sari-sari* stores were particularly located in regions of export crops, especially sugar, abaca and tobacco. For example, after the end of the government monopoly in 1880, Chinese moved into the tobacco trade in Northern Luzon, establishing *sari-sari* stores in Cagayan Valley towns. With Aparri at the mouth of the Cagayan River as their initial settlement, Chinese buyers made three-month trips up-river towards Isabela. Establishing shops, they sold groceries, palm wine and textiles, and bought up tobacco. Even the most obscure places were regarded as suitable for shops, such as the eighteen *sari-sari* stores established by 1889 in Gamú, a town in Isabela. By mid-1886 there were thirty-six Chinese shops in Tuguegarao, the capital of Isabela. The Chinese also moved into the buying up of other crops which had previously been Chinese mestizo perquisites. Indigo was one example.[44] Wherever they went they remained aloof from the Chinese mestizos, assuming the latter's role as itinerant pedlars and driving them into agriculture. In Cebu City they established their own quarter which grew from a population of thirty in 1857 to about 1,400 in the 1890s, while operating the *cabecilla*-agent system throughout the island.[45] Similarly in Iloilo Chinatown numbers grew from thirty-two in 1857 to 1,994 in the 1890s.[46]

The Chinese in the Philippines were very homogeneous. By the end of the nineteenth century the Cantonese were probably no more than 5 per cent of the total Chinese population. The vast majority came from four counties in Southern Fujian in the vicinity of Quanzhou and Zhangzhou. A similar pattern was true for Iloilo.[47] Jacques Amyot's study covers the lifespan of those who were members of Manila's Chinese community in 1958–59 and shows that immigration was an economic venture spanning several generations. The community in China, in fact, was supported from abroad, the migrant coming to specific enterprises started, staffed and continued in the Philippines. Although Amyot's sample families had sent members to the Philippines for several generations, until 1941 members of each succeeding generation were born in China. The situation until the late 1930s was often as if families lived in China, and as many males as could be spared commuted to the Philippines to work. The home remained the emigrant community in China. Boys were brought over to the Philippines to begin their careers between the ages of 12 and 16. Later their own children joined them when they came of age.[48]

These immigration patterns dominated in the American period. Despite the Chinese Exclusion Act and the American policy of 'The Philippines for Filipinos', the Chinese population increased slowly and there were no restrictions on where in the archipelago Chinese could reside. Chinese *sari-sari* stores spread to all corners of the archipelago. Prior to the Japanese War it was estimated that 70 per cent of all retail and semi-retail trade was carried on by Chinese. By 1934 the total Chinese population was roughly 80,000, whilst the 1939 census gave them a population of 117,987.[49] Because of lack of American restrictions on Chinese trade and business during that administration, the Chinese had become involved in almost every phase of the Philippine economy by 1946. They were very close to the Americans in the total share of the commerce of the archipelago by the end of the American regime.[50]

In addition, Chinese traders became involved in industrial entrepreneurship by the close of the American period. Before 1941, as a consequence of natural evolution, many Chinese had entered manufacturing through trading, establishing enterprises such as rice-milling, wood-processing, alcohol-distilling, coconut products, tobacco, shoes and containers.[51] They were extremely important in the milling and marketing end of the rice industry and it was recorded that during the early 1940s the Chinese owned no less than 75 per cent of the 2,500 rice mills in the islands, in addition to controlling most of the rice warehouses in the archipelago. In commercialized localities, such as the huge rice region of Central Luzon which furnished rice to Manila and other trade centres, the Chinese played a leading role in the processing and distribution of the grain. Most of the milling of rice was done by the Chinese, since much Filipino capital was tied up in the sugar industry and was not available to operate big rice mills. Often the Chinese mill was the only buyer of rice in the locality.[52] The Chinese were also active in the lumber industry as millers; around 1940 the Chinese milled nearly 40 per cent of the timber annually put on the market, and they were also involved in the manufacture of lumber for the retail trade.[53] They did not have the capital to finance centrifugal sugar mills, but the optimum scale of production in tobacco and coconut oil was much smaller and their careers as intermediaries in this trade led them eventually to be able to process the products. Entry into manufacturing from trading has of course been a common pattern for all the communities dealt with here, and in the Philippines the percentage of Chinese entrepreneurs who opened manufacturing establishments after 1945 and who had been traders prior to that date was close to 90 per cent.[54]

The backbone of Chinese business was the individual merchant, family or firm. The largest Chinese houses in Manila lent out money or goods on credit, based on personal relationships of kinship or friendship.[55] In Iloilo certain individuals and businesses, because of their large size and communal leadership positions, served as backers for large numbers of immigrants, loans being specifically directed towards townmates, dialect groups and others.[56] Although many immigrants came from the same village and were of one lineage, the urban environment of Manila did not favour the development of the lineage form quite as it existed in China. Most of the functions of the lineage were taken over by the clan association, which gave some form of solidarity to its members in business when it became obvious that regional or lineage groups could not recruit a sufficiently large membership to undertake corporate action. Amyot describes the clan hall, oriented around an ancestral shrine, as a ritual centre. Ancestor worship took place once or twice a year; a day devoted not only to this but also to social and business purposes. The day of ancestor worship was a day devoted to the affirmation of clan familism, of which the ancestor worship ceremony was the symbolic expression *par excellence*. Amyot notes that further research is required on the religious nature of ancestor worship, but he is at one with Durkheim sociologically that its function includes the realization of clan solidarity, so that the consciousness of the communion of clansmen with their ancestors leads to an awareness of common origins and a common history.[57]

While the prerequisites for business confidence are here, clan associations did not engage in business ventures, nor were association funds available to individual clan members to invest in private business. But funds springing from friendships made among clan members were used for business endeavours, and non-family companies were formed with close friends. Further coordination of economic activity was by general and local chambers of commerce and individual trade associations. There were also mutual aid societies and occupational associations.[58] In the American period the ties of the Chinese community with China were close, underlining the community's cultural distinctiveness. Compared to Filipino business elites, the core of the Chinese business community was not affected strongly by American civilization and the Chinese instead adopted a policy of organization and sinification of their community.[59]

The most powerful Chinese in the Philippines at the end of the Spanish period was Carlos Palanca Tan Quien-sien or Tan Chueco. Born to a poor family in a south Fujian county in 1844, he migrated to the Philippines in about 1856. A relative initiated him into the textile business and he advanced himself through hard work and personal connections. His business interests expanded to include general importing, sugar exporting, coolie brokerage, monopoly tax contracting and rice importing. He also had at least some interest in a wider range of businesses, through investments if not actual participation. He was also active in community affairs, though his attitude to Chinese mestizos was one of contempt.[60] He was a member, as has been said of Iloilo's Chinese community, of 'a closed ethnic community under tight rein'.[61]

Changing Chinese Enterprise in Java

From approximately 1870 the Netherlands state began to withdraw from the supervision of crop production and the operation of state monopolies, to establish instead the political and economic conditions for the expansion of Dutch and other Western capital in Indonesia. Under a changed legal regime, the Dutch industrial and financial entrepreneurial classes invested in capitalist agriculture both in Java and the Outer Islands, leasing land, clearing, planting, building mills and hiring wage labour. The Chinese expanded into areas which fed off this activity, including retailing, credit and distribution: enterprises known as 'the intermediate trade'.[62] They functioned as a link between European firms and the Javanese population. After 1904 many of the travel and abode regulations pertaining to them were relaxed, and from 1914 the entire system was dismantled. Immigration restrictions were relaxed too, so that the total number of Chinese admitted to the Indies between 1900 and 1930 was 871,113, many destined for work as coolies on estates in the Outer Islands. In 1815 the number of Chinese in Java had been estimated to be only 94,000. In 1900 the corresponding figure was 280,000 and by the 1930 census it was 582,000 or 1.4 per cent of Java's population. Upwards of 30,000 Javanese villages counted a Chinese contingent among their population.[63]

The Chinese in Java lived largely in the cities, however, and were still predominantly of Hokkien-speaking origin and Java-born.[64] G.W. Skinner has concluded that in no sense were the peranakans undergoing a process of assimilation; they constituted rather, in every major city of Java, a community bearing a distinct culture that was also stable and internally creative, certainly no longer in the process of Indonesianization. Skinner argues that at the end of the nineteenth century there was only one Chinese community on Java, that of the peranakans, who were almost wholly of Hokkien extraction.[65] A study of Semarang has also shown considerable differences between the peranakans and the *totok* or China-born, and certainly both communities felt themselves culturally distinct.[66]

The economic basis of peranakan life changed towards the end of the nineteenth century. The opium farms were abolished when public opinion turned against them. In any case, with the influx of new groups of Chinese, the farms' social and economic structures were no longer capable of absorbing newcomers in the traditional manner. The major *kongsis* reneged on their government obligations and left large unpaid debts. There was also a wave of failures among Chinese businesses which depended on the commercial networks associated with the farms. The Chinese officer system was another casualty of the passing of the opium farms, although it survived to 1931.[67] But while the *cabang atas* never recovered their dominant economic position, there was a release of money into the community which gave business opportunities to a range of peranakan in new proto-industries which opened up at the turn of the century. While peranakans played a modest role in big concerns, which were largely European-dominated, they played an important role in medium-size industries such as rice mills, batik businesses and cigarette production. Here where organization was not particularly complicated, mechanization not well developed and the share of labour great compared to the share of capital, peranakans with their mercantile talent played an important role.

Peranakan movement into Java's batik industry was spectacular.[68] Up to the middle of the nineteenth century there existed two major centres of batik enterprise and trade in Java, the north central coast and the princely courts of Yogyakarta and Surakarta. The batik produced in these centres was the so-called *batik tulis*, in which the wax which secured the design was applied to the cloth by hand, using a *canting* or wax-applicator, generally made of copper. Production was overwhelmingly in the hands of women, working in their own homes, although at the princely courts there were also larger batik workshops, again operated by women. The fine cloth used for batik-making was not a product of Java, but was imported into the north Javanese ports from India, a trade long in the hands of Indian Muslims and later of Arab settlers at the main harbours.

A series of economic and technical changes affected the batik industry in the nineteenth century, beginning with changes in Dutch commercial policy towards Java in the early part of the century. The first was an attempt to find markets in Java for newly manufactured textiles of Netherlands factories, which encouraged batik-makers to investigate industrial methods which would enable them to compete with the imported cloth. A very simple stamp for applying wax in the batik process was recorded early in the century, and by mid-century a copper stamp (*cap*) had been invented, probably somewhere along the north coast. In 1859 metal stamps were already being used in Pekalongan, and by 1872 in Batavia. The major subsequent technical change was the introduction of synthetic (aniline) dyes, which allowed traditional colours to be imitated at far greater speed and with less effort and skill, and which began to be imported into Java from Germany in the late nineteenth century. The material used for batik also changed; since European printed cottons could not withstand the gains made by the revitalized batik industry, the European private firms which multiplied on Java from the 1870s began importing plain European manufactured cloth which gradually superseded Indian cloth as the basic material for batik.

It was as a consequence of these changes that Chinese in possession of varying amounts of capital, released due to the ending of the monopoly lease system, were able to enter an industry which provided clothing for almost the entire female population of Java and for males other than in West Java. The adoption of the *cap* meant a considerable increase in output. A month's work was often required to produce one *kain* (piece of cloth) of *batik tulis*, as batik could only be a side occupation for a village woman when she had no more pressing tasks. In

1873 it was reported that by using a selection of *cap*, some with fine patterns and others with less attractive patterns, one fine *kain* could be printed within one day and four coarser ones in the same space of time. In a reasonably short time a large number of *batik kain* could be made from one pattern and, if there was a sudden demand for a particular pattern, it could be satisfied relatively quickly.

The field was open for Chinese entrepreneurs with disposable capital. With a small amount of capital a few *cap* could be acquired, although considerably more was required to purchase the whole sets needed for large patterns. A comparatively effective business needed to use about twenty patterns of fairly different character, with additional capital required for the acquisition of workshop space. In the same year fourteen Chinese workshops were already operating in Surabaya, side by side with twenty-three Javanese 'ateliers', and from that decade *batik cap* workshops mushroomed on Java.

Just as the introduction of the *cap* meant that traditional skills could be superseded by new ones, so too did synthetic dyes break down reliance on age-old Javanese techniques, as the long-standing cachets of various local dyes could be easily and speedily imitated. Traditional dyeing took much time and only after weeks could the required colour be achieved. With the new German dyes the professional secrets of the batik worker no longer played a role, and the way was now open to the Chinese entrepreneur. He was further advantaged by Chinese dominance of the retail trade of Java. A Javanese entering the *cap* business and able to supply a large range of batik fabrics was at a disadvantage when compared to Chinese competitors with better connections to assist in finding markets. This close connection with the market also enabled a Chinese entrepreneur to obtain the latest intelligence of patterns in demand, which he could then quickly reproduce and place for sale. Chinese entered the industry, too, just at the time when transport was being vastly improved throughout Java, the new rail and tram routes sometimes leading to a decline in traditional batik areas and the rise of new ones.

But the greatest advantage possessed by the Chinese in their entry to the world of batik was the gradual dominance they achieved over the trade in batik ingredients. With the change to European ingredients – cloth, dyes and paraffin which came to be added to the wax – came a virtual Chinese monopoly in these particulars. This monopolistic access was achieved as a simple extension of the long-standing Chinese role as a middleman minority for European commercial interests, so that by the 1920s it was reported that about 90 per cent of this trade was in Chinese hands. Chinese had a considerable history of acting as the 'second hand' for the European cloth trade. The failure of the trade in European printed cottons coincided with the inauguration of the Liberal Policy, the encouragement of European private enterprise in the Indies and a rise in Dutch immigration. With the *cap* came the changeover from the fine cottons of India essential for the *canting* to a much wider range of plain coarser cloth which the European market could supply. From the 1870s European manufacturers and import houses zealously rushed to supply the market, competing thereby for the favours of Chinese distributors and offering generous credits even to those who may not have been creditworthy. As late as the 1930s it was reported that Chinese intermediate traders with a capital of not more than 5,000 guilders sometimes enjoyed credit of more than 100,000 guilders with various wholesale dealers. The chain extended right down to the individual Chinese in the marketplace, with his shop for selling cloth.

The process whereby the Chinese managed to obtain a dominant position in what had been a completely Javanese industry differed by region and even by city and cannot be fully investigated here. A few examples should suffice. In Batavia *batik tulis* was an old industry with a considerable clientele for certain local specialities such as red and white headcloths. Chinese initially entered this hand industry, the first recorded business being that of The Yoe Hok founded in the 1860s, which by 1869 was already making headcloths for the Padang market by hand. At some period in the 1870s and 1880s the changeover to *cap* took place and the Chinese, because of their greater access to capital, began to achieve considerable success in these new ventures. By the early 1890s it was reported that the Chinese were dominating the industry and by 1909 the batik industry in Batavia was said to be completely in Chinese hands. *Batik tulis* began to die out in the early part of the century until by 1929 there was only one *batik tulis* workplace left in Batavia. The number of *batik cap* workshops grew from 105 in 1910 to 197 in 1914; declined in 1915–1917 due to the difficulties in obtaining imported goods from Europe; stabilized at 101 in 1918; and grew to 288 in 1924. By 1929 there were 264 Chinese batik workshops in Batavia, compared with 93 Javanese businesses, strongly competing with the traditional batik areas of Yogyakarta and Surakarta, particularly in the West Java market.

The bases of Chinese success were several. In the first place numerous Chinese possessed *toko* where they were readily supplied by the Chinese intermediate trade with batik ingredients such as cloth, wax, dyes, paraffin, resin, etc. The key, however, was the availability of a vast workforce due to the desperate economic condition of many Javanese in the kampungs surrounding Batavia, together with the Chinese ability to organize this workforce. A census of 1929 estimated that for Batavia as a whole 13,063 women and girls were working in the kampung for Chinese batik entrepreneurs, while 2,101 worked regularly in a workshop. This census took place in a period of downturn, and it was estimated that in normal times 6,000 women probably worked in the workshops.

Although the term 'Chinese' has been used so far, most businesses were run by peranakan Chinese well acculturated to Java and barely able to write Chinese, employing as *tukang cap* fellow peranakan who often lived with the *taokeh* and helped in the evening with other work. The largest businesses were run by commercial *kongsis* made up of family members and friends, who pooled capital for a particular venture. One large batik workshop in Paal Merah belonging to a *kongsi* made batiks for Java, Celebes, Palembang, the Straits and Rangoon. These businesses were in a position to organize women to work in a workshop but they could also take advantage of women who wanted to work but could not leave the kampung, and who might not finish their work for a considerable time owing to other activities.

Women working at home were required to complete work after the contour lines had been stamped on the cloth by the *tukang cap*. Between the contour lines were whole areas which, when placed in the indigo, must not be allowed to become blue; and these areas must be thickly covered with wax, a task which village women could perform at home with a type of pencil or thick brush. The Chinese *taokeh* maintained good relations with the village head, the *kain* were delivered and collected by brokers, and the women were in a position to work for more than one batik business at a time. Even more loosely connected with the Chinese *taokeh*, but still enmeshed in his economic control, were the hundreds of women who merely wished to make batiks on their own account and at their own expense in the hope of finding a buyer. Perhaps starting out independently, such women would need to buy ingredients from the *toko* (which successful batik *taokeh* generally owned); they would gradually buy on credit and ultimately find themselves so committed that they would make and sell batiks at a fixed price like a wage-labourer.

Similar examples of Chinese penetration of the batik industry throughout Java abound. Two more will suffice. In Banyumas Residency at the time of the Batik Inquiry of 1929–31 there were seventy-seven Chinese workshops, twenty-one Javanese and three European. All the Javanese businesses were under Chinese economic control, working on commission for Chinese entrepreneurs. Nearly all of the businesses were *batik tulis* operations and yet in the space of a few years between 1914 and 1918, without introducing the *cap*, Chinese had been able to take over an industry which had a Java-wide reputation. Interest first began to be shown by the Chinese batik merchants of Bandung, and gradually Chinese already settled in Banyumas town and Sukaraja encouraged their wives to learn patterns from Javanese women and acquired experienced workers from existing operations. These Chinese were generally highly regarded peranakan, well established in the locality and regarded as *alus* (refined) by the local people.

The background to Chinese success was similar to that in Batavia. Improvements in transport, particularly the opening of the Yogya–Bandung railway line, accompanied the changeover to imported cloth. Chinese, well supplied with capital and cushioned by other enterprises, were able to maintain themselves in the industry even in periods of contraction in a manner impossible for their Javanese competitors. The Chinese also began very early on to introduce aniline dyes, so taking control by the early 1920s of the dyeing business associated with batik-making. But again the key to success was the ample reservoir of workers.

Banyumas in the early twentieth century was a region of agricultural poverty, isolated from markets, where even those with some land could often only harvest enough paddy for two months of the year. In these circumstances batik was a way of life; there was no other residency in Java where batik-making was so widespread, with many localities having their own specialities and own techniques and with even men using the *canting*. The common saying was: 'Batik prolongs our life.'[69] Chinese entrepreneurs would issue 'contractors' with money, cloth and wax, and these would advance small amounts to village women with the commission to make batiks at either a fixed price or a price subsequently to be fixed, turning such women into wage-labourers for the entrepreneur in the town.

> This manner of conducting business has advantages for the *taokèhs*. The wages are generally lower than those paid in an atelier, the batik women in the desas are required i.a. to provide their own charcoal and lighting; no outlay need be made on supervision, space for ateliers and accommodation for workers. The Chinese even avoids having to give advances to the batik women. They are not in his service, but work rather for the contractor. Moreover, it is the contractor and not the commissioning agent who bears the risk of spoilt work and theft.[70]

By the late 1920s in Banyumas it had become more common for women to want to work in a town workshop, where there was plenty of material, no lack of firewood and wax, and ample work. Initially, however, in the two main towns of Banyumas and Sukaraja a type of bonding had grown up based on the advance system. The *batik tulis* business always required a steady supply of experienced workers, which could only be achieved in the case of the entrepreneur who was just starting out by keeping good workers perpetually in debt not only by advances on wages by also by selling on credit. What was required from the woman was work, not repayment of the debt, and village administrations were enlisted to return defaulting batik women.

This was the situation in many parts of Java as Chinese expanded into the batik industry. Even in areas such as Pekalongan, where Javanese businesses still appeared to be flourishing by the late 1920s, Chinese – and also Arab – inroads had been made in ways which were not superficially apparent. At the time of the Batik Inquiry there were sixty Chinese and 1,107 Javanese batik enterprises in Pekalongan Residency, stretching from the coast to the mountains in the interior. The changeover to the *cap* dated from the 1860s, and batik workshops spread out along the roads which bound the district capitals and even penetrated distant hamlets, using the labour of family members to produce a cheap product.

The whole system rested on Chinese, and to some extent Arab, credit. Everything – working capital, cloth, wax – was supplied by entrepreneurs in the town, usually advanced on credit to a contractor who operated in the same way as outlined for Banyumas. None of the small batik workplaces scattered over the Residency could really be regarded as independent enterprises, and batiks were generally fashioned for a price agreed at the time the ingredients were advanced to the workplace, thus freeing the small business from the need to find a market.

A similar use for capital released from the opium farms was found in the *kretek* (Javanese cigarette) industry, where there appears to have been considerable peranakan investment, although the background of the proprietors is not altogether clear.[71] *Kretek*, a cigarette containing a mixture of tobacco and cloves, was popularized in the North Java town of Kudus in about 1870. The taste for this innovation spread through Central and East Java and, as the industry's profitability was demonstrated, Chinese started *kretek* enterprises which they extended into the Brantas Valley of East Java, where the main centres – all Chinese-dominated – were Malang, Tulungagung, Blitar and Kediri.[72] The Brantas industry started in 1909 and expanded in 1918–19, offering serious competition to Kudus. In a few years the Brantas towns gained markets in Central and West Java and some owners of the most important factories began exporting to Sumatra, Borneo, Celebes and Bali.[73]

Labour organization was arranged somewhat differently in the two localities. In Kudus, where there were successful Chinese entrepreneurs, village workers rolled the cigarettes for intermediaries who called regularly at the owner's head-quarters to collect the mixture of tobacco and cloves and returned with the finished cigarettes a week later. Each inter-mediary had his own workers in his home village, a number averaging from eight to ten, whilst the larger entrepreneurs had hundreds of intermediaries. This system in Kudus was slowly replaced by a rudimentary factory system, so that by 1929 a total of 10 per cent of the workers were in factories, increasing to 36 per cent by 1933. This gave the entrepreneur greater control over quality and output, a contemporary necessity in the face of new challenges. In East Java, where the industry was under Chinese domination, factory workers outnumbered household workers by more than two to one by 1929.[74] There the industry had previously been organized on similar principles to those of Kudus, making use of intermediaries to reach the workers in the villages. In the Brantas Valley, however, the Chinese *taokeh* did not give these intermediaries contracts but relied on a system of trust, whereby they employed their own acquaintances or family members.[75]

The basic equipment required for a *kretek* factory was fairly cheap and simple. The major tool, the roller to place the ingredients firmly in the wrapping, was cheap. A machine was also needed to chop or grind the cloves; and another machine was required to shred the tobacco. More expensive equipment could also be acquired, such as drying ovens, but it was possible to begin *kretek* manufacture at a low level of production with very little capital, though firms operating on a sufficiently large scale to justify the purchase of the more expensive items of equipment had a great advantage. Fixed capital could be small, but demands for working capital could be rather large, particularly to supply credit to new distributors. The industry failed to mechanize until after the war, partly due to government policies to maintain employment levels.[76]

The Chinese eventually came to dominate the industry in Kudus too, specializing in larger enterprises. By about 1933 in the whole industry there were more Chinese than Javanese enterprises. The Chinese were more willing to advance credit, which gave them a better distributive network. They also had greater mutual trust, enabling them to borrow funds necessary to see them over periods of high clove prices and other difficult conditions. They were also more willing to adopt corporate forms of organization, although these companies were largely still family firms.[77] They also had the advantage of close ties to the peranakan tobacco dealers in the tobacco-growing areas of Java. In Kedu, the centre of so-called 'people's tobacco', peranakans had been living there and acquiring the crop since at least the eighteenth century, supplying Kudus and other places.[78]

Turning to other industries, it is not altogether possible to separate the peranakan and *totok* investment in medium-scale mechanical production. Both were involved in a large variety of industries including beverages, foodstuffs and the processing of agricultural products. Rice mills were particularly important.[79] Richard Robison argues that the *totok* were more successful in penetrating the capitalist manufacturing sector.[80] One example is the Chinese penetration of the nascent West Java weaving industry in the 1930s. Bandung from the turn of the century had become a centre for Chinese batik traders, some of whom had arrived in Java as poor *totok* and moved there to participate in the vast profits made by importing Princely States' batik.[81] These traders became active in the weaving industry which arose in a region adjacent to their head-quarters.

The West Java weaving industry arose as a result of the Netherlands Indies government's concern at the decline of the Javanese weaving industry in the late nineteenth century, coupled with a desire to introduce a technique that was sufficiently modern to be competitive but which was appropriate to conditions of heavy rural overpopulation. The result was a decision to seek technical improvements in the existing simple Javanese loom, leading in the 1920s to the production by the Textile Institute of Bandung of an improved handloom with automatic shuttle. Known as the TIB-loom, this was a combination of an old Dutch loom and one used in India; it altered the relationship between hand and machine loom production from 1:50 to about 1:5.[82]

The new loom was quickly adopted in the Bandung Regency, particularly in the southeastern part, so that by 1938 a textile industry had developed in Java which was providing approximately 80 per cent of the entire Indies requirements in woven sarongs. The number of TIB-handlooms in the area rose from 257 in 1930 to 3,919 in 1935 and to 30,028 in 1938. In 1938, 80 per cent of the weaving factories of Java – kept small by government regulations – were located in the Majalaya area of the Bandung plateau, consisting of 1,600 businesses employing more than 30,000 workers.[83] The Sundanese took up the challenge readily, possessed as they were of a tradition of cloth-weaving coupled with large-scale agrarian underemployment.

Chinese were already commercially active in textiles in the city of Bandung. Playing no role in the batik production industry, Bandung was from the mid-nineteenth century the central batik market for the whole of Java, attracting batik traders from as far away as Banjarmasin, Makassar and Padang. From the early years of the twentieth century the batik market, which had previously been in the hands of an Islamicized network of traders operating between Bandung and the Principalities, came to be dominated by Chinese traders with superior business practices. With the increase in the sarong trade, this part of the market also fell into Chinese hands.[84]

From the mid-1930s these Chinese textile traders penetrated the sarong-weaving industry and in 1936 the first factory,
owned by a Chinese, was built in Majalaya town. By 1939
about 29 per cent of the businesses in the Bandung region
belonged to Chinese or Arabs, including several other factories.
Not only did they open their own premises, they also took
over existing Sundanese businesses, a trend which continued
for some years after 1945. Moreover, as with the batik industry,
Chinese traders dominated the sarong industry in a more
profound way, by financing it in its many aspects through a
system of advances.[85] As late as 1965 researchers were able to
confirm the existence of this pattern of dominance,
commenting that Chinese were the financing contractors to a
large part of the indigenous textile industry.[86]

The system of advances operated in the same way as in
the batik industry, and for the same reasons the Bandung
Chinese had most of the advantages. In the first place, the cost
of yarn made up about 70 per cent of the cost price of the
sarong, and this yarn was imported. In addition the sarong was
very prone to changes in fashion, so that relationships to the
market were very close. This was particularly important for the
Majalaya region, where production was far in excess of
regional consumption, increasing dependence on Chinese
marketing contacts throughout Java. The methods used by the
Chinese to exercise their control were also similar to those in
the batik industry. The Chinese Bandung textile merchant was
able to keep the small weaver in a continuous state of debt:
yarn was supplied in accordance with the number of looms,
but while the production process from start to finish took three
weeks, yarn was supplied only in quantities sufficient to keep
the looms busy for one week. With one week required for
preparation and one for finishing, new yarn could not be
advanced when the finished sarongs were delivered. Rather,
when sarongs made from the yarn that had been advanced
three weeks previously were delivered, the weaver had already
obtained two new deliveries of yarn.

The existence of government regulations limiting the size
of sarong factories meant that on the eve of the Second World

War only about 18 per cent of Chinese factories were mecha-nized. Even by the mid-1960s there were still no large mills by international standards, the tradition labour-intensive tech-niques based on the TIB-loom dominating the industry.[87]

While there were limited *totok* Chinese innovations in the weaving industry, particularly in the 1930s with the move to machines,[88] the peranakans produced the first Chinese-community corporate businessman in Java, originating from the Chinese opium farmer class and from the long peranakan connection with sugar production. This was the famous Oei Tiong Ham, son of the Fujian-born Oei Tjie Sien who arrived in Semarang in 1858 at the age of 23. He married into a locally-established family and joined the peranakan-dominated economy of Semarang. In 1863 Oei Tjie Sien founded a small business buying and selling local produce such as tobacco and gambier and specializing in sugar. Named the Kian Gwan *kongsi*, the enterprise was expanded following European penetration of the export crop economy. In 1886 his son Oei Tiong Ham, then about 20, was named Chinese lieutenant of Semarang and the family subsequently moved into opium-farming, taking over farms which had been declared bankrupt. Oei Tjie Sien retired in about 1890, his son having married the daughter of a rich peranakan merchant of Semarang who advanced him money to found his own company. Subsequent marriages were all into distinguished peranakan families.

The opium farms were only part of Oei's growing commercial empire. In 1893 he incorporated the Kian Gwan *kongsi* to form the Handel Maatschappij Kian Gwan, which cornered the Java sugar market and the Central Java opium market. He then expanded his company by establishing branches throughout Java; the Kian Gwan soon traded in virtually every important export crop in Indonesia. Following this, he added shipping facilities to his corporation by gaining a controlling interest in both the Semarang Steamship Navigation Company and the Heap Eng Moh Steamship Company of Singapore, a city that became his secondary base of operations.[89]

In 1906 Oei Tiong Ham created his own bank and in 1911 his own transport company, with five ships travelling between Batavia and Singapore. Among the main products exported were coffee, tapioca, maize, peanuts, kapok and, above all, sugar (Oei Tiong Ham's main concern). He acquired successively five large sugar factories and the land on which they depended; ultimately the Concern came to control 60 per cent of Java's production. In 1911–12 the sugar exports of the Concern amounted to 200,000 tons, while at the same time the internal market for sugar was developing. The volume of the Concern's internal sugar trade rose to more than 200,000 tons and the export of agricultural and forestry products was expanded. During the 1930s Kian Gwan was the largest exporter of maize to Japan, whilst the establishment of an office in Bangkok assisted in the appropriation of a sizeable share of the Indies' rice import trade. Industrial branches underwent expansion. The Redjo Agung sugar factory became the first electrified sugar factory in the Indies. In Malang a modern tapioca factory was established with a 17,000 ton annual capacity. Other branches of the Concern were established at Calcutta, Bombay, Karachi, Hong Kong and Shanghai.[90]

Oei Tiong Ham was an example of how peranakans involved in the nascent industrialization process in Java were able to appropriate a dual identity. He adhered to both a paternal model in his enterprises and to modern practices. He was probably one of the first Chinese in Java to cut his queue; he adopted European dress and he gained authorization to live outside the Chinese quarter. These 'ambiguous tendencies', as Denys Lombard calls them,[91] were evident in his business, which up to certain limits he forged on modern Western principles. He insisted the ownership of his company remain with the family, disinherited a number of his sons, and employed many non-family members in key positions, including considerable numbers of European managers, engineers and Western-trained accountants. He also sent some of his younger employees to study in the Netherlands and Germany, but he refused to delegate his authority and the room for initiative among lower managerial groups was small.[92] His style of life was eclectic. His vast fortune amounted to 200 million guilders at his death and he lived in a large house in Semarang resembling a fairytale palace. It was guarded by four large Africans, there were no less than 40 servants, and huge banquets specializing in different cuisines were given.[93]

Two of Oei Tiong Ham's sons succeeded him, but only one, Oei Tjong Hauw born in 1904, led the business through the difficulties of the Depression and the Second World War. Faced with considerable obstacles, he sought to diversify his operations by extending them outside the Netherlands Indies. He acquired several latex remilling factories, while also importing machinery and heavy equipment. In 1934 he decided to invest in China itself. He had received a good Dutch education but, while maintaining a great admiration for the West, he asserted his peranakan identity and, imbued with family spirit, tried to include in the concern many of his brothers and half-brothers whom Oei Tiong Ham had deliberately put aside. He died in 1950.[94]

Just as the Kian Gwan Concern gave evidence of peranakan innovation and the desire for achievement, so too did the peranakan community in this period show considerable flexibility and ability to change identity. In 1920 the peranakan Chinese formed 70 per cent of the Chinese population in Java; ten years later the numbers dropped to 63.5 per cent.[95] Dutch liberalization measures made it possible for peranakans to enjoy the fruits of Dutch civilization. In 1908 Dutch Chinese Schools (the first Dutch language schools for the Chinese modelled on the Dutch schools for Europeans) were set up in Batavia and other cities. In 1910 the Dutch Nationality Law was issued, under which peranakan Chinese were regarded as Dutch subjects. More peranakan children attended Dutch schools, and Dutch policy proved to be effective in making a significant number of peranakans Indies-oriented.[96] *Cabang atas* sons, Dutch-educated where possible, moved increasingly into white-collar occupations and Western professions. Many of them carried on family businesses with varying degrees of success and shrewdly invested in urban real estate. Few, except Oei Tiong Ham, amassed fortunes of the old kind, but everywhere they became self-consciously modern.[97]

This striving for modernity led to the continuation of the peranakans' symbiotic relation with the Dutch, which had existed since the seventeenth century. In 1928 a peranakan political party, the Chung Hwa Hui, was established, originating in a movement among peranakan students in the Netherlands who were able to gain the collaboration of peranakan business firms competing against Europeans and Japanese. It was primarily an organ of the Dutch-educated Chinese elite, peranakan businessmen such as Oei Tjong Hauw, and the remaining Chinese officers. There were many clauses in its constitution which reflected the goals of peranakan entrepreneurs, and reflected too their sympathy towards the Dutch colonial regime under which they felt safe. The organization, North Central Java based, was criticized as an organ of landlords and capitalists and branded 'the Packard Group Party' after the expensive Packard cars the representatives drove to meetings.[98]

Many peranakans remained active of course in the intermediate trade. In the period after the war, Clifford Geertz summed up in his work on the East Javanese town of 'Modjokuto' the position of these peranakans:

> The fourth market group, the Chinese, was at this time still small, and it too was fairly traditionalized. Mostly it was composed of Chinese born in the Netherlands Indies rather than in China, usually for several generations back – that is they were *peranakans* rather than recently migrant *singkèhs*. The *peranakans* ran small retail stores, leased certain monopolies, sold opium, managed gambling dens, and built rice mills and warehouses. In contrast to the *singkèhs*, who began to come in increasing strength to Modjokuto in the boom period, the *peranakans* were a static group with a well-defined though not necessarily wholly secure position in the plural society, a position which had developed over the course of several centuries from the days when Chinese rented whole villages to rule and exploit from the East India Company, or when they leased a whole range of functional monopolies ... from the Company's

Cultural System successors. Their economic activity ... thus lay along well-developed, stabilized lines, and their culture was a curious amalgam of Javanese aristocratic patterns with Chinese Mandarin patterns, so that they have often been said to be both more Javanese and more Chinese than the *singkèhs*.[99]

The remainder of the Chinese community in Java in this period was however strongly sinicized.[100] The numbers of *totok* in the Chinese population increased considerably, although largely in the Outer Provinces. However, Batavia – with its commercial ties to Singapore – came to be much more of a *totok* city. As in the contemporary Philippines, cultural associations, clan structures and popular cults assisted in sinicization, and Chinese chambers of commerce helped in retaining close ties to China. Chinese-language schools and newspapers flourished and the emigration of women assisted communal solidarity. Assimilation to peranakan society was further discouraged by a shift in the proportion of speech groups among immigrants, away from Hokkiens and in favour of Hakkas and Cantonese. True *totok* communities formed in all the major cities, establishing dialect-group and regional associations for mutual aid, including financial assistance and economic cooperation.[101]

While peranakans were noted for their attraction to the batik and *kretek* industries, both they and *totok* Chinese by the 1920s played a modest role in industries which tied Java more clearly to the world-economy. Approximately 10.6 per cent of the total capital invested in large concerns in Indonesia in 1921 was Chinese, of which a little over half was committed to large-scale plantation enterprise and half to wholesale trade, industry, transport and banking.[102] But the story of these businesses is not well known; Chinese capital was always short, and by 1943 it was reported that there were few Chinese entrepreneurs in large businesses, the majority devoting their capital to medium or small concerns or becoming financiers of Javanese small businesses.[103] Chinese business life was not well suited to well-organized, permanent associations of capital; much use was made of *kongsis* to raise credit. Friendship and kinship was the basic economic principle, the major objective of the *kongsi* being to create an association of persons rather

CHANGING CHINESE ENTERPRISE IN THE PHILIPPINES AND JAVA 189

than what might be called the indiscriminate mobilization of capital.[104] Few Chinese could therefore be concerned with large enterprises which required an extensive association of capital. Of the fifty-five Chinese limited liability companies established in Semarang in the years 1922 and 1923, thirty-three were formed by two persons, eighteen by three or four, and only four by more than four persons.[105]

Nevertheless, there was considerable Chinese business activity centred on those crops which had long attracted Chinese commercial attention. In the 1920s and 1930s Chinese had large interests as inland rice-dealers, owners of rice-hulling mills and holders of rice-growing estates. In Krawang district near Batavia, one of the most important rice-growing areas in Java, there were in the 1920s seventy large and small rice mills, almost all in Chinese hands.[106] Cassava was a major secondary crop in the Priangan area centred on Bandung. In 1920, 44 of Java's 78 cassava factories were in Priangan and 52 of these were Chinese.[107] The Chinese, of course, had long-standing connections with the sugar crop. European banks financed Chinese exports to foreign countries. The three major sugar trading companies to which sugar harvests were sold were Kwik Hoo Tong, Kian Gwan and Oei Tjoe. These were powerful, well-capitalized firms exporting to China, Hong Kong, India, America and Europe; they were generally financed by buyers in foreign countries. A further major modern trade was that in timber, based in Surabaya.[108] It was at this time that the creator of one of the largest financial empires in Southeast Asia came to Java from Fujian and began life trading in agricultural commodities. Liem Sioe Liong, born in Fujian in 1916, arrived in Java about 1936 and established himself in Kudus where his uncle had a business in peanut oil. With his older brother Sioe Hie he began to help this uncle and then became involved in the importation of cloves, heavily consumed by the *kretek* factories of Kudus.[109] His later career is legendary.

Whether these Chinese economic activities of the 1920s and 1930s were truly innovatory has been the object of some contention. Lea Williams' argument that the Chinese and their funds gravitated towards economic activities in the main concerned with the exchange rather than the production of goods[110] seems to be challenged by the considerable success of the peranakan batik and *kretek* industries, where knowledge of Javanese society and mores paid remarkable dividends. Moreover these industries were innovative, using new dyes, new production techniques and new ways of organizing labour. The Siauw Giap formulates an answer:

> It is hardly possible to conceive the people who developed the three largest ethnic-Chinese-owned cigarette factories in present-day Indonesia (Gudang Garam, Karum, and Bentool) into enterprises employing tens of thousands of labourers as other than entrepreneurs. The period 1900–1940 can perhaps be regarded as the formative stage of Chinese entrepreneurial history.[111]

Reprise

In this chapter we have been dealing with what Philip Curtin calls an 'aging trade diaspora'.[112] Curtin argues that diasporas have a life history which evolves to the point where they 'tend to work themselves out of existence',[113] moving eventually from trade to other sectors of the economy. He sees the root cause of the 'twilight of the diasporas'[114] as the birth of the industrial age.[115] Edna Bonacich too puts forth the notion that trade – implying liquidity of assets – is the primary characteristic of a middleman minority; such a group, she argues, is absent from industrial entrepreneurship.[116]

Our argument is different, and stresses continuity. All of the conjoint communities discussed here have moved, sooner or later, into some form of industrial enterprise. But in doing so they have not, in general, lost their dual identity. Rather, this has assisted them to face several ways, serve several masters, and seize new economic opportunities.

An example will serve from the subject matter of this chapter. The Netherlands Indies Government's 1931 inquiry into the batik industry of Java – an industry in which we have seen local Chinese making use of their access to Western-imported ingredients to organize a large Javanese workforce – concluded that in, for example, the core areas of Yogyakarta and Surakarta, one reason for business success was the good relations between Javanese operatives and peranakan Chinese entrepreneurs:

> The probable explanation for this is that the Chinese of the Princely States is 'aloes', i.e. refined not coarse, although this should not be taken to mean that the remainder of the Chinese population of Java should be characterized as coarse.
>
> The Chinese of the Princely States has incontestably adopted much that is Javanese, probably ascribed to the Javanese blood that 'courses through the veins' of many of them.
>
> His language, his manner of speaking, his mode of thought is Javanese, his form of entertainment is the gamelan and wayang where he is on a par with the Javanese.
>
> He is in general patient, accommodating, in short 'aloes' as the Javanese says. And these are the characteristics which make the Princely States Chinese a good employer in the eyes of the Javanese worker.[117]

This dynamic was apparent to Werner Sombart when he wrote *The Jews and Modern Capitalism*. Denying Weber's claim that Jews had not succeeded as industrialists, Sombart catalogued a range of industrial activities in which they had become prominent over the centuries.[118] Then, in an eternal depiction of the dual identity, he wrote:

> To my mind, the best picture of the modern capitalistic under-taker [entrepreneur] is that which paints him as the combina-tion of two radically different natures in one person. Like Faust, he may say that two souls dwell within his breast; unlike Faust's, however, the two souls do not wish to be sepa-rated, but rather, on the contrary, desire to work harmoniously together. What are these two natures? The one is the under-taker ... and the other is the trader ... The undertaker becomes a capitalistic undertaker when he combines his origi-nal activities with those of the trader.[119]

Notes

1. Wickberg, 'The Chinese Mestizo', pp. 84, 90–91.
2. *Ibid.*, pp. 92–93; Wickberg, *The Chinese*, p. 143.

3. Wickberg, 'The Chinese Mestizo', p. 79.

4. *Ibid.*, pp. 79–80.

5. Wickberg, *The Chinese*, p. 134.

6. *Ibid.*, pp. 136–138; Wickberg, 'The Chinese Mestizo', pp. 83–84, 95–96.

7. Wickberg, *The Chinese*, pp. 129–131; B. Dahm, *José Rizal. Der National-held der Filipinos*, Göttingen, Muster-Schmidt Verlag, 1988, pp. 21–24.

8. Larkin, *Pampangans*, pp. 94–97; Owen, 'The Principalia', pp. 321–324.

9. Dahm, *Rizal*, pp. 18–19; Wickberg, *The Chinese*, pp. 33–34.

10. Wickberg, *The Chinese*, p. 132.

11. Larkin, *Sugar and Philippine Society*, pp. 46–47, 99.

12. *Ibid.*, p. 100, Yoshihara, *Philippine Industrialization*, p. 32.

13. Larkin, *Pampangans*, p. 77; see also Larkin, *Sugar and Philippine Society*, pp. 91–92.

14. Larkin, *Sugar and Philippine Society*, pp. 55–59.

15. K. Yoshihara, *The Rise of Ersatz Capitalism in South-East Asia*, Singapore, Oxford University Press, 1988, pp. 153–165.

16. Larkin, *Sugar and Philippine Society*, pp. 99, 147, 168–170.

17. Quoted in K.K.M. Jensen, 'The Chinese in the Philippines during the American Regime: 1898–1946', Ph.D., University of Wisconsin, 1956, p. 299.

18. Quoted in *ibid.*, p. 301.

19. Yoshihara, *Philippine Industrialization*, pp. 115–116; Larkin, *Sugar and Philippine Society*, pp. 169–170.

20. G. Hawes, 'Marcos, his Cronies, and the Philippines' Failure to Develop', in McVey (ed.), *Southeast Asian Capitalists*, pp. 148–149.

21. A.W. McCoy, 'Review of Sugar and the Origins of Modern Philippine Society', *Journal of Asian Studies* 53, no. 2 (1994): 637.

22. Cullinane, 'Cebu Urban Elite', pp. 268, 270.

23. Wickberg, *The Chinese*, p. 77.

24. Cullinane, 'Cebu Urban Elite', pp. 272–273, 277–278, 280.

25. *Ibid.*, pp. 270–271, 284.

26. Wickberg, 'The Chinese Mestizo', pp. 91–92; Larkin, *Sugar and Philippine Society*, p. 62; A.W. McCoy, *Priests on Trial*, Ringwood, Penguin Books, 1984, pp. 86–87.

27. McCoy, 'Iloilo City', p. 302.

28. V.B. Lopez-Gonzaga, *The Negrense. A Social History of an Elite Class*, Bacolod, University of St. la Salle, 1991, p. 11.

29. Quoted in *ibid.*, p. 13.

30. McCoy, 'Iloilo City', pp. 308, 315–316, 324.

31. Lopez-Gonzaga, *The Negrense*, p. 21.

32. McCoy, 'Iloilo City', p. 320.

33. *Ibid.*, p. 326; Lopez-Gonzaga, *The Negrense*, pp. 35–36, 42–43.
34. Wickberg, *The Chinese*, pp. 23–24, 147.
35. Diaz-Trechuelo, 'Economic Background', p. 26.
36. Wickberg, *The Chinese*, pp. 48, 52.
37. Bowring, *Philippine Islands*, p. 183.
38. Wickberg, *The Chinese*, pp. 169–170.
39. J. Amyot, *The Manila Chinese. Familism in the Philippine Environment*, Quezon City, Institute of Philippine Culture, 1973, p. 26.
40. Wickberg, *The Chinese*, pp. 62–63, 121–122.
41. *Ibid.*, pp. 69–70, 122–123.
42. *Ibid.*, p. 71.
43. *Ibid.*, pp. 72–74, 106–107; J.T. Omohundro, *Chinese Merchant Families in Iloilo. Commerce and Kin in a Central Philippine City*, Quezon City, Ateneo de Manila University Press, 1981, p. 55.
44. Wickberg, *The Chinese*, pp. 98–101.
45. Cullinane, 'Cebu Urban Elite', pp. 273–274, 278; Larkin, *Sugar and Philippine Society*, pp. 86–87.
46. McCoy, 'Iloilo City', p. 310.
47. Amyot, *Manila Chinese*, p. 26; Wickberg, *The Chinese*, p. 177; Omohundro, *Chinese Merchant Families*, pp. 23–26.
48. Amyot, *Manila Chinese*, pp. 40–42.
49. Jensen, 'Chinese in the Philippines', pp. 58–59, 149–150.
50. *Ibid.*, p. 248.
51. Yoshihara, *Philippine Industrialization*, pp. 46–47, 86.
52. Jensen, 'Chinese in the Philippines', pp. 216–219.
53. *Ibid.*, pp. 222–223.
54. Yoshihara, *Philippine Industrialization*, pp. 89–92.
55. Jensen, 'Chinese in the Philippines', p. 248; Amyot, *Manila Chinese*, p. 66.
56. Omohundro, *Chinese Merchant Families*, p. 67.
57. Amyot, *Manila Chinese*, pp. 62–63, 85–86, 90, 94, 98–100.
58. *Ibid.*, pp. 13, 101–102, 136–141; Yoshihara, *Philippine Industrialization*, pp. 103–105; Wickberg, *The Chinese*, pp. 75–76.
59. Yoshihara, *Philippine Industrialization*, p. 101; Wickberg, *The Chinese*, pp. 148–150, 203–205.
60. Wickberg, *The Chinese*, pp. 199–201.
61. Omohundro, *Chinese Merchant Families*, p. 84.
62. Robison, *Rise of Capital*, pp. 6, 20; for an account of the 'intermediate trade' see Liem Twan Djie, *Die Distribueerende Tusschenhandel der Chineezen op Java*, 2nd ed., The Hague, Martinus Nijhoff, 1952, *passim*.
63. Cator, *Economic Position*, pp. 33–34, 38–39, 98–99.

194   ASIAN ENTREPRENEURIAL MINORITIES

64. *Ibid.*, pp. 100–101.

65. Skinner, 'Java's Chinese Minority', pp. 356–357.

66. Willmott, *Chinese of Semarang*, pp. 103–105, 108–109.

67. Rush, *Opium to Java*, pp. 195–197, 242–244.

68. See Dobbin, 'Middleman Minorities to Industrial Entrepreneurs', pp. 112–117; the following material, taken from my article, is based on the survey P. De Kat Angelino, *Batikrapport*, 3 vols, Weltevreden, Landsdrukkerij, 1930–1931. References to the *Batikrapport* can be found in the article.

69. *Batikrapport* 2, p. 11.

70. *Ibid.*, pp. 12–13.

71. The Siauw Giap, 'Socio-Economic Role of the Chinese', p. 174.

72. L. Castles, *Religion, Politics and Economic Behavior in Java: the Kudus Cigarette Industry*, New Haven, Yale University Southeast Asia Studies, 1967, p. 38.

73. B. van der Reijden, *Rapport Betreffende een Gehouden Enquête naar de Arbeidstoestanden in de Industrie van Strootjes en Inheemsche Sigaretten op Java*, 3 vols. Bandung, Kantoor van Arbeid, 1934–1936, vol. 3, pp. 15, 113–115, 123.

74. Castles, *Kudus Cigarette Industry*, p. 34.

75. Van der Reijden, *Strootjes en Inheemsche Sigaretten* 3, pp. 15–16.

76. Castles, *Kudus Cigarette Industry*, pp. 22–24, 92.

77. *Ibid.*, pp. 85–88.

78. J.L. Vleming, *Tabak. Tabakscultuur en Tabaks-producten van Nederlandsch-Indië*, Weltevreden, Landsdrukkerij, 1925, pp. 8, 65–68, 76–77, 83, 198; J.L. Vleming, *Het Chineesche Zakenleven in Nederlandsch-Indië*, Weltevreden, Landsdrukkerij, p. 220.

79. Ong Eng Die, *Chineezen in Nederlandsch-Indië. Sociografie van een Indonesische Bevolkingsgroep*, Assen, Van Gorcum and Co., 1943, p. 151; Robison, *Rise of Capital*, pp. 26–27.

80. Robison, *Rise of Capital*, p. 29.

81. *Batikrapport* 1, pp. 95–99.

82. G. Schwencke, 'De Weefindustrie in het Regentschap Bandoeng', *Koloniaal Tijdschrift* 23 (1939): 159–160; W. van Warmelo, 'Ontstaan en Groei van de Handweefnijverheid in Madjalaja', *Koloniale Studiën* 23 (1939): 5–8.

83. Schwencke, 'De Weefindustrie', pp. 160–161; van Warmelo, 'Handweefnijverheid in Madjalaja', p. 9.

84. *Batikrapport* 1, pp. 95–98.

85. Van Warmelo, 'Handweefnijverheid in Madjalaja', pp. 11, 17; Schwencke, 'De Weefindustrie', p. 163; H. Antlöv and T. Svensson, 'From Rural Home Weavers to Factory Labour: The Industrialization of Textile Manufacturing in Majalaya', in P. Alexander *et al.* (eds), *In the Shadow of Agriculture*.

Non-farm Activities in the Javanese Economy, Past and Present, Amsterdam, Royal Tropical Institute, 1991, p. 116.

86. I. Palmer and L. Castles, 'The Textile Industry', in B. Glassburner (ed.), *The Economy of Indonesia: Selected Readings*, Ithaca, Cornell University Press, 1971, p. 322, ftn. 18.

87. Van Warmelo, 'Handweefnijverheid in Madjalaja', pp. 16–17; Schwencke, 'De Weefindustrie', p. 164; H. Hill, 'The Economics of Recent Changes in the Weaving Industry', *Bulletin of Indonesian Economic Studies* 16, no. 2 (1980): 83–84.

88. Schwencke, 'De Weefindustrie', p. 164.

89. Rush, *Opium to Java*, pp. 231, 248–249; J. Panglaykim and I. Palmer, 'Study of Entrepreneurship in Developing Countries: the Development of One Chinese Concern in Indonesia', *Journal of Southeast Asian Studies* 1, no. 1 (1970): 85–87; M. Godley, *The Mandarin-Capitalists from Nanyang. Overseas Chinese Enterprise in the Modernization of China*, Cambridge, Cambridge University Press, 1981, pp. 18–19; C. Salmon, 'Les marchands chinois en Asie du Sud-est', in Lombard and Aubin (eds), *Marchands et hommes d'affaires*, p. 340.

90. Panglaykim and Palmer, 'Study of Entrepreneurship', p. 90; Lombard, *Carrefour Javanais* 2, pp. 245–246.

91. Lombard, *Carrefour Javanais* 2, p. 245.

92. Rush, *Opium to Java*, p. 250; Lombard, *Carrefour Javanais* 2, p. 245; Panglaykim and Palmer, 'Study of Entrepreneurship', p. 88; Willmott, *Chinese of Semarang*, p. 49.

93. Lombard, *Carrefour Javanais* 2, p. 246.

94. *Ibid.*, pp. 246–248; Panglaykim and Palmer, 'Study of Entrepreneurship', pp. 91–93.

95. L. Suryadinata, *Peranakan Chinese Politics in Java 1917–1942*, Singapore, Singapore University Press, 1981, pp. xiv–xv.

96. *Ibid.*, pp. 10–11.

97. Rush, *Opium to Java*, pp. 248, 252.

98. Suryadinata, *Peranakan Chinese Politics*, pp. 39–50, 61, 75, 82.

99. C. Geertz, *The Social History of an Indonesian Town*, Cambridge, The MIT Press, 1965, pp. 91–92.

100. Lombard, *Carrefour Javanais*, pp. 211–212.

101. Suryadinata, *Peranakan Chinese Politics*, pp. 82–84; Skinner, 'Java's Chinese Minority', pp. 357–358; Willmott, *Chinese of Semarang*, pp. 27, 101–102; Cator, *Economic Position*, pp. 95–96.

102. Cator, *Economic Position*, pp. 63–64.

103. Ong Eng Die, *Chineezen in Nederlandsch-Indië*, p. 144.

104. Cator, *Economic Position*, pp. 59, 80; Willmott, *Chinese of Semarang*, pp. 52–53.

105. Vleming, *Chineesche Zakenleven*, pp. 74–77.

106. *Ibid.*, p. 204; Cator, *Economic Position*, pp. 65–66.

107. Vleming, *Chineesche Zakenleven*, p. 212.

108. *Ibid.*, pp. 145–146, 203.

109. Lombard, *Carrefour Javanais* 2, p. 251.

110. L.E. Williams, 'Chinese Entrepreneurs in Indonesia', *Explorations in Entrepreneurial History* 5, no. 1 (1952): 37.

111. The Siauw Giap, 'Socio-Economic Role of the Chinese', pp. 177–178.

112. Curtin, *Cross-Cultural Trade*, p. 50.

113. *Ibid.*, p. 230; see also p. 3.

114. *Ibid.*, p. 230.

115. *Ibid.*

116. Bonacich, 'Middleman Minorities', pp. 79, 83.

117. *Batikrapport 2*, pp. 129–130.

118. Sombart, *The Jews*, pp. 161–162.

119. *Ibid.*

8

Conclusion: Creativity and Identity

The aim throughout this book has been to keep what have been called conjoint communities as the central theme. It has been their role in the growth of the world-economy since the sixteenth century that has provided the focus of attention. Several other explorations could have been made, in particular in respect to the policies of the European powers with which these entrepreneurial communities led their conjoint life and in respect, too, to the reactions of the local populations to others holding the commanding heights of the economy. To have attempted these explorations would have resulted in an unwieldy piece of work. The earliest policies towards the minorities, have in fact been discussed because they led in so many cases to a tampering with identity. But no attempt at a deeper methodological investigation of policy has been ventured on.

Indeed, how could it be? Dutch policy at Batavia, for example, constituted myriad twists and turns. The Chinese were welcome, but they were soon regulated in their right to reside, in their movements by sea and by land, and in many other aspects of their life. Every decade new regulations were introduced and old ones were altered. It would be unprofitable to concentrate on policy as such, other than where there were major initiatives, and so limit the story to, say, Chinese manoeuvring and adaptability within imperial boundaries. Similarly, the commercial and entrepreneurial focus has been on the minority community itself. Wallerstein talks of the late eighteenth-century development of the India–China–Britain triangular trade in cotton and opium as 'an invention of the East India Company'.[1] Our emphasis has been on the role of the Parsis as financial backers of the Company's traders and as a community which possessed the networks which could bring both cotton and opium on to the market.

Outside of the focus, too, has been the reaction of the local population to the strangers in their midst. This is an extensive story in itself, bound up with the rise of nationalism in an imperial environment. Whatever the state of the current controversy over the nature of the Sarekat Islam[2] – the first real Indonesian nationalist movement – it represented in large part Javanese opposition to Chinese penetration of various indigenous commercial preserves in the early part of the twentieth century. Similarly the Burmese Saya San rebellion of 1930–31 represented in part peasant grievances against the controlling power of the Chettiar moneylenders.[3] But the emergence of nationalism in the guise of opposition to minority commercial communities is a large subject and not one that can be dealt with here. The questions we have asked focus on the communities themselves and other parts of the story have had to be left aside.

With centrality given to the conjoint communities themselves, we see expanding Western commerce and shipping in our period resting on a bedrock of Indian and Chinese money, commercial expertise and diaspora connections: Indian and Chinese firms both collaborating and competing with Western companies.[4] Economic symbiosis, as Chris Bayly says, had created lines of mutual economic interdependence and ultimately dependence. In the case of India, everywhere on the subcontinent the British secured the acquiescence and often the financial support of groups of indigenous merchants, financiers and revenue farmers; an alliance of convenience was cemented between Indian capitalists and entrepreneurs and the East India Company.[5] Elsewhere it was the same. Loans to Western merchants formed an important part of Indian financial operations in Zanzibar, for example, although the borrowing was to some extent mutual.[6]

These Asian communities were conjoint to an even deeper extent; they not only helped to finance European economic endeavours in new markets flung across Asia, but they developed marketing networks, supplying credit for indigenous producers and traders and investing in local processing industries, so establishing essential links between what had formerly been primarily subsistence economies and the world-economy emerging since the sixteenth century.[7] Ronald Robinson has called this use of local collaborating groups – whether merchants, ruling elites or landlords – the most important mechanism of European management of the non-European world.[8] Robinson sees the collaborating classes as mediators between the European and the indigenous political and economic systems. However, he underplays the role of commercial collaborators, and collaboration theory in general gives stress to political forms of collaboration.[9] Our own theory remains that it was certain conjoint communities – members of India's and Southeast Asia's sophisticated minority commercial diasporas – which enabled European powers to operate at all in the region.

What was it that made members of these diasporas so successful at interlocking their interests with those of the incoming Europeans? We began with Simmel. Simmel speaks of the stranger's chief characteristic as being the possession of objectivity, 'a particular structure composed of distance and nearness, indifference and involvement'.[10] One of our aims has been to show that the members of our conjoint communities displayed their objectivity, their nearness and distance, by creating more than one identity for themselves or, in extreme cases such as the Philippines, by having an extra identity foisted on them. Erik Erikson defines identity as 'a subjective sense of an invigorating sameness and continuity'.[11] Our argument has been rather that our conjoint communities – strangers in essence – possessed dual or multiple identities. For them everything represented not continuity but a question to be posed and a problem to be solved. The stranger enters on 'a field of adventure, not a matter of course but a questionable topic of investigation ... a problematic situation itself and one hard to master'.[12]

In relation, then, to the spirit of nascent capitalist world-economy, the economic creativity of the members of a conjoint community is tied to a spirit of business confidence founded on the ability to seize opportunities while facing in a number of directions. Enlarging upon Weber, we may say that the spirit of capitalism in South and Southeast Asia can be discovered in as many spiritual sources as make up an identity, under conditions of stranger status. Where more than one spiritual source makes up an identity, economic creativity would appear to be heightened.

In addressing this thesis, the historical material has sometimes been thinner than we would have wished; where the material might be said to be ample, the labourers in the vineyard have been few. It is important at this point to indicate that there is in fact material available which can cast light on the dimmer corners of our approach. Just as we commenced sociologically with Georg Simmel, historically we began with the Iberian peninsula. From the early days of Iberian expansion there was one epithet above all which was applied to our conjoint communities. Garcia da Orta, a Portuguese doctor visiting Diu and travelling through India in the sixteenth century, wrote of the Parsis: 'We Portuguese call them Jews, but they are not so.'[13] Further again to the east, Edmund Scott in Banten in 1603–04 spoke of the Chinese as living among the Javanese like Jews.[14] All other communities received at some time the same appellation.[15]

What was meant were the Sephardic Jews of the Iberian peninsula, particularly Portugal. From the sixteenth century these Portuguese Jews formed an extensive diaspora tied together by certain leading families throughout Western Europe, parts of South America and the Caribbean and also eastwards in the Indian Ocean. Termed 'New Christians' because of their forced conversion in the fifteenth century, they were popularly known as Marranos. In Portugal it was axiomatic that New Christian and merchant were one and the same. These New Christians were tied together in the major commercial towns of

Western Europe by bonds of family and identity; in the
sixteenth century they flourished in particular at Antwerp,
Rouen, Seville and Geneva.[16] They were involved in the spice
trade in Europe and, as a result, developed centres throughout
the Portuguese possessions in Asia, as far east as Malacca.[17]
After 1570, when the geography of the Portuguese empire
moved from the Indian Ocean to Brazil, they involved themselves in the Brazilian enterprise. Their economic interests
centred in particular on the cultivation of and commerce in
sugar cane; for this and other Brazilian products they ensured a
passage across the Atlantic and distribution networks in
Europe, re-exporting to Brazil in the same manner wheat,
wine, oil and salt.[18]

We have here quite clearly a stranger trading diaspora, but
our interest is particularly to find a strongly researched
exemplar of an identity deriving from more than one spiritual
source. Portuguese Jews were forced to convert to Catholicism
en masse in 1497. As knowledge of the Hebrew Scriptures
gradually faded and Hebrew books themselves disappeared,
from the mid-sixteenth century the faith of Marranism evolved.
At its core was the doctrine that salvation was possible through
the law of Moses and not through the law of Christ; but,
outwardly, attendance at church took place, chapels and altars
were endowed, religious confraternities were formed and
fasting duties were assumed. Nevertheless, Judaism as a rule of
life rather than a mere creed was maintained beneath this crust
of Catholicism, and there was no belief in the efficacy of the
Catholic sacraments.[19] Marranism, states one writer, was 'a
collective, clandestine denial of the Catholic mentality'.[20] At the
base of Marranism, therefore, was 'a fundamental duplicity'.[21]
Having only access to Catholic culture and the Catholic
mentality, which counted for nothing in their eyes, the New
Christians clung to the outward form of the law of Moses
without the ability to give depth to its content. They lived a
public and outward life of insincerity, balanced by an obstinate
and internal desire to be attached to Jewish tradition.[22]

Marranism, moreover, was handed down in families. It
maintained a tradition in these families, and therefore in

Europe, of a denial of Christianity, while forming a spiritual base on which rested a hugely successful commercial and financial bourgeoisie organized as a diaspora right across the known world.[23] Later, in the post-1590 Amsterdam phase of this community's life – and all that Amsterdam means for Sephardic commercial endeavour – it has been argued that, although it was not possible to experience life as a Jew, a dual identity was maintained; what marked the Portuguese Jews of Amsterdam was their identity as 'Iberians'. This continuity of 'Iberian descent' gave birth to Sephardic ethnic exclusiveness and it was this, not Judaism, which formed the underpinning of the community's commercial solidarity. The persistence of Iberian modes of thought and Iberian patterns of behaviour cemented the community.[24]

The phenomenon just explained lies at the core of this book. Despite the paucity of material, we see the Chinese mestizos of the Philippines rising as a group from a deliberate act of Spanish policy, which overlaid an earlier identity with Catholicism and Hispanic culture generally. The peranakans of Java achieved a somewhat similar outcome by a different route. The Parsis from their earliest days in India stressed their nearness to Hinduism, but distanced themselves with the coming of the British, while the Ismailis possessed several religious identities consecutively before their Anglicization in the early twentieth century. The Nattukottai Chettiars were able to combine asceticism in their commercial life with manifestations of ecstatic practices in their religion. What is clear, as Stonequist says, is that 'a dual self-consciousness and identification'[25] can give rise to a creative type of personality[26] and, further, that it is the creative response in business which is coterminous with entrepreneurship.[27] Involvement in a duality of cultures produces in an individual a duality of both personality and culture.[28] The individual then becomes the Schumpeterian entrepreneurial archetype, a person not sharing in the basic assumptions of society, placing everything in question, constantly facing problematic situations.[29]

As well as individuals, it is diasporas which are important. We have mentioned at the beginning the importance to this work of the concept of the trading diaspora as outlined by Abner Cohen. Such a diaspora, according to Cohen, develops an integrated ideological scheme, usually a 'universal' religion,[30]

> which is related to the basic problems of man, his place in society and in the universe ... An ideology ... is a blue-print for the organization of a polity in dispersal. Ideologies differ in their comprehensiveness, flexibility, and in the potency of their symbols. A diaspora may develop its own ideology. This is a long process of trial and error, of cultural innovations and of meditation and symbolic formulation by 'experts'.[31]

It is fruitful at this point to return to Max Weber and to note that he too had something of interest to say about commercial diasporas. While we have challenged Weber in many areas – among others arguing for the universality of spirit which can motivate capitalist enterprise and the importance of the family as opposed to the individual in entrepreneurial success – it is always possible to find in his writings something which strikes a new cord. His treatment of the Baptists in *The Protestant Ethic* is interesting, because he recognized them as a religious group 'whose ethics rest upon a basis differing in principle from the Calvinistic doctrine',[32] although he went on to develop his argument to find ascetic virtues in the community too.[33] What is interesting here is Weber's recognition that the Baptist community, in the right situation, could form a commercial diaspora in a manner that promoted business confidence and success.

It was Weber's contact with the United States and its vast immigrant masses in 1904 which led him to some interesting reflections on the connection between religious affiliation and credit relations in business and social life. His interest was aroused in how religion was tied to the needs of a commercial diaspora. Weber writes, concerning a Baptist congregation he observed in North Carolina:

> Admission to the congregation is recognized as an absolute guarantee of the moral qualities of a gentleman, especially of those qualities required in business matters. Baptism secures to the individual the deposits of the whole region and unlimited

credit without any competition. He is a 'made man' ... In general, only those men had success in business who belonged to the Methodist or Baptist or other *sects* or sect-like conventicles. When a sect member moved to a different place, he carried the certificate of his congregation with him; and thereby he found credit everywhere.[34]

Weber did not elaborate much further his ideas on the commercial diaspora, but he certainly associated it with minority status and with an ideological underpinning. His sect members, organized in their commercial diaspora, in his eyes possessed nothing more than an inner-worldly form of asceticism,[35] so that diaspora ideology as he observed it meant individual members were certified as to their morals and, particularly, their business morals.[36] *The Protestant Ethic* thesis is repeated to a considerable extent, despite his earlier recognition of the difference between Calvinist and Baptist ethics. However, the ideology and organization of the trading diaspora as we have observed it through our five communities is much more adaptable and flexible than this; certainly religion has played an important part, but there are aspects of greater complexity.

Much of what we would like to elaborate on this point is not possible because of the paucity of source materials from the seventeenth, eighteenth and nineteenth centuries. It is very difficult to investigate the ideological underpinning of the diaspora. We read, for example, of the tightly-knit Chinese mestizo community of Cebu, but do not know where in the Amoy region its members originated, what the nature of the village ties they brought with them to Cebu was, and how their family agents were organized for commercial purposes outside the city. Much more needs to be known, too, of their religious mentality. What we do know is that we do not need to attribute their commercial success to a particular form of 'puritan' morality and we must look beyond this to the nature of the moral community of the diaspora itself.

Fortunately one excellent study on this theme exists for Java in 1919. This is an investigation of the so-called *cina mindering*, a group of China-born moneylenders who specialized in making small loans in the Javanese countryside based

on a system of periodic repayments. The members formed a
true diaspora. They originated from three areas adjacent to the
city of Fuzhou in northern Fujian and received in Java from
these origins the appellations Hok Tsjia, Hok Tsjioe and Hing
Hoa. The vast majority practised no profession other than
moneylending, and they returned regularly to China.[37] In Java
they gradually spread from their core area of business –
Magelang and the region around Yogyakarta and Surakarta –
towards the east, especially Surabaya, Kediri, Madiun and
Pasuruan. In the west, by 1919, they had gone no further than
Bandung. In Madiun whereas by about 1909 there were 20–30
cina mindering, in 1919 there were 115–120 Hok Tsjia and 45–
50 Hing Hoa.[38]

No member of these communities emigrated from China
without coming to join a family member or a village connection. Each needed a patron in whom he was obliged to
place unconditional trust to assist him to get a good economic
start. He would learn his new business by accompanying his
patron on his loan-collecting expeditions to the marketplace
and into the village. If, as was common, the moneylender sold
cloth as a means of acquiring debtors, he would act as a
messenger or coolie.[39]

> In addition, in accordance with Chinese custom he is housed
> by his patron. In the latter case he is naturally included in the
> household of the toko. However if he begins as the apprentice
> of an ordinary 'toekang mindering', he comes to live with the
> latter in what is colloquially called 'the kongsi-house'. This
> inaccurate and misleading appellation refers to an ordinary
> dwelling-house which is rented jointly by a number of 'mind-
> ering' Chinese in the name of one of them who, through con-
> siderable proficiency in the local language and greater
> familiarity with local conditions, can act as a representative in
> relations with the outside world, although this does not neces-
> sarily mean that this individual is the head or leader of the
> communal household. The number of inhabitants of these
> houses varies markedly, from 3 or 4 to 25 to 30 men. It goes
> without saying that grouping into 'houses' rests on kinship, on
> village of origin or on personal recommendation by a trusted,
> mutual friend ...

> The appointments of these houses – and this applies also to the manner of life of the 'Tjina mindering' – are invariably of the most extreme simplicity ... In their manner of life, their food etc., etc. these Hok Tsjia, Hing Hoa and Hok Tsjioe Chinese, like all other sien khehs, also practise a rare frugality and thrift. They pay the minimum possible for their daily necessities and practically nothing for pleasure or relaxation ... In their social relations they limit themselves almost exclusively to their own counterparts. They have nothing to do with the peranakans or with other sien khehs.[40]

The role of the patron was crucial. He provided the apprentice with board, clothing, food and accommodation. Of approximately 1,000 Hok Tsjias in Surabaya by 1919, some had become very successful and were either running businesses as importers of cloth, or were active in the *toko* trade; Hok Tsjia patrons had access to this cloth on credit and packages of the cloth could be passed on to the apprentice, also on credit. There was a close connection between the moneylending trade and the cloth trade, the latter being a means of getting a foot in the door to build up credit-purchasing in the village.[41] Without going further into this system, we can note that the Hok Tsjias have been reported to be extraordinarily prominent in business in Indonesia after the Second World War.[42]

Here, then, we have a moral community although, as in so many of our earlier cases, the religious dimensions is not clear. Nevertheless, we do not simply have to look for guidance to Weber and the diasporas he found among Puritan sects, bound together by a particular type of ethical conduct arising from inner-worldly asceticism. The *cina mindering* diaspora has its own internal consistency originating in north Fujian. The patron provides a form of patriarchal environment, and around him a collectivist society is created in which the individual is attached to a group. In the group personal relationships, which are extremely important, at all levels are modelled on Chinese familial relationships. Paternalism is a key dimension of both personal and business existence. In the moral community we see shared values, ideas and symbolic systems. Personalized social networks emphasizing trustworthiness and loyalty are pre-eminent.[43] In this case, and in the case of the other religious communities dealt with in this work, mentalities and institutions rooted in their own cultures have proved sufficient to allow them to enter the world-economy at the appropriate time; in many places to make its arrival possible, and to prosper from it.

The final issue of the problematic with which we started is that posed by Gunder Frank. The developing world-economy has as its concomitant a developing metropolis and an underdeveloping periphery. This periphery, in turn characterized by metropolis and satellites, is condemned to underdevelopment among its domestic peripheral satellite regions and sectors.[44] This is not to say that the metropolises of the periphery cannot be highly developed; but, using Chile as an example, for this thesis, Gunder Frank notes: 'The most powerful interest groups of the Chilean metropolis were interested in policies producing underdevelopment at home because their metropolis was at the same time a satellite.'[45]

We can certainly say that the conjoint communities dealt with here – or at least their leading families – developed their peripheral metropolises. Indeed, European incomers were dependent on them for commercial intelligence, capital, the opening up of internal networks and for commercial administration. But whether in the course of this they underdeveloped peripheral satellite regions and sectors is a question to which contradictory answers might be given; only research in a multitude of localities could provide some insight region by region and sector by sector.

The batik industry of Java may be taken as an example. Chinese batik bosses certainly prospered, acting to tie the Javanese textile industry into the world-economy by their access to the new European and Japanese cloth used as the basic industry ingredient and their virtual monopoly over new European dyestuffs. But the consequences in the various batik regions of Java were not similar. For example, the infamous case of Lasem on the north coast was certainly not typical. Here the incorporation into the world-economy brought hopeless underdevelopment for the batik workers. A government inquiry over the period 1928–29 and 1930–31 painted a horrifying picture of conditions in Chinese-owned batik workplaces, where workers were physically mistreated and forced to remain continuously in the workplace under a form of debt bondage based on advancing needed items to them on credit, a system government investigators felt could 'be compared with slavery'.[46] Yet a similar inquiry in the old and prestigious batik cities of Yogyakarta and Surakarta found a quite different situation in the Chinese-owned or -controlled batik workplaces. In Surakarta considerable prosperity was reported among many of the batik workers, particularly those who worked with the innovatory batik stamp. They took part in many city amusements and some had even become interested in European political philosophies.[47] The report noted:

> Although wages are low and work security is minimal, the worker quite clearly feels himself fortunate in this milieu ... He feels himself in his element there, he is free, he knows his employer as well as he knows his fellow workers, he is at home and he takes what he can into the bargain.[48]

Similar contradictions are to be found in the agricultural sector. The case of the sugar-growers of Negros in the Philippines parallels that of the batik-workers of Lasem. Alfred McCoy considers their plantation economy, which was instituted by Chinese mestizos from Iloilo, to be a social system without parallel elsewhere in the Philippines. McCoy calls the sugar-worker a debt slave and indeed, like the batik-worker of Lasem, his movements were restricted and his accumulated debts could be so large that they were inherited by his children. The Negros sugar-workers evolved into a rural proletariat without the savings, agricultural skills or the entrepreneurial ability to fashion any sort of livelihood off the plantation. McCoy traces this development to the Chinese mestizos' familiarity with work relationships of debt bondage in the Iloilo textile industry from which the original sugar-investment money sprang, but the sugar economy, tied as it was to world demand, caused a marked decline in even these imperfect conditions.[49] After forty years of sugar exports, the

1896 census showed that only 324 planters controlled almost 80 per cent of the cultivated land in Negros Occidental, while 75 per cent of the province's population were landless labourers.[50]

Yet very different conditions obtained in other regions which had been incorporated into the periphery of the world-economy and which profited markedly from the success of the local conjoint community. Cotton poured out of Gujarat at the time of the American Civil War and beyond, partly organized by members of the Parsi diaspora headquartered in Bombay who either wished to export it or to use it in their nascent cotton textile industry. These cotton districts, far from becoming underdeveloped, produced, with the assistance of favourable government administrative measures, a substantial class of independent cultivators with capital for agricultural improvement. Best known among them is the Patidar community of Kheda district near Ahmadabad in Gujarat, which grew cotton benefiting from new irrigation works and the opening of the railway. Some regions of Kheda were famous for their prosperity, and the cultivation of cotton, along with other labour-intensive crops, gradually increased Patidar wealth. Much of this was invested in agricultural improvements and in building up outstanding cattle herds.[51]

It is possible to continue this line of argument endlessly. A striking contrasting example could be produced from the region of Nattukottai Chettiar activity and that of the Ismailis. James Scott has shown how in Lower Burma, with the Depression, reasonably secure subsistence peasants were swept into an existence as either tenants or wage labourers – the tenant being vulnerable to losing his crop, his savings and his plough animals to his landlord creditor; the labourer to losing his job altogether. Economic guarantees which existed before the spread of the world-oriented rice economy were simply swept away.[52] In Kenya in the same period, by contrast, the Kikuyu farmers prospered, brought into the periphery of the world-economy by Indian – including Ismaili – shop-owners who settled the area, promoting marketing networks and the spread of the monetary economy, and so facilitating long-distance trade in Kikuyu agricultural products and encouraging the Kikuyu to buy up Western goods. Kikuyu farmers eagerly embraced new commercial opportunities and began to substitute higher-quality crops for traditional products, particularly maize for millets and sorghums. By the 1920s some farmers had become modern and efficient, exporting high-quality maize; efficient farmers expanded their holdings and practised extensive cash-crop farming.[53]

But the world-economy is only our framework. In this study it has been certain classical sociologists who have posed the questions that have enabled us to confront the historical evidence. Much of the evidence available concerning entrepreneurial minorities in South and Southeast Asia in the age of the emerging world-economy cannot offer satisfactory responses to the questions asked. However, the weight of the evidence – particularly when conjoined to evidence from a deeply researched European exemplar – is sufficient for us to attempt some generalizations about the communities which have played such an important role in the union of Asia and Europe since the sixteenth century. We have argued that our conjoint communities have owed their position to entrepreneurial creativity, a creativity stemming from both spiritual and material sources, from the constant duality of 'nearness and distance' which marked their identity. Part of this dual identity is 'spirit' in the more conventional sense, and here we have argued that it is not necessary to look in these communities for analogies of the 'puritan' spirit; rather, all five can be seen to possess their own spiritual sources which have served them as creative wellsprings. We have seen these spiritual sources underlie the form taken by each community's trading diaspora, and we have observed the renewed creativity of an ageing diaspora. Further, we have seen the important role the leading families of all communities have played, using the concept of business confidence as the emotional climate which sets these families apart.[54]

But it would be an intellectual disservice to imply that the phenomena we have discussed are peculiarly Asian. In the sixteenth and seventeenth centuries, as Henry Kamen writes:

> In England, in Holland, in Germany, in Switzerland, it was the foreigner and stranger who came to settle and to develop his business which religious strife had forced him to abandon in his own land. It is easier to describe this phenomenon than to explain it.[55]

Kamen sees in these strangers the main force for capitalist development in Europe.[56] It is important to close a book concerning conjoint communities on a note which signals the uniting forces of both civilizations.[57]

Notes

1. Wallerstein, *Modern World-System III*, p. 167.

2. A.P.E. Korver, *Sarekat Islam 1912–1916. Opkomst, bloei en structuur van Indonesië's eerste massabeweging*, Amsterdam, Universiteit van Amsterdam, 1982, pp. 17–18.

3. J.C. Scott, *The Moral Economy of the Peasant. Rebellion and Subsistence in Southeast Asia*, New Haven/London, Yale University Press, 1976, p. 154.

4. W.G. Clarence-Smith, 'Indian Business Communities in the Western Indian Ocean in the Nineteenth Century', *Indian Ocean Review* 2, no. 4 (1989): 18–21.

5. C.A. Bayly, 'Beating the Boundaries: South Asian History, c. 1700–1850', in S. Bose (ed.), *South Asia and World Capitalism*, Delhi, Oxford University Press, 1990, p. 37.

6. Clarence-Smith, 'Indian Business Communities', pp. 18–21.

7. Adas, *Burma Delta*, p. 385.

8. R. Robinson, 'Non-European Foundations of European Imperialism: Sketch for a Theory of Collaboration', in R. Owen and B. Sutcliffe (eds), *Studies in the Theory of Imperialism*, London, Longman, 1972, p. 117.

9. Robinson, 'Non-European Foundations', pp. 129–130, 133.

10. Simmel, 'The Stranger', p. 404.

11. D. Capps *et al.*, *Encounter with Erikson. Historical Interpretation and Religious Biography*, Missoula, Scholars Press, 1977, p. 281.

12. A. Schuetz, 'The Stranger: An Essay in Social Psychology', *American Journal of Sociology* 49 (1944): 506; see also p. 502.

13. Paymaster, *Early History of the Parsees*, p 37.

14. Lombard, *Carrefour Javanais* 2, p. 35.

15. See, for example, Jain, *Indigenous Banking*, p. 37.

16. F. Mauro, *Études économiques sur l'expansion Portugaise (1500–1900)*, Paris, Fundação C. Gulbenkian, 1970, pp. 18–19; I.S. Revah, 'L'Hérésie Marrane dans l'Europe Catholique du 15ᵉ au 18ᵉ siècle', in J. Le Goff, *Hérésies et sociétés dans l'Europe pre-industrielle 11ᵉ-18ᵉ siècles*, Paris and The Hague, Mouton, 1968, p. 333.

17. M.A.P. Meilink-Roelofsz, *Asian Trade and European Influence in the Indonesian Archipelago between 1500 and about 1630*, The Hague, Nijhoff, 1962, pp. 131–132.

18. Mauro, *Études économiques*, p. 19; J. Lockhart and S.B. Schwartz, *Early Latin America. A History of Colonial Spanish America and Brazil*, Cambridge, Cambridge University Press, 1983, p. 226.

19. Revah, 'L'Hérésie Marrane', p. 328; C. Roth, *Gleanings. Essays in Jewish History, Letters and Art*, New York, Hermon Press, 1967, pp. 121–123; *ibid.*, *A History of the Marranos*, 4th ed., New York, Hermon Press, 1974, pp. 168–177, 193–194; H. Pohl, *Die Portugiesen in Antwerpen (1567–1648). Zur Geschichte einer Minderheit*, Wiesbaden, Franz Steiner, 1977, pp. 342–346.

20. Revah, 'l'Hérésie Marrane', p. 328.

21. *Ibid.*

22. *Ibid.*, pp. 328–329.

23. *Ibid.*, pp. 332, 336.

24. D.M. Swetschinski, 'The Portuguese Jewish Merchants of Seventeenth-Century Amsterdam: A Social Profile', Ph.D., Brandeis University, 1980, pp. 549, 554–556.

25. Stonequist, *The Marginal Man*, p. 146.

26. *Ibid.*, p. 156.

27. Schumpeter, 'Creative Response', p. 150.

28. Stonequist, *The Marginal Man*, p. 217.

29. A. Schuetz, 'The Stranger', pp. 502, 506.

30. Cohen, 'Cultural Strategies', p. 277.

31. *Ibid.*, p. 276.

32. Weber, *Protestant Ethic*, p. 144.

33. *Ibid.*, pp. 144–153.

34. Weber, 'The Protestant Sects and the Spirit of Capitalism', in H.H. Gerth and C. Wright Mills (eds), *From Max Weber: Essays in Sociology*, London, Routledge and Kegan Paul, 1958, p. 305.

35. *Ibid.*, pp. 320–321.

36. *Ibid.*, p. 305.

37. V.B. van Gutem, 'Tjina Mindering. Eenige aanteekeningen over het Chineesche geldschieterswezen op Java', *Koloniale Studien* 3, no. 1 (1919): 113–114.

38. *Ibid.*, p. 115.

39. *Ibid.*, pp. 120–121.

40. *Ibid.*, pp. 121–122.

41. *Ibid.*, pp. 116, 119, 122–124.

42. J. Mackie, 'Changing Patterns of Chinese Big Business in Southeast Asia', in McVey (ed.), *Southeast Asian Capitalists*, p. 178, ftn. 47.

43. G. Redding and G.Y.Y. Wong, 'The Psychology of Chinese Organizational Behaviour', in M.H. Bond (ed.), *The Psychology of the Chinese People*, Hong Kong, Oxford University Press, 1986, pp. 280–282.

44. A.G. Frank, *Capitalism and Underdevelopment*, p. 53.

45. *Ibid.*, p. 94.

46. *Batikrapport* 2, p. 283; see also pp. 276, 289, 302.

47. *Ibid.*, pp. 109–111, 113, 130.

48. *Ibid.*, p. 146.

49. McCoy, *Priests on Trial*, pp. 69, 84–86; McCoy, 'Iloilo City', p. 325.

50. McCoy, *Priests on Trial*, p. 86.

51. D. Hardiman, *Peasant Nationalists of Gujarat. Kheda District 1917–1934*, Delhi, Oxford University Press, 1981, pp. 5–6, 25, 38; K.L. Gillion, *Ahmadabad. A Study in Indian Urban History*, Canberra, Australian National University Press, 1969, pp. 160–162; Government of Gujarat, *Gujarat State Gazetteers. Kheda District*, Ahmadabad, Government Printing Gujarat State, 1977, p. 265.

52. Scott, *Moral Economy*, pp. 86–88.

53. R.L. Tignor, *The Colonial Transformation of Kenya: The Kamba, Kikuyu, and Maasai from 1900 to 1939*, Princeton, Princeton University Press, 1976, pp. 295–297, 299, 305–307; B. Berman, *Control and Crisis in Colonial Kenya. The Dialectic of Domination*, London, James Currey, 1990, p. 54.

54. I am grateful to Margo Lyon and Jack Barbalet for discussing this with me.

55. H. Kamen, *The Iron Century. Social Change in Europe 1550–1660*, New York, Praeger Publishers, 1971, p. 89.

56. *Ibid.*, pp. 89–102.

57. T. Svensson, 'The Euro-Asian Connection', *NIASnytt* 1994, no. 1, p. 3.

Glossary

adathi	Nattukottai Chettiar elite 'parent' banker.
arak	spirituous liquor distilled from the coconut palm or from rice and sugar.
batik	a type of dyed cloth using stamps or pens to make patterns in molten wax, followed by steeping in dye.
bhakti	medieval Hindu spiritual movement stressing fervent devotion to god.
cabang atas	peranakan Chinese elite in Java, literally 'the upper branch'.
cabecilla	nineteenth-century Chinese chief agent in Manila who consigned goods to provincial sub-agents; also head of an occupational *gremio*.
canting	metal applicator for wax in the batik process.
cap	wooden or metal stamp for applying wax in the batik process.
cina mindering	a group of Chinese hawkers-cum-moneylenders in Java.
compadrazgo	co-parenthood; term describing the ritual relationship acquired by acting as sponsors in a Catholic baptism, confirmation or wedding.
creole	person born in Spanish colonies both of whose parents were Spanish.
crore	ten million (India).
desa	Javanese village.
dharma	proper way of life or code of conduct in Hinduism.

duka	Gujarati shop in East Africa.
firman	for the Ismailis, a decree of the Aga Khan, read out in their *jamatkhana*.
gobernadorcillo	Spanish administrative term in the Philippines used to designate a local official assigned or elected to administer a town or *parian*.
gremio	a municipal ward or local administrative unit legally recognized by the Spanish in the Philippines.
hacienda	in the Philippines a large, unified agricultural property.
ilustrado	literally 'enlightened'; a late nineteenth-century term for a non-Spanish resident of the Philippines who had acquired some tertiary education.
imam	an Islamic spiritual and/or temporal leader.
indio	Spanish colonial terminology in the Philippines for a Christian of Filipino descent.
jamatkhana	place of prayer and community administration for Ismailis.
kain	untailored cloth used as a garment (Java).
kamaria	accountant in the Ismaili *jamatkhana*.
karma	the principle of universal causality resulting from action; one of the basic constituents of the Hindu philosophical system.
kongsi	a Chinese commercial society in Java; usually a syndicate or partnership formed to capitalize and manage a particular enterprise.
kretek	Javanese cigarette containing a mixture of tobacco and cloves.
mestizo	a person of mixed-race parentage; in the Philippines the usual implication was Chinese mestizo descent.
mukhi	treasurer in the Ismaili *jamatkhana*.
obras pias	Catholic so-called 'pious foundations' whose funds were administered for charitable purposes.
panchayat	a council, in India, of at least five persons from a caste, village or other group which arbitrates matters such as group disputes.
pacto de retrovento	a form of mortgage agreement used to secure loans, facilitating foreclosure.

parian	part of a town area designated by the Spanish regime in the Philippines as a place of residence for Chinese.
peranakan	individuals born from unions between Hokkien Chinese and Javan women; also the Chinese-Indonesian culture that predominated among the Javan Chinese from the eighteenth century.
principalia	a nineteenth-century term in the Philippines for the municipal political elite, comprising a range of officials.
reconquista	Christian reconquest of Spain from the Muslims.
rial	originally a Spanish coin, *real de ocho*, widely in circulation in Southeast Asia.
Saivism	the religion devoted to the worship of the god Siva and his symbols (Hinduism).
sari-sari store	Chinese general store in the Philippines.
shet	in Bombay a merchant, banker or trader who was the head or leading member of a trading body or caste.
shetia	in Bombay, the head of a caste or trading body, distinguished by his great wealth.
Shia	the general name for a large group of Muslim sects, the starting point of all of which is the recognition of Ali, the son-in-law of Muhammad, as the legitimate caliph after the death of the Prophet.
singkeh	a new Chinese immigrant in Indonesia.
taokeh	in Java a Chinese financier of an enterprise or an employer of labour.
taqiya	Islamic Shia practice of permitting dissimulation of real belief in difficult situations.
toko	in Java, a Chinese shop.
totok	China-born or full-blood Chinese in Indonesia.
tukang cap	workman who handled the stamps (*cap*) in batik business.
Vaishnavism	Hindu religious beliefs surrounding the god Vishnu.
vituti	Nattukottai Chettiar communal lodging house.
wayang	Javanese puppet theatre.

Select Bibliography

Primary Sources

Alphen, M. van, 'Iets over den oorsprong en de eerste uitbreiding der Chineesche Volkplanting te Batavia', *Tijdschrift voor Nederlandsch Indië* 4, no. 1 (1842): 70–100.

'Bishop Salazar's Report to the King', in A. Felix Jr. (ed.), *The Chinese in the Philippines 1570–1770*, vol. 1, Manila, Solidaridad Publishing House, 1966, pp. 119–132.

Blair, E.H. and J.A. Robertson (eds), *The Philippine Islands 1493–1898*, 55 vols, Cleveland, Arthur Clark Co., 1903–07.

Bowring, J., *The Philippine Islands*, London, Smith, Elder and Co., 1859.

Burma, *Report of the Burma Provincial Banking Inquiry Committee, 1929–30*, vols 1 and 2, Rangoon, Superintendent of Government Printing, 1930.

Colenbrander H.T., (ed.), *Jan Pietersz. Coen. Bescheiden Omtrent Zijn Bedrijf in Indië*, 4 vols, The Hague, Martinus Nijhoff, 1919–22.

Comyn, T. de, *State of the Philippines in 1810*, Manila, Filipiniana Book Guild, 1969.

De Kat Angelino, P., *Batikrapport*, 3 vols, Weltevreden, Landsdrukkerij, 1930–31.

Enthoven, R.E., *The Tribes and Castes of Bombay*, 3 vols, Delhi, Cosmo Publications Reprint, 1975 (original publication Bombay, 1920–22).

Fawcett, C., *The English Factories in India*, vol. 1 *(New Series) 1670–1671*, Oxford, Clarendon Press, 1936.

Forbes, J., *Oriental Memoirs*, 2 vols, 2nd edn, London, Bentley, 1834.

Forrest, G.W. (ed.), *Selections from the Letters, Despatches, and Other State Papers Preserved in the Bombay Secretariat, Home Series*, vol. 1, Bombay, Government Central Press, 1887.

Hooyman, J., 'Verhandeling over den Tegenwoordigen Staat van den Land-Bouw in de Ommelanden van Batavia', *Verhandelingen van het Bataviaasch Genootschap der Kunsten en Wetenschappen* 1 (1779): 173–262.

Huiser, P.C., 'Iets over de assistent-residentie Blitar', *Tijdschrift voor Nederlandsch Indië*, New Series, 3, no. 1 (1874): 319–324.

Imperial Gazetteer of India, *Baroda*, Calcutta, Superintendent of Government Printing, 1908.

Jain, L.C., *Indigenous Banking in India*, London, Macmillan, 1929.

Jonge, J.K.J. de, *et al.* (eds), *De Opkomst van het Nederlandsch Gezag in Oost Indië*, 13 vols, The Hague, Martinus Nijhoff, 1862–88.

Karaka, D.F., *History of the Parsis including their Manners, Customs, Religion, and Present Position*, 2 vols, London, Macmillan, 1884.

Nes, J.F. van, 'De Chinezen op Java', *Tijdschrift voor Nederlandsch Indië* 13, no. 1 (1851): 239–254, 292–314.

Phoa Liong Gie, 'De Economische Positie der Chineezen in Nederlandsch Indië', *Koloniale Studiën* 20, no. 5 (1936): 97–119.

Raffles, T.S., *The History of Java*, 2 vols, London, 1817; reissued Kuala Lumpur, Oxford in Asia Historical Reprints, 1965.

Reijden, B. van der, *Rapport Betreffende een Gehouden Enquête naar de Arbeidstoestanden in de Industrie van Strootjes en Inheemsche Sigaretten op Java; Deel I. West Java; Deel II. Midden-Java; Deel III. Oost Java*, Bandung, Kantoor van Arbeid, 1934–36.

Schwencke, G., 'De Weefindustrie in het Regentschap Bandoeng', *Koloniaal Tijdschrift* 23 (1939): 159–170.

Stanley, H.M., *Through the Dark Continent*, 2nd edition, 2 vols, London, George Newnes, 1899.

The Memoirs of Aga Khan: World Enough and Time, London, Cassell, 1954.

Thurston, E., *Castes and Tribes of Southern India*, vol. 5, Madras, Government Press, 1909.

Valentijn, F., *Oud en Nieuw Oost-Indien*, The Hague, H.C. Susan, 1858, first edition, 1724–26.

Vleming, J.L., *Het Chineesche Zakenleven in Nederlandsch-Indië*, Weltevreden, Landsdrukkerij, 1926.

——, *Tabak, Tabakscultuur en Tabaksproducten van Nederlandsch-Indië*, Weltevreden, Landsdrukkerij, 1925.

Warmelo, W. van, 'Ontstaan en Groei van de Handweefnijverheid in Madjalaja', *Koloniale Studiën* 23 (1939): 5–25.

Zuñiga, J.M. de, *Status of the Philippines in 1800*, Manila, Publications of the Filipiniana Book Guild, 1973.

Other Sources

Abercrombie, N., S. Hill and B.S. Turner, *Sovereign Individuals of Capitalism*, London, Allen and Unwin, 1986.

Abeyasekere, S., *Jakarta. A History*, revised edition, Singapore, Oxford University Press, 1989.

Abraham, J.H., *Origins and Growth of Sociology*, Harmondsworth, Penguin Books, 1973.

Abrams, P., *Historical Sociology*, London, Open Books, 1982.

Adas, M., 'Immigrant Asians and the Economic Impact of European Imperialism: The Role of the South Indian Chettiars in British Burma', *Journal of Asian Studies* 33, no. 3 (1974): 385–401.

——, *The Burma Delta. Economic Development and Social Change on an Asian Rice Frontier, 1852–1941*, Madison, The University of Wisconsin Press, 1974.

Ahmed, T., *Religio-Political Ferment in the N.W. Frontier during the Mughal Period. The Raushaniya Movement*, Delhi, Idarah-i Adabiyat-i Delli, 1982.

Alexeiev, B.M., *The Chinese Gods of Wealth*, London, School of Oriental Studies, 1928.

Amyot, J., *The Manila Chinese. Familism in the Philippine Environment*, Quezon City, Institute of Philippine Culture, 1973.

Antlöv, H. and T. Svensson, 'From Rural Home Weavers to Factory Labour: The Industrialization of Textile Manufacturing in Majalaya', in P. Alexander, P. Boomgaard and B. White (eds), *In the Shadow of Agriculture. Non-farm Activities in the Javanese Economy, Past and Present*, Amsterdam, Royal Tropical Institute, 1991, pp. 113–126.

Arasaratnam, S., *Merchants, Companies and Commerce on the Coromandel Coast 1650–1740*, Delhi, Oxford University Press, 1986.

——, 'Society, Power, Factionalism and Corruption in Early Madras 1640–1746', *Indica* 23 (1986): 113–134.

Ardener, S., 'The Comparative Study of Rotating Credit Associations', *Journal of the Royal Anthropological Institute of Great Britain* 94 (1964): 201–229.

Bader, Z., 'The Contradictions of Merchant Capital 1840–1939', in A. Sheriff and E. Ferguson (eds), *Zanzibar under Colonial Rule*, London, James Currey, 1991, pp. 163–187.

Bagchi, A.K., 'European and Indian Entrepreneurship in India, 1900–30', in E. Leach and S.N. Mukherjee (eds), *Elites in South Asia*, Cambridge, Cambridge University Press, 1970, pp. 223–256.

Baker, H.D.R., *Chinese Family and Kinship*, London, Macmillan, 1979.

Baks, C., 'Chinese Communities in Eastern Java: A Few Remarks', *Asian Studies* 8, no. 2 (1970): 248–259.

Barbalet, J.M., 'Confidence: Time and Emotion in the Sociology of Action', *Journal for the Theory of Social Behaviour* 23, no. 3 (1993): 229–247.

Bayly, C.A., 'Beating the Boundaries: South Asian History, c. 1700–1850', in S. Bose (ed.), *South Asia and World Capitalism*, Delhi, Oxford University Press, 1990, pp. 27–39.

——, *Indian Society and the Making of the British Empire*, Cambridge, Cambridge University Press, 1988.

——, *Rulers, Townsmen and Bazaars. North Indian Society in the Age of British Expansion, 1770–1870*, Cambridge, Cambridge University Press, 1983.

Bellah, R.N. *Tokugawa Religion. The Values of Pre-Industrial Japan*, Glencoe, The Free Press, 1957.

Bendix, R., *Max Weber. An Intellectual Portrait*, London, Methuen and Company, 1966.

Benedict, B., 'Family Firms and Economic Development', *Southwestern Journal of Anthropology* 24, no. 1 (1968): 1–19.

Bennett, G., *Kenya. A Political History*, London, Oxford University Press, 1963.

Berger, P.L., 'An East Asian Development Model?', in P.L. Berger and H.H.M. Hsiao (eds), *In Search of an East Asian Development Model*, New Brunswick and Oxford, Transaction Books, 1988, pp. 3–11.

—— and B. Berger, *Sociology: A Biographical Approach*, Harmondsworth, Penguin Books, 1972.

Berghe, P.L. van den, *The Ethnic Phenomenon*, New York, Elsevier, 1981.

Berman, B., *Control and Crisis in Colonial Kenya. The Dialectic of Domination*, London, James Currey, 1990.

Berna, J.J., *Industrial Entrepreneurship in Madras State*, Bombay, Asia Publishing House, 1960.

Bernal, R., 'The Chinese Colony in Manila, 1570–1770', in A. Felix Jr. (ed.), *The Chinese in the Philippines 1570–1770*, vol. 1, Manila, Solidaridad Publishing House, 1966, pp. 40–66.

Bharati, A., 'A Social Survey', in D.P. Ghai (ed.), *Portrait of a Minority: Asians in East Africa*, Nairobi, Oxford University Press, 1965, pp. 13–43.

Blussé, L., *Strange Company. Chinese Settlers, Mestizo Women and the Dutch in VOC Batavia*, Dordrecht and Riverton, Foris Publications, 1986.

Bonacich, E., 'A Theory of Middleman Minorities', in N.R. Yetman and C.H. Steele (eds), *Majority and Minority: The Dynamics of Racial and Ethnic Relations*, 2nd edn, Boston, Allyn and Bacon, 1975, pp. 77–89.

—— and J. Modell, *The Economic Basis of Ethnic Solidarity. Small Business in the Japanese American Community*, Berkeley and Los Angeles, University of California Press, 1980.

Boomgaard, P., 'Buitenzorg in 1805: The Role of Money and Credit in a Colonial Frontier Society', *Modern Asian Studies* 20, no. 1 (1986): 33–58.

Braudel, F., *Civilization and Capitalism 15th–18th Century*, vol. 3, *The Perspective of the World*, London, Collins/Fontana Press, 1984.

Budd, S., *Sociologists and Religion*, London, Collier-Macmillan, 1973.

Cady, J.F., *Southeast Asia: Its Historical Development*, New York, McGraw-Hill, 1964.

Capps, D., W.H. Capps and M.G. Bradford, *Encounter with Erikson. Historical Interpretation and Religious Biography*, Missoula, Scholars Press, 1977.

Carey, P., 'Changing Javanese Perceptions of the Chinese Communities in Central Java, 1755–1825', *Indonesia* 37 (1984): 1–47.

Carroll, J., *The Filipino Manufacturing Entrepreneur*, Ithaca, Cornell University Press, 1965.

Castles, L., *Religion, Politics and Economic Behavior in Java: the Kudus Cigarette Industry*, New Haven, Yale University Southeast Asia Studies, 1967.

Cator, W.J., *The Economic Position of the Chinese in the Netherlands Indies*, Oxford, Basil Blackwell, 1936.

Chakravarti, N.R., *The Indian Minority in Burma: The Rise and Decline of an Immigrant Community*, London, Oxford University Press, 1971.

Chaudhuri, K.N., *Trade and Civilisation in the Indian Ocean. An Economic History of the Rise of Islam to 1750*, Cambridge, Cambridge University Press, 1985.

Chaudhuri, N.C., *Hinduism*, Oxford, Oxford University Press, 1979.

Chaunu, P., 'Les "Cristãos Novos" et l'effondrement de l'empire portugais dans l'Océan Indien au début du xviie siècle', *Revue des études juives* 4, no. 2 (xcii) (1963): 188–190.

——, *Les Philippines et le Pacifique des Ibériques (xvie, xviie, xviiie siècles). Introduction methodologique et indices d'activité*, Paris, S.E.V.P.E.N., 1960.

Cheong, W.E., 'Canton and Manila in the Eighteenth Century', in J. Ch'en and N. Tarling (eds), *Studies in the Social History of China and Southeast Asia*, Cambridge, Cambridge University Press, 1970.

Clarence-Smith, W.G., 'Indian Business Communities in the Western Indian Ocean in the Nineteenth Century', *Indian Ocean Review* 2, no. 4 (1989): 18–21.

Cohen, A., 'Cultural strategies in the organization of trading diasporas', in C. Meillassoux (ed.), *The Development of Indigenous Trade and Markets in West Africa*, London, Oxford University Press, 1971, p. 266–280.

—— (ed.), *Urban Ethnicity*, London, Tavistock Publications, 1974.

Coppell, C.A., 'Mapping the *Peranakan* Chinese in Indonesia', *Papers in Far Eastern History* 8 (1973): 143–167.

Cullinane, M., 'The Changing Nature of the Cebu Urban Elite in the 19th Century', in A.W. McCoy and E.C. de Jesus (eds), *Philippine Social History: Global Trade and Local Transformations*, Sydney, George Allen & Unwin, and Manila, Ateneo de Manila University Press, 1982, pp. 251–296.

Curtin, P.D., *Cross-Cultural Trade in World History*, Cambridge, Cambridge University Press, 1984.

Cushman, J.W., *Family and State. The Formation of a Sino-Thai Tin-mining Dynasty*, Singapore, Oxford University Press, 1991.

——, 'The Khaw Group: Chinese Business in Early Twentieth-Century Penang', *Journal of Southeast Asian Studies* 17, no. 1 (1986): 58–79.

Dahm, B., *José Rizal. Der Nationalheld der Filipinos*, Göttingen, Muster-Schmidt Verlag, 1988.

Das Gupta, A., *Indian Merchants and the Decline of Surat c. 1700–1750*, Wiesbaden, Steiner, 1979.

——, *Malabar in Asian Trade 1740–1800*, Cambridge, Cambridge University Press, 1967.

——, 'The Merchants of Surat, c. 1700–50', in E. Leach and S.N. Mukherjee (eds), *Elites in South Asia*, Cambridge, Cambridge University Press, 1970, pp. 201–222.

De Glopper, D.R., 'Doing Business in Lukang', in A.P. Wolf (ed.), *Studies in Chinese Society*, Stanford, Stanford University Press, 1978, pp. 291–320.

Desai, A.V., 'The Origins of Parsi Enterprise', *Indian Economic and Social History Review* 5, no. 4 (1968): 307–317.

Diaz Trechuelo, L., 'The Economic Background', in A. Felix Jr. (ed.), *The Chinese in the Philippines*, vol. 2, Manila, Solidaridad Publishing House, 1969, pp. 18–44.

——, 'The Role of the Chinese in the Philippine Domestic Economy (1570–1770)', in A. Felix Jr. (ed.), *The Chinese in the Philippines*

1570–1770, vol. 1, Manila, Solidaridad Publishing House, 1966, pp. 175–210.

Dobbin, C., *Basic Documents in the Development of Modern India and Pakistan, 1835–1947*, London, Van Nostrand Reinhold, 1970.

——, 'Competing Elites in Bombay City Politics in the Mid-Nineteenth Century (1852–83)', in E. Leach and S.N. Mukherjee (eds), *Elites in South Asia*, Cambridge, Cambridge University Press, 1970, pp. 79–94.

——, 'From Middleman Minorities to Industrial Entrepreneurs: The Chinese in Java and the Parsis in Western India 1619–1939', *Itinerario* 13, no. 1 (1989): 109–132.

——, *Islamic Revivalism in a Changing Peasant Economy. Central Sumatra, 1784–1847*, London and Malmö, Curzon Press, Scandinavian Institute of Asian Studies Monograph Series No. 47, 1983, repr. 1987.

——, 'The Parsi Panchayat in Bombay City in the Nineteenth Century', *Modern Asian Studies* 4, no. 2 (1970): 149–164.

——, *Urban Leadership in Western India. Politics and Communities in Bombay City 1840–1885*, London, Oxford University Press, 1972.

Duara, P., 'Superscribing Symbols: The Myth of Guandi, Chinese God of War', *Journal of Asian Studies* 47, no. 4 (1988): 778–795.

Durkheim, E., *The Elementary Forms of Religious Life*, New York, The Free Press, 1965.

Eitzen, D.S., 'Two Minorities: The Jews of Poland and the Chinese of the Philippines', *Jewish Journal of Sociology* 10, no. 2 (1968): 221–240.

Elson, R.E., *Javanese Peasants and the Colonial Sugar Industry. Impact and Change in an East Java Residency, 1830–1940*, Singapore, Oxford University Press, 1984.

——, *Village Java under the Cultivation System 1830–1870*, Sydney, Allen and Unwin, 1994.

Erikson, E., *Identity. Youth and Crisis*, New York, W.W. Norton, 1968.

Evers, H.D., 'Chettiar Moneylenders in Southeast Asia', in D. Lombard and J. Aubin (eds), *Marchands et hommes d'affaires asiatiques dans l'Océan Indien et la Mer de Chine 13ᵉ–20ᵉ siècles*, Paris, Éditions de l'École des Hautes Études, 1987, pp. 199–219.

—— and J. Pavadarayan, *Asceticism and Ecstasy: The Chettiars of Singapore*, University of Bielefeld, Sociology of Development Research Centre Working Paper No. 79 (1986).

—— and J. Pavadarayan, 'Religious Fervour and Economic Success. The Chettiars of Singapore', in K.S. Sandhu and A. Mani (eds), *Indian Communities in Southeast Asia*, Singapore, Institute of Southeast Asian Studies, 1993, pp. 847–865.

Fairbank, J.K., *Trade and Diplomacy on the China Coast. The Opening of the Treaty Ports, 1842–1854*, Stanford, Stanford University Press, 1964.

Farquhar, J.N., *Modern Religious Movements in India*, London, Macmillan, 1929.

Fasseur, C., *The Politics of Colonial Exploitation. Java, the Dutch, and the Cultivation System*, Ithaca, Cornell University Studies on Southeast Asia, 1992.

Felix, A. Jr. (ed.), *The Chinese in the Philippines 1570–1770*, 2 vols, Manila, Solidaridad Publishing House, 1966–69.

Fernando, M.R. and D. Bulbeck, *Chinese Economic Activity in Netherlands India. Selected Translations from the Dutch*, Singapore. Institute of Southeast Asian Studies, 1992.

Frank, A.G., *Capitalism and Underdevelopment in Latin America*, New York and London, Monthly Review Press, 1967.

——, *Lumpenbourgeoisie: Lumpendevelopment. Dependence, Class and Politics in Latin America*, New York and London, Monthly Review Press, 1972.

Freedman, M., *Chinese Lineage and Society: Fukien and Kwangtung*, 2nd edn, London, The Athlone Press, 1971.

Freund, J., *The Sociology of Max Weber*, Harmondsworth, Penguin Books, 1972.

Frisby, D., *Sociological Impressionism. A Reassessment of Georg Simmel's Social Theory*, London, Heinemann, 1981.

Fruin, T.A., 'Kerftabak op Java', *Koloniale Studiën* 7, no. 2 (1923): 347–385.

Furnivall, J.S., *Colonial Policy and Practice*, New York, New York University Press, 1956.

——, *The Fashioning of Leviathan. The Beginnings of British Rule in Burma*, Reprint, Canberra, Australian National University, 1991.

Gallagher, J. and R. Robinson, 'The Imperialism of Free Trade', *Economic History Review*, Second Series, 6, no. 1 (1953): 1–15.

Geertz, C., 'The Rotating Credit Association: A "Middle Rung" in Development', *Economic Development and Cultural Change* 10, no. 3 (1962): 241–263.

——, *The Social History of an Indonesian Town*, Cambridge, Mass., The M.I.T. Press, 1965.

Gellner, E., *Muslim Society*, Cambridge, Cambridge University Press, 1981.

Gerth, H.H. and C. Wright Mills (eds), *From Max Weber: Essays in Sociology*, London, Routledge and Kegan Paul, 1948.

Gibb, H.A.R. and J.H. Kramers, *Shorter Encyclopaedia of Islam*, Leiden/ London, Brill/Luzac, 1961.

Giddens, A., 'Introduction', in M. Weber, *The Protestant Ethic and the Spirit of Capitalism*, London, George Allen and Unwin, 1976, pp. 1–12.

Gillion, K.L., *Ahmedabad. A Study in Indian Urban History*, Canberra, Australian National University Press, 1969.

Godley, M., *The Mandarin-Capitalists from Nanyang. Overseas Chinese Enterprise in the Modernization of China*, Cambridge, Cambridge University Press, 1981.

Golas, P.J., 'Early Ch'ing Guilds', in G.W. Skinner, *The City in Late Imperial China*, Stanford, Stanford University Press, 1977, pp. 555–580.

Goody, J., *The Oriental, the Ancient and the Primitive. Systems of Marriage and the Family in the Pre-industrial Societies of Eurasia*, Cambridge, Cambridge University Press, 1990.

Gordon, A.D.D., *Businessmen and Politics. Rising Nationalism and a Modernising Economy in Bombay, 1918–1933*, New Delhi, Manohar, 1978.

Government of Gujarat, *Gujarat State Gazetteers. Kheda District*, Ahmadabad, Government Printing Gujarat State, 1977.

——, *Gujarat State Gazetteers. Kutch District*, Ahmadabad, Government Printing Gujarat State, 1971.

Government of Tamil Nadu, *Tamil Nadu District Gazetteers. Ramanathapuram*, Madras, Director of Stationery and Printing, 1972.

Greenow, L.L., 'Spatial Dimensions of the Credit Market in Eighteenth Century Nueva Galicia', in D.J. Robinson (ed.), *Social Fabric and Spatial Structure in Colonial Latin America*, Ann Arbor, University of Michigan, 1979, pp. 227–279.

Guerrero, M.C., 'The Chinese in the Philippines, 1570–1770', in A. Felix Jr. (ed.), *The Chinese in the Philippines 1570–1770*, vol. 1, Manila, Solidaridad Publishing House, 1966, pp. 15–39.

Guha, A., 'Parsi Seths as Entrepreneurs, 1750–1850', *Economic and Political Weekly* 5 (1970): M-107, M-115.

——, 'The Comprador Role of Parsi Seths, 1750–1850', *Economic and Political Weekly* 5 (1970): 1933–1936.

Gutem, V.B. van, 'Tjina Mindering. Eenige aanteekeningen over het Chineesche geldschieterswezen op Java', *Koloniale Studiën* 3, no. 1 (1919): 106–150.

Haan, F. de, *Oud Batavia*, Batavia, Kolff, 1922.

Hagen, E.E., 'British Personality and the Industrial Revolution: The Historical Evidence', in T. Burns and S.B. Saul (eds), *Social Theory and Economic Change*, London, Tavistock Publications, 1967, pp. 35–66.

——, *The Economics of Development*, Homewood and Nobleton, Richard D. Irwin, 1968.

Hall, D.G.E., *Burma*, 3rd edn, London, Hutchinson University Library, 1960.

Hao Yen-p'ing, *The Commercial Revolution in Nineteenth-Century China. The Rise of Sino-Western Mercantile Capital*, Berkeley and Los Angeles, University of California Press, 1986.

Hardiman, D., *Peasant Nationalists of Gujarat. Kheda District 1917–1934*, Delhi, Oxford University Press, 1981.

Harris, F.R., *Jamsetji Nusserwanji Tata. A Chronicle of his Life*, 2nd edn, Bombay, Blackie and Son, 1958.

Hawes, G., 'Marcos, his Cronies, and the Philippines' Failure to Develop', in R. McVey (ed.), *Southeast Asian Capitalists*, Ithaca, Cornell University Southeast Asia Program, 1992, pp. 145–160.

Haynes, D.E., 'From Tribute to Philanthropy: The Politics of Gift Giving in a Western Indian City', *Journal of Asian Studies* 46, no. 2 (1987): 339–360.

Higgins, B., *Economic Development. Principles, Problems and Policies*, New York, W.W. Norton and Company, 1959.

Hill, H., 'The Economics of Recent Changes in the Weaving Industry', *Bulletin of Indonesian Economic Studies* 16, no. 2 (1980): 83–103.

Hinnells, J.R., 'Anglo-Parsi Commercial Relations in Bombay Prior to 1847', *Journal of the K.R. Cama Oriental Institute* 46 (1978): 5–17.

——, 'Bombay, Persian Communities of', *Encyclopaedia Iranica* 4, no. 4, London, Routledge and Kegan Paul, 1985–1993, pp. 340–346.

——, 'British Accounts of Parsi Religion, 1619–1843', *Journal of the K.R. Cama Oriental Institute* 46 (1978): 20–41.

——, 'Parsis and British Education, 1820–1880', *Journal of the K.R. Cama Oriental Institute* 46 (1978): 42–59.

——, 'Zoroastrianism', in J.R. Hinnells (ed.), *The Penguin Dictionary of Religions*, Harmondsworth, Penguin Books, 1984.

——, *Zoroastrianism and the Parsis*, London, Ward Lock Educational, 1981.

Hirschmeier, J., *The Origins of Entrepreneurship in Meiji Japan*, Cambridge, Mass., Harvard University Press, 1964.

Hoadley, M.C., 'Javanese, Peranakan, and Chinese Elites in Cirebon: Changing Ethnic Boundaries', *Journal of Asian Studies* 47, no. 3 (1988): 503–517.

Hoetink, B., 'Chineesche Officieren te Batavia Onder de Compagnie', *Bijdragen tot de Taal-, Land- en Volkenkunde van Nederlandsch Indië* 78 (1922): 1–136.

——, 'Ni Hoekong. Kapitein der Chineezen te Batavia in 1740', *Bijdragen tot de Taal-, Land- en Volkenkunde van Nederlandsch Indië* 74 (1918): 447–518.

——, 'So Bing Kong. Het Eerste Hoofd der Chineezen te Batavia (1629–1636)', *Bijdragen tot de Taal-, Land- en Volkenkunde van Nederlandsch Indië* 73 (1917): 344–385.

Hsiao, H.H.M., 'An East Asian Development Model: Empirical Explorations', in P.L. Berger and H.H.M. Hsiao (eds), *In Search of an East Asian Development Model*, New Brunswick and Oxford, Transaction Books, 1988, pp. 12–23.

Hutchison, J., 'Class and State Power in the Philippines', in K. Hewison, R. Robison and G. Rodan (eds), *Authoritarianism, Democracy and Capitalism*, Sydney, Allen and Unwin, 1993, pp. 193–212.

Ito, S., 'A Note on the "Business Combine" in India – with Special Reference to the Nattukottai Chettiars', *Developing Economies* 4 (1966): 367–380.

——, 'On the Basic Nature of the Investment Company in India', *Developing Economies* 16 (1978): 223–238.

Jash, P., *History of Saivism*, Calcutta, Roy and Chaudhury, 1974.

Kamen, H., *The Iron Century. Social Change in Europe 1550–1660*, New York, Praeger Publishers, 1971.

Kennedy, R.E., 'The Protestant Ethic and the Parsis', *American Journal of Sociology* 68 (1962–63): 11–20.

Klausner, S.Z., 'Introduction', in W. Sombart, *The Jews and Modern Capitalism*, New Brunswick and London, Transaction Books, 1982, pp. xv–cxxv.

Kochanek, S.A., 'Briefcase Politics in India. The Congress Party and the Business Elite', *Asian Survey* 27, no. 12 (1987): 1278–1301.

Kondapi, C., *Indians Overseas*, New Delhi, Oxford University Press, 1951.

Korver, A.P.E., *Sarekat Islam 1912–1916. Opkomst, bloei en structuur van Indonesië's eerste massabeweging*, Amsterdam, Universiteit van Amsterdam, 1982.

Kulke, E., *The Parsees in India. A Minority as Agent of Social Change*, Munich, Weltforum Verlag, 1974.

Kumar, A.L., 'Islam, the Chinese, and Indonesian Historiography – A Review Article', *Journal of Asian Studies* 46, no. 3 (1987): 603–615.

Lamb, H.B., 'The Indian Business Communities and the Evolution of an Industrialist Class', *Pacific Affairs* 28, no. 2 (1955): 101–116.

Larkin, J.A., *Sugar and the Origins of Modern Philippine Society*, Berkeley and Los Angeles, University of California Press, 1993.

——, *The Pampangans. Colonial Society in a Philippine Province*, Berkeley and Los Angeles, University of California Press, 1972.

Lehmann, D., *Dependencia: An Ideological History*, Brighton, IDS University of Sussex, 1986.

Levine, D.N., 'Simmel at a Distance: On the History and Systematics of the Sociology of the Stranger', in D. Frisby (ed.), *Georg Simmel. Critical Assessments*, vol. 3, London and New York, Routledge, 1994, pp. 174–189.

Lewis, S.R., *Pakistan. Industrialization and Trade Policies*, London, Oxford University Press, 1970.

Liem Twan Djie, *De Distribueerende Tusschenhandel der Chineezen op Java*, 2nd edn, The Hague, Martinus Nijhoff, 1952.

Lockhart, J. and S.B. Schwartz, *Early Latin America. A History of Colonial Spanish America and Brazil*, Cambridge, Cambridge University Press, 1983.

Lombard, D., *Le Carrefour Javanais. Essai d'histoire globale*, vol. 2 *Les réseaux asiatiques*, Paris, Éditions de l'École des Hautes Études en Sciences Sociales, 1990.

——, 'Y-a-t-il une continuité des réseaux marchands asiatiques?', in D. Lombard and J. Aubin (eds), *Marchands et hommes d'affaires asiatiques dans l'Océan Indien et la Mer de Chine 13ᵉ–20ᵉ siècles*, Paris, Éditions de l'École des Hautes Études, 1988, pp. 11–18.

—— and J. Aubin (eds), *Marchands et hommes d'affaires asiatiques dans l'Océan Indien et la Mer de Chine 13ᵉ–20ᵉ siècles*, Paris, Éditions de l'École des Hautes Études, 1988.

—— and C. Salmon, 'Islam et sinité', *Archipel* 30 (1985): 73–94.

Lopez-Gonzaga, V.B., *The Negrense. A Social History of An Elite Class*, Bacolod, University of St la Salle, 1991.

Loycke, A. (ed.), *Der Gast, Der Bleibt. Dimensionen von Georg Simmels Analyse des Fremdseins*, Frankfurt, Campus Verlag, 1992.

Lugard, Lord, *The Dual Mandate in British Tropical Africa*, London, Frank Cass, 1965.

Lütt, J., 'Max Weber and the Vallabhacharis', *International Sociology* 2, no. 3 (1987): 277–287.

McClelland, D.C., *The Achieving Society*, New York, The Free Press, 1967.

McCoy, A.W., 'A Queen Dies Slowly: The Rise and Decline of Iloilo City', in A.W. McCoy and E.C. de Jesus (eds), *Philippine Social History:*

Global Trade and Local Transformations, Sydney, George Allen &
Unwin, and Manila, Ateneo de Manila University Press, 1982,
pp. 297–358.

——, *Priests on Trial*, Ringwood, Penguin Books, 1984.

——, 'Review of Sugar and the Origins of Modern Philippine Society',
Journal of Asian Studies 53, no. 2 (1994): 636–638.

—— and E.C. de Jesus (eds), *Philippine Social History: Global Trade and
Local Transformations*, Sydney, George Allen & Unwin, and Manila,
Ateneo de Manila University Press, 1982.

Mackie, J., 'Changing Patterns of Chinese Big Business in Southeast Asia',
in R. McVey (ed.), *Southeast Asian Capitalists*, Ithaca, Cornell
University Southeast Asia Program, 1992, pp. 161–190.

McVey, R., 'The Materialization of the Southeast Asian Entrepreneur', in
R. McVey (ed.), *Southeast Asian Capitalists*, Ithaca, Cornell
University Southeast Asia Program, 1992, pp. 7–34.

Mahadevan, R., 'Immigrant Entrepreneurs in Colonial Burma – An
Exploratory Study of the Role of the Nattukottai Chettiars of Tamil
Nadu, 1880–1930', *Indian Economic and Social History Review* 15,
no. 3 (1978): 329–358.

Mamdani, M., *Politics and Class Formation in Uganda*, New York and
London, Monthly Review Press, 1976.

Mangat, J.S., *A History of the Asians in East Africa c. 1886 to 1945*,
Oxford, Clarendon Press, 1969.

——, 'Was Allidina Visram a robber baron or a skilful and benevolent
commercial pioneer?', *East Africa Journal* 2 (1968): 33–35.

Mann, S., *Local Merchants and the Chinese Bureaucracy, 1750–1950*,
Stanford, Stanford University Press, 1987.

Markovits, C., *Indian Business and Nationalist Politics 1931–39. The
Indigenous Capitalist Class and the Rise of the Congress Party*,
Cambridge, Cambridge University Press, 1985.

——, 'Les grands capitalistes indiens', in D. Lombard and J. Aubin (eds),
*Marchands et hommes d'affaires asiatiques dans l'Océan Indien et
la Mer de Chine 13ᵉ–20ᵉ siècles*, Paris, Éditions de l'École des Hautes
Études, 1988, pp. 311–329.

——, 'Les hommes d'affaires musulmans dans la première moitié du xxᵉ
siècle', *Puruṣārtha* 9 (1986): 111–126.

Masselos, J., 'Changing Definitions of Bombay: City State to Capital City',
in I. Banga (ed.), *Ports and Their Hinterlands in India (1700–
1950)*, New Delhi, Manohar, 1992, pp. 273–316.

Mathias, P., *The First Industrial Nation. An Economic History of Britain
1700–1914*, New York, Charles Scribner's Sons, 1969.

Mauro, F., *Études économiques sur l'expansion portugaise (1500-1900)*, Paris, Fundação C. Gulbenkian, 1970.

——, 'Marchands et marchands-banquiers portugais au xviie siècle', *Revista portuguesa de história* 9 (1961): 63–78.

Mehta, S.D., *The Cotton Mills of India 1854 to 1954*, Bombay, The Textile Association, 1954.

Meilink-Roelofsz, M.A.P., *Asian Trade and European Influence in the Indonesian Archipelago between 1500 and about 1630*, The Hague, Nijhoff, 1962.

Mendels, F.F., 'Proto-industrialization. The First Phase of the Industrialization Process', *Journal of Economic History* 32, no. 1 (1972): 241–261.

Merino, J., 'The Chinese Mestizo: General Considerations', in A. Felix Jr. (ed.), *The Chinese in the Philippines*, vol. 2, Manila, Solidaridad Publishing House, 1969, pp. 45–66.

Mill, J.S., *On Liberty*, London, Oxford University Press, 1963.

Morris, H.S., 'The Divine Kingship of the Aga Khan: A Study of Theocracy in East Africa', *Southwestern Journal of Anthropology* 14 (1958): 454–472.

——, *The Indians in Uganda*, Chicago, University of Chicago Press, 1968.

Nafziger, E.W., *Class, Caste, and Entrepreneurship. A Study of Indian Industrialists*, Honolulu, University Press of Hawaii, 1987.

Neue Deutsche Biographie, vol. 10, Berlin, Duncker and Humblot, 1974.

Ng Chin-Keong, *Trade and Society: The Amoy Network on the China Coast 1683-1735*, Singapore, Singapore University Press, 1983.

Nightingale, P., *Trade and Empire in Western India 1784-1806*, Cambridge, Cambridge University Press, 1970.

Omohundro, J.T., *Chinese Merchant Families in Iloilo. Commerce and Kin in a Central Philippine City*, Quezon City, Ateneo de Manila University Press, and Athens, Ohio, Ohio University Press, 1981.

Ong Eng Die, *Chineezen in Nederlandsch-Indië: Sociografie van een Indonesische Bevolkingsgroep*, Assen, Van Gorcum and Co., 1943.

Owen, N.G., 'The Principalia in Philippine History: Kabikolan, 1790–1898', *Philippine Studies* 22 (1974): 297–324.

Palmer, I. and L. Castles, 'The Textile Industry', in B. Glassburner (ed.), *The Economy of Indonesia: Selected Readings*, Ithaca, Cornell University Press, 1971, pp. 315–336.

Panglaykim, J. and I. Palmer, 'Study of Entrepreneurship in Developing Countries: the Development of One Chinese Concern in Indonesia', *Journal of Southeast Asian Studies* 1, no. 1 (1970): 85–95.

Papanek, G.F., 'Pakistan's Industrial Entrepreneurs – Education, Occupational Background, and Finance', in W.P. Falcon and G.F. Papanek (eds), *Development Policy II – The Pakistan Experience*, Cambridge, Mass., Harvard University Press, 1971, pp. 237–259.

——, 'The Development of Entrepreneurship', *American Economic Review* 52 (1962): 48–58.

Papanek, H., 'Pakistan's Big Businessmen: Muslim Separatism, Entrepreneurship, and Partial Modernization', *Economic Development and Cultural Change* 21, no. 1 (1972/73): 1–32.

Park, R.E., 'Human Migration and the Marginal Man', *American Journal of Sociology* 32, no. 6 (1928): 881–893.

Paymaster, R.B., *Early History of the Parsees in India from their Landing in Sanjan to 1700 A.D.*, Bombay, Zartoshti Mandli, 1954.

Peacock, J.L., *Muslim Puritans. Reformist Psychology in Southeast Asian Islam*, Berkeley and Los Angeles, University of California Press, 1978.

Pearn, B.R., *A History of Rangoon*, Rangoon, American Baptist Mission Press, 1939.

Pearson, M.N., 'Brokers in Western Indian Port Cities. Their Role in Servicing Foreign Merchants', *Modern Asian Studies* 22, no. 3 (1988): 455–472.

——, *Merchants and Rulers in Gujarat. The Response to the Portuguese in the Sixteenth Century*, Berkeley and Los Angeles, University of California Press, 1976.

Penrad, J.C., 'La présence isma'ilienne en Afrique de l'est. Note sur l'histoire commerciale et l'organisation communautaire', in D. Lombard and J. Aubin (eds), *Marchands et hommes d'affaires asiatiques dans l'Océan Indien et la Mer de Chine 13ᵉ–20ᵉ siècles*, Paris, Éditions de l'École des Hautes Études, 1988, pp. 221–236.

Phelan, J.L., *The Hispanization of the Philippines. Spanish Aims and Filipino Responses 1565–1700*, Madison, University of Wisconsin Press, 1959.

Poensen, C., 'Naar en op de Pasar', *Mededeelingen van wege het Nederlandsche Zendelinggenootschap* 26 (1882): 1–27.

Pohl, H., *Die Portugiesen in Antwerpen (1567–1648). Zur Geschichte einer Minderheit*, Wiesbaden, Franz Steiner, 1977.

Prakash, O., *The Dutch East India Company and the Economy of Bengal, 1630–1720*, Princeton, Princeton University Press, 1985.

Quiason, S.D., 'The Sampan Trade, 1570–1770', in A. Felix Jr. (ed.), *The Chinese in the Philippines 1570–1770*, vol. 1, Manila, Solidaridad Publishing House, 1966, pp. 160–174.

Ray, R.K., 'Chinese Financiers and Chetti Bankers in Southern Waters: Asian Mobile Credit during the Anglo-Dutch Competition for the Trade of the Eastern Archipelago in the Nineteenth Century', *Itinerario* 11, no. 1 (1987): 209–234.

Raychaudhuri, T., 'The Commercial Entrepreneur in Pre-Colonial India: Aspirations and Expectations. A Note', in R. Ptak and D. Rothermund (eds), *Emporia, Commodities and Entrepreneurs in Asian Maritime Trade. c.1400–1750*, Stuttgart, Franz Steiner Verlag, 1991, pp. 339–352.

Redding, G. and G.Y.Y. Wong, 'The Psychology of Chinese Organizational Behaviour', in M.H. Bond (ed.), *The Psychology of the Chinese People*, Hong Kong, Oxford University Press, 1986, pp. 266–295.

Reid, A., *Southeast Asia in the Age of Commerce 1450–1680*, vol. 1 *The Lands Below the Winds*, vol. 2 *Expansion and Crisis*, New Haven, Yale University Press, 1988 and 1993.

Revah, I.S., 'L'Hérésie Marrane dans l'Europe catholique du 15ᵉ au 18ᵉ siècle', in J. Le Goff (ed.), *Hérésies et sociétés dans l'Europe préindustrielle 11ᵉ–18ᵉ siècles*, Paris and The Hague, Mouton, 1968, pp. 327–339.

Ricklefs, M.C., *A History of Modern Indonesia c.1300 to the Present*, London, Macmillan, 1981.

Risso, P., *Oman and Muscat. An Early Modern History*, London and Sydney, Croom Helm, 1986.

Rizvi, S.S.A. and N.Q. King, 'Some East African Ithna-Asheri *Jamaats* (1840–1967)', *Journal of Religion in Africa* 5, no. 1 (1973): 12–22.

Roberts, J.G., *Mitsui. Three Centuries of Japanese Business*, 2nd edn, New York and Tokyo, Weatherhill, 1989.

Robinson, R., 'Non-European Foundations of European Imperialism: Sketch for a Theory of Collaboration', in R. Owen and B. Sutcliffe (eds), *Studies in the Theory of Imperialism*, London, Longman, 1972, p. 117–141.

——, and J. Gallagher, *Africa and the Victorians. The Official Mind of Imperialism*, London, Macmillan, 1961.

Robison, R., *Indonesia: The Rise of Capital*, Sydney, Allen and Unwin, 1986.

Rodinson, M., *Islam and Capitalism*, Harmondsworth, Penguin Books, 1977.

Roth, C., *A History of the Marranos*, 4th ed., New York, Hermon Press, 1974.

——, *Gleanings. Essays in Jewish History, Letters and Art*, New York, Hermon Press, 1967.

Roth, D.M., 'Church Lands in the Agrarian History of the Tagalog Region', in A.W. McCoy and E.C. de Jesus (eds), *Philippine Social History: Global Trade and Local Transformations*, Sydney, George Allen & Unwin, and Manila, Ateneo de Manila University Press, 1982, pp. 131–153.

Rudner, D.W., 'Religious Gifting and Inland Commerce in Seventeenth-Century South India', *Journal of Asian Studies* 46, no. 2 (1987): 361–379.

——, *Caste and Capitalism in Colonial India. The Nattukottai Chettiars*, Berkeley and Los Angeles, University of California Press, 1994.

Rush, J.R., *Opium to Java. Revenue Farming and Chinese Enterprise in Colonial Indonesia, 1860–1910*, Ithaca and London, Cornell University Press, 1990.

Salmon, C., 'Les marchands chinois en Asie du Sud-est', in D. Lombard and J. Aubin (eds), *Marchands et hommes d'affaires asiatiques dans l'Océan Indien et la Mer de Chine 13ᵉ–20ᵉ siècles*, Paris, Éditions de l'École des Hautes Études, 1988, pp. 331–351.

——, *Literature in Malay by the Chinese of Indonesia*, Paris, Editions de la Maison des Sciences de l'Homme, 1981.

——, 'The Han Family of East Java. Entrepreneurship and Politics (18th–19th Centuries)', *Archipel* 41 (1991): 55–87.

——, 'The Three Kingdoms in the Malay World – Religion and Literature', *Asian Culture* 16 (1992): 14–34.

—— and D. Lombard, *Les Chinois de Jakarta. Temples et vie collective*, Paris, Editions de la Maison des Sciences de l'Homme, 1977.

Santamaria, A., 'The Chinese Parian (El Parian de los Sangleyes)', in A. Felix Jr. (ed.), *The Chinese in the Philippines 1570–1770*, vol. 1, Manila, Solidaridad Publishing House, 1966, pp. 67–118.

Schipper, K.M., 'Neighbourhood Cult Associations in Traditional Tainan', in G.W. Skinner (ed.), *The City in Late Imperial China*, Stanford, Stanford University Press, 1977, pp. 651–678.

Schrader, H., *Chettiar Moneylenders. An Indian Minority in Burma*, University of Bielefeld Sociology of Development Research Centre Working Paper No. 121 (1989).

——, 'The Socioeconomic Function of Moneylenders in Expanding Economies: the Case of the Chettiars', *Savings and Development* 15, no. 1 (1992): 69–72.

Schuetz, A., 'The Stranger: An Essay in Social Psychology', *American Journal of Sociology* 49 (1944): 499–507.

Schumacher, J.N., *Readings in Philippine Church History*, Quezon City, Ateneo de Manila University, 1979.

Schumpeter, J.A., *Capitalism, Socialism and Democracy*, London, George Allen and Unwin, 1943.

——, *Essays of J.A. Schumpeter*, Cambridge, Mass., Addison Wesley Press, 1951.

——, 'The Creative Response in Economic History', *Journal of Economic History* 7, no. 2 (1947): 149–159.

——, *The Theory of Economic Development*, Cambridge, Mass., Harvard University Press, 1949.

Schurz, W.L., *The Manila Galleon*, New York, E.P. Dutton, 1939.

Scott, J.C., *The Moral Economy of the Peasant. Rebellion and Subsistence in Southeast Asia*, New Haven and London, Yale University Press, 1976.

Seal, A., *The Emergence of Indian Nationalism. Competition and Collaboration in the Later Nineteenth Century*, Cambridge, Cambridge University Press, 1968.

See, T.A. and Go Bo Juan, 'Religious Syncretism among the Chinese in the Philippines', in T.A. See (ed.), *The Chinese in the Philippines. Problems and Perspectives*, Manila, Kaisa Para Sa Kaunlaran, Inc., 1990, pp. 54–67.

Sen, A., 'Economics and the Family', *Asian Development Review* 1, no. 2 (1983): 14–26.

Sheldon, C.D., *The Rise of the Merchant Class in Tokugawa Japan 1600–1868. An Introductory Survey*, New York, Association for Asian Studies, 1958.

Sheriff, A., *Slaves, Spices and Ivory in Zanzibar. Integration of an East African Commercial Empire into the World Economy, 1770–1873*, London, James Currey, 1987.

Shiba, Y., 'Ningpo and its Hinterland', in G.W. Skinner (ed.), *The City in Late Imperial China*, Stanford, Stanford University Press, 1977, pp. 391–439.

Shivapadasundaram, S., *The Saiva School of Hinduism*, London, George Allen and Unwin, 1934.

Siem Bing Hoat, 'Het Chineesch Kapitaal in Indonesië', *Chung Hwa Hui Tsa Chih* 8, no. 1 (1930): 7–17.

Simmel, G., 'The Stranger', in K.H. Wolff (ed.), *The Sociology of Georg Simmel*, New York, The Free Press, 1950, pp. 402–408.

Singer, M., *When a Great Tradition Modernizes. An Anthropological Approach to Indian Civilization*, London, Pall Mall Press, 1972.

Skinner, G.W., 'Introduction: Urban Social Structue in Ch'ing China', in G.W. Skinner (ed.), *The City in Late Imperial China*, Stanford, Stanford University Press, 1977, pp. 521–523.

——, 'Java's Chinese Minority: Continuity and Change', *Journal of Asian Studies* 20 (1960–61): 253–262.

——, 'The Chinese Minority', in R.T. McVey, *Indonesia*, New Haven, Yale University Press, 1963, pp. 97ff.

Smith, D., *The Rise of Historical Sociology*, Oxford, Polity Press, 1991.

Smith, T.C., *The Agrarian Origins of Modern Japan*, Stanford, Stanford University Press, 1959.

Sombart, W., *The Jews and Modern Capitalism*, New Brunswick and London, Transaction Books, 1982.

Spear, P., *The Nabobs. A Study of the Social Life of the English in Eighteenth Century India*, London, Oxford University Press, 1963.

Steensgaard, N., *The Asian Trade Revolution of the Seventeenth Century. The East India Companies and the Decline of the Caravan Trade*, Chicago and London, University of Chicago Press, 1974.

Stein, B., 'The Economic Function of a Medieval South Indian Temple', *Journal of Asian Studies* 19 (1959–60): 163–176.

Stonequist, E.V., *The Marginal Man. A Study in Personality and Culture Conflict*, New York, Russell and Russell, 1961.

Subrahmanyam, S., *The Political Economy of Commerce*, Cambridge, Cambridge University Press, 1990.

Suryadinata, L., *Peranakan Chinese Politics in Java 1917–1942*, Singapore, Singapore University Press, 1981.

The Siauw Giap, 'Religion and Overseas Chinese Assimilation in Southeast Asian Countries', *Revue du sud-est asiatique* (1965): 67–83.

——, 'Socio-Economic Role of the Chinese in Indonesia, 1820–1940', in A. Maddison and G. Prince (eds), *Economic Growth in Indonesia, 1820–1940*, Dordrecht and Providence, Foris, 1989, pp. 159–183.

Thompson, G., 'The Ismailis in Uganda', in M. Twaddle (ed.), *Expulsion of a Minority. Essays on Ugandan Asians*, London, Athlone Press, 1975, pp. 30–52.

Tignor, R.L., *The Colonial Transformation of Kenya: The Kamba, Kikuyu, and Maasai from 1900 to 1939*, Princeton, Princeton University Press, 1976.

Timberg, T.A., *The Marwaris. From Traders to Industrialists*, New Delhi, Vikas, 1978.

Tindall, G., *City of Gold. The Biography of Bombay*, London, Temple Smith, 1982.

Tribe, M.A., 'Economic Aspects of the Expulsion of Asians from Uganda', in M. Twaddle (ed.), *Expulsion of a Minority. Essays on Ugandan Asians*, London, Athlone Press, 1975, pp. 141–176.

Trimingham, J.S., *Islam in East Africa*, Oxford, Clarendon Press, 1964.

Turner, B., *Weber and Islam. A Critical Study*, London, Routledge and Kegan Paul, 1974.

Tsai Mauw-Kuey, *Les Chinois au Sud-Vietnam*, Paris, Bibliothèque Nationale, 1968.

Vermeulen, J.T., *De Chineezen te Batavia en de Troebelen van 1740*, Leiden, Eduard Ijdo, 1938.

Walker, B., *The Hindu World. An Encyclopedic Survey of Hinduism*, 2 vols, New York and Washington, Frederick A. Praeger, 1968.

Wallerstein, I., *The Modern World-System I. Capitalist Agriculture and the Origins of the European World-Economy in the Sixteenth Century*, New York, Academic Press, 1974.

——, *The Modern World-System II. Mercantilism and the Consolidation of the European World-Economy, 1600–1750*, New York, Academic Press, 1980.

——, *The Modern World-System III. The Second Era of Great Expansion of the Capitalist World-Economy, 1730–1840s*, New York, Academic Press, 1989.

Wang Gungwu, 'Merchants without Empire: The Hokkien Sojourning Communities', in J.D. Tracy (ed.), *The Rise of Merchant Empires. Long-Distance Trade in the Early Modern World, 1350–1750*, Cambridge, Cambridge University Press, 1990, pp. 400–421.

——, 'Trade and Cultural Values: Australia and the Four Dragons', *Asian Studies Association of Australia Review* (1988): 1–10.

Wang Yeu-Farn, *Chinese Entrepreneurs in Southeast Asia: Historical Roots and Modern Significance*, Stockholm Center for Pacific Asia Studies Working Paper 34, 1994.

Ward, R. and R. Jenkins (eds), *Ethnic Communities in Business: Strategies for Economic Survival*, Cambridge, Cambridge University Press, 1984.

Weber, M., *Economy and Society. An Outline of Interpretive Sociology*, New York, Bedminster Press, 1968.

——, *The Protestant Ethic and the Spirit of Capitalism*, 2nd edn, London, George Allen and Unwin, 1976.

——, 'The Protestant Sects and the Spirit of Capitalism', in H.H. Gerth and C. Wright Mills (eds), *From Max Weber: Essays in Sociology*, London, Routledge and Kegan Paul, 1948, pp. 302–322.

——, *The Religion of China. Confucianism and Taoism*, New York, The Free Press, 1951.

——, *The Religion of India. The Sociology of Hinduism and Buddhism*, New York, The Free Press, 1958.

——, *The Sociology of Religion*, Boston, Beacon Press, 1963.

Wertheim, W.F., *East-West Parallels. Sociological Approaches to Modern Asia*, The Hague, W. van Hoeve, 1964.

——, *Indonesian Society in Transition. A Study of Social Change*, The Hague, W. van Hoeve, 1964.

Wickberg, E., *The Chinese in Philippine Life 1850-1898*, New Haven and London, Yale University Press, 1965.

——, 'The Chinese Mestizo in Philippine History', *Journal of Southeast Asian History* 5, no. 1 (1964): 62–100.

Williams, L.E., 'Chinese Entrepreneurs in Indonesia', *Explorations in Entrepreneurial History* 5, no. 1 (1952): 34–60.

Willmott, D.E., *The Chinese of Semarang: A Changing Minority Community in Indonesia*, Ithaca, Cornell University Press, 1960.

Wills, J.E., 'De VOC en de Chinezen in China, Taiwan en Batavia in de 17 de en de 18 de eeuw', in M.A.P. Meilink-Roelofsz, *De VOC in Azië*, Bussum, Fibula-Van Dishoeck, 1976, pp. 157–192.

Wink, A., *Al-Hind. The Making of the Indo-Islamic World*, vol. 1. *Early Medieval India and the Expansion of Islam, 7th-11th Centuries*, Leiden, E.J. Brill, 1991.

——, 'The Jewish diaspora in India: eighth to thirteenth centuries', *Indian Economic and Social History Review* 24, no. 4 (1987): 349–366.

Wolf, E.R., *Europe and the People Without History*, Berkeley and Los Angeles, University of California Press, 1982.

Yambert, K.A., 'Alien Traders and Ruling Elites: The overseas Chinese in Southeast Asia and the Indians in East Africa', *Ethnic Groups* 3 (1981): 173–198.

Yang, C.K., 'Introduction', in M. Weber, *The Religion of China. Confucianism and Taoism*, New York, The Free Press, 1951, pp. ix–xliii.

Yoshihara, K., *Philippine Industrialization. Foreign and Domestic Capital*, Quezon City, Ateneo de Manila University Press and Singapore, Oxford University Press, 1985.

——, *The Rise of Ersatz Capitalism in South-East Asia*, Singapore, Oxford University Press, 1988.

Zaehner, R.C., *Hinduism*, London, Oxford University Press, 1962.

Zarco, R.M., 'The Chinese Family Structures in the Philippines', in A. Felix Jr. (ed.), *The Chinese in the Philippines 1570-1770*, vol. 1, Manila, Solidaridad Publishing House, 1966, pp. 211–222.

Unpublished Theses

Jensen, K.K.M., 'The Chinese in the Philippines during the American Regime: 1898–1946', Ph.D., University of Wisconsin, 1956.

Nagtegaal, L., 'Rijden op een Hollandse Tijger. De noordkust van Java en de V.O.C. 1680–1740', Ph.D., Utrecht University, 1988.

Rudner, D.W., 'Caste and Commerce in Indian Society: A Case Study of Nattukottai Chettiars, 1600–1930', Ph.D. University of Pennsylvania, 1985.

Siegelman, P., 'Colonial Development and the Chettyar: A Study in the Ecology of Modern Burma, 1850–1941', Ph.D., University of Minnesota, 1962.

Swetschinski, D.M., 'The Portuguese Jewish Merchants of Seventeenth-Century Amsterdam: A Social Profile', Ph.D., Brandeis University, 1980.

Walji, S.R., 'A History of the Ismaili Community in Tanzania', Ph.D., University of Wisconsin, 1974.

Weightman, G.H., 'The Philippine Chinese: A Cultural History of a Marginal Trading Community', Ph.D., Cornell University, 1960.

Index

For Product Safety Concerns and Information please contact our EU
representative GPSR@taylorandfrancis.com
Taylor & Francis Verlag GmbH, Kaufingerstraße 24, 80331 München, Germany

9 780700 704439